To

Mrs. Chalmers Hadley

with gratitude
for her goodwill.

[signature] Guy Murray Shipler

Dec. 14, 1954.

Sermons of Goodwill

Sermons of Goodwill

Edited by Guy Emery Shipler

The Churchman's first series

on Brotherhood and Goodwill

ASSOCIATION PRESS — NEW YORK

1948

145

PREFACE

THIS VOLUME presents evidence that the Protestant clergymen of America know that confusion of values has created a widespread mental paralysis and that the resulting chaos demands a new reformation—a revolution rooted in the principles of religion applied to the social order.

There is no better index to the danger implicit in the mental confusion of today than current statements of our leading scientists, particularly those who have worked in developing the atom bomb and biological warfare. Long considered our "realists" they have now become also our "idealists." They have aligned themselves, willy-nilly, with the American pulpit by stressing their conviction that civilization is headed for an abyss unless men of good will and understanding succeed in remolding our social relations nearer to the pattern of brotherhood.

The sermons in this volume were written to help "promote goodwill and better understanding among all peoples." They have been selected from hundreds of sermons on this basic theme preached to local congregations and then submitted to *The Churchman* for its "Sermon-of-the-Week" project. Each sermon in the collection was broadcast on a Sunday morning over Station WOR, New York, and each writer was given a citation.

In the early part of the present century, Walter Rauschenbusch wrote: "The essential purpose of Christianity was to transform human society into the Kingdom of God by regenerating all human relations and reconstituting them in accordance with the will of God." While the clergymen of several Protestant denominations whose sermons appear in this volume may have varying theological reactions to this Rauschenbusch statement,

5

it is obvious that they hold deep convictions on the social implications of the principles laid down by the prophets of Israel and
by Jesus, and the importance of those principles for the world
of today and tomorrow.

We asked clergymen who were to submit sermons to speak
bluntly on social relations and to give concrete examples of what
had been or could be accomplished in their local communities
and elsewhere by goodwill in action. We said that we were not
interested in "perfume sprinkling." We said that we wanted to
know "what kind of practices should be condemned—in your
community and the world—in order to promote better race
relations," and all other group relations. We asked for stories
of individuals who had done constructive things for the social
order, "how they have done them, what kind of people they are,
what was their motivation. Community relations, international
relations, race relations, church relations—the good and the bad—
are things we want discussed forthrightly."

In making plans to have these sermons broadcast, we hoped
to reach people who were not regular church attendants and who
did not ordinarily listen to sermons which were broadcast. That
is why we decided to have the sermons read on the air by laymen
who were well-known in the fields of business, the theatre, and
various professions. Their co-operation was not only generous
but enthusiastic—so much so, in fact, that we charged many of
them with having had a secret yearning to preach at least one
sermon, an impeachment which they readily admitted. To each
of this group whose names are listed elsewhere in this volume,
we wish to record the gratitude of *The Churchman* and the radio
congregation.

The sermons have been edited, and many of them condensed,
to meet the requirements for broadcasting.

Perhaps the most appreciated compliment a clergyman ever
receives is: "You have changed my thinking about many things."
In the hundreds of letters from listeners commenting on the
sermons now appearing in this volume, that statement has been
found frequently. It is our hope that similar reactions may be
inspired in many of those who read this book.

GUY EMERY SHIPLER
Editor, *The Churchman*

New York, 1948

SERMONS OF GOODWILL

The Churchman's First Series on Brotherhood
and Goodwill

7

2. The Consequences of Denial

3. The Narrow Path

4. Brotherhood Affirmed

5. That They All May Be One

6. Am I My Brother's Keeper?

7. The Church and Brotherhood

8. He Whom a Dream Had Possessed

9. The False Slogan:
"The Jews Killed Jesus"

10. Mother's Day

11. The Way of Understanding

12. The Kingdom Is Coming

13. The Healing of the Nations

Notes on Broadcasters

Warren R. Austin—U. S. Senator from Vermont, 1931-40. Now permanent U. S. delegate to the United Nations.

Raymond E. Baldwin—Republican U. S. Senator from Connecticut. Former governor of Connecticut, 1939-41 and 1943-46.

Roger Baldwin—Director of the American Civil Liberties Union, New York, since 1917. Served a prison term during World War I as a pacifist conscientious objector. Author of books and pamphlets on civil liberties.

Ralph Bellamy—Actor of stage and screen. Appeared in the play *Tomorrow the World* and *The State of the Union*.

William Rose Benet—Contributing editor to the *Saturday Review of Literature*. Winner of Pulitzer prize for poetry, 1942. Author of many books of poetry.

Chester Bowles—Established Benton & Bowles, Inc., New York advertising firm. General Manager of OPA in 1943. Appointed Price Administrator by President Roosevelt in 1943-46. Member of American National Commission for UNESCO, 1946-7.

John Roy Carlson—Writer and lecturer on subversive activities. With Friends of Democracy since 1940. Author of *Under Cover* and *The Plotters*.

Carl Carmer—Author, lecturer. President of the Poetry Society of America. Author of *Stars Fell on Alabama, Listen to the Lonesome Drum, For the Rights of Men,* etc.

Bennett Cerf—President of Modern Library and Random House. Contributor to the *Saturday Review of Literature*. Editor of many books.

Benjamin A. Cohen—Assistant Secretary General of the United Nations in charge of Public Information. In diplomatic service of Chile for many years. Recipient of many international honors.

Norman Corwin—First radio playwright to receive grant from the Academy of Arts and Letters, 1942. Recipient of the first Wendell Willkie *One World* Award. Radio drama writer, director, producer.

13

editorial board of the Overseas Bureau of the Office of War Information.

Norman Cousins—Editor *Saturday Review of Literature.* Former chairman of

Jane Cowl—Actress who starred in many plays including *Lilac Time, Information Please, Anthony and Cleopatra,* and more recently *The Second Mrs. Frazer.* Also co-author of *Daybreak* and *Lilac Time.*

George V. Denny, Jr.—President of Town Hall, Inc. since 1937. Founder and director of Town Meeting of the Air.

Florence Eldridge—Screen and stage actress. Has appeared in numerous plays and many films. Wife of Frederic March.

José Ferrer—Producer, director, actor. Directed and produced the stage play *Strange Fruit* in 1945. Also acted in and produced *Cyrano de Bergerac,* 1946.

John Garfield—Distinguished star of stage and screen. Appeared in the Academy Award winning picture *Gentleman's Agreement.* Active in Experimental Theatre Group.

Peter Grimm—President and director of William A. White & Sons, 1929-44. Ex-president of the Real Estate Board of New York. Chairman of many boards.

Lillian Hellman—Playwright. Wrote such successful plays as *The Children's Hour, Watch on the Rhine, The Searching Wind, The Little Foxes,* and *Another Part of the Forest.*

Fannie Hurst—Internationally known authoress whose works have been translated into twelve languages. Many of these have been made into motion pictures.

Harold L. Ickes—Lawyer, writer. Secretary of Interior in cabinets of President Roosevelt and President Truman, 1933-46. Awarded Louis D. Brandeis medal for service to humanity.

Eric Johnston—President of the Motion Picture Association of America since 1945. Director of the Chamber of Commerce of the U. S., 1934-41; president, 1942-46.

Henry J. Kaiser—Industrialist. Organizer and chairman of Kaiser-Frazer Corp. Prominent during the war for his ship-building and organizational capacity.

Arthur Kennedy—Stage actor. Distinguished for his work in *All My Sons.*

Harley M. Kilgore—U. S. Senator from West Virginia since 1940.

Freda Kirchwey—Editor of *The Nation* since 1932. Chevalier, French Legion of Honor, 1946. Vice-chairman of International Rescue and Relief Committee.

Joseph Wood Krutch—Dramatic critic of *The Nation* since 1937. Professor of Dramatic Literature at Columbia University since 1943. Author of several books.

Fiorello LaGuardia—Mayor, New York, 1934-45. Director Office of Civilian Defense, 1941. Lawyer, writer, commentator.

Canada Lee—Actor noted for his parts in many Broadway hits, including the role of Bigger Thomas in *Native Son.* At one time leading contender for the welterweight championship.

Herbert H. Lehman—Former governor of New York, 1932-42. Director General, United Nations Relief and Rehabilitation Administration, 1943-46.

Percy Mackaye—Poet, dramatist. Translator of many classics. Received Shelley Memorial prize award for poetry. Author of many books and volumes of verse.

Frederic March—Distinguished screen and stage star. Won acting award of Academy of Motion Picture Arts and Sciences in 1932 and 1947.

Raymond Massey—Actor and producer. Among the plays he has appeared in and directed are *Saint Joan, The Constant Nymph, Abe Lincoln of Illinois,* etc.

Robert A. Millikan—Internationally famous physicist, author. Vice-president of the Board of Trustees of California Institute of Technology in Pasadena, since 1946. Awarded Nobel prize in physics in 1923. Honorary member of twenty-one foreign scientific societies and recipient of many honors.

Newbold Morris—Lawyer. President of the Henry Street Settlement. Also president and director of Children's Welfare Federation, New York City. Active in many civic enterprises.

Arnold Moss—Stage actor. Had leading role in *The Front Page* and *The Temper.*

Paul Muni—Stage and screen star. Awarded medal for best work of year by the Motion Picture Academy of Arts and Sciences for his role in *Life of Louis Pasteur* (1936).

William O'Dwyer—Mayor of New York City since 1945. Former Brigadier General of the U. S. Army. Representative of Foreign Economic Administration in Italy, 1944.

Harry Overstreet—College professor, lecturer, and author of many philosophical books, among them *Influencing Human Behaviour, The Enduring Quest* and numerous other books and technical papers.

Claude Pepper—U. S. Senator from Florida since 1936. Participant in many liberal causes and frequent contributor to periodicals.

Owen J. Roberts—Justice of the Supreme Court of the U. S. Chairman of the War Department Advisory Board on Clemency, 1945-47. Director of many commercial enterprises.

Albert Rusted—Former National Chaplain of the American Legion.

William Shirer—Veteran radio commentator and foreign correspondent. Author of *Berlin Diary* and *End of a Berlin Diary.* War correspondent, 1939-45.

Harrison Smith—Editor and publisher. President of the Saturday Review of Literature.

Kate Smith—Singer, actress. Has had own radio program since 1936. Also appeared in several motion pictures.

Harold E. Stassen—Governor of Minnesota. Resigned in 1943 to enter U. S. Navy. Active in young people's groups.

Meier Steinbrink—Justice of Supreme Court of New York, and National Chairman of the Anti-Defamation League of B'nai B'rith.

Herbert Bayard Swope—Journalist, war correspondent. Winner of Pulitzer prize for best reporting of year, 1917. Awarded Poor Richard Medal.

Glen H. Taylor—U. S. Senator from Idaho. Vice-presidential candidate on the Progressive Party ticket with Henry Wallace.

Ordway Tead—Chairman of the Board of Higher Education of New York City. Author of many technical books. Editor, teacher. Director of Harper & Bros.

Carl Van Doren—Pulitzer Prize winner for the biography of Benjamin Franklin (1938). Editor of the Living Library since 1946. Author of many books.

Margaret Webster—Actress, director. Started American Repertory Theatre with Eva La Gallienne and Cheryl Crawford (1946). Formerly a member of the Old Vic Company. Directed Theatre Guild Production, *Twelfth Night.*

Walter White—Secretary of the National Association for Advancement of Colored People since 1931. Author of *A Rising Wind* and other articles and books. Fellow of the John Simon Guggenheim Memorial Foundation, for creative writing in prose.

INTRODUCTION

IN ONE of his challenging essays, Professor George E. Woodberry declared: "Democracy is a prophecy and looks to the future." That statement was made many years ago, but it is still true. America still moves too often heavy-footed, toward those ideals of fellowship and brotherly goodwill envisioned by the founding fathers, and so clearly and emphatically stated in her Declaration of Independence. This "dream to be accomplished" fired the imaginations and determination of our great leaders of the past and brought them sturdily to the defense of our ideals when they were challenged—men of the calibre of Washington and Lincoln; of William Lloyd Garrison and Wendell Phillips.

No one who has read the story can forget a night in Faneuil Hall in Boston, in 1837, when a mass meeting had been called to denounce the mob murder in Alton, Illinois, of the first martyr to a free press in America, the Rev. Elijah Parish Lovejoy. He was the editor of a religious journal, and, because he had continously denounced slavery, his press three times had been destroyed by mobs. Because he believed in the rights and dignity of every human being of whatever race or color, and because he was a fearless, crusading editor, he was shot and killed as he was attempting once more to establish his printing press. On that night in Boston the Attorney General had denounced Lovejoy. It was that denunciation which brought Wendell Phillips to his feet to make an extemporaneous and immortal address in defense of a free press and freedom of speech. Interrupted by catcalls and roars of defiance, he persisted to the end, determined to be heard.

It is to such spirit that we must look if the fulfillment of our American dream of democracy is to be accomplished—a dream which has at its center and as its inspiration the conviction that every individual is sacred in the sight of God.

No day in the year could be more appropriate for the launching of *The Churchman's* Sermon-of-the-Week broadcasts than this Race Relations Sunday. All over America today clergymen of all denominations are pleading with their congregations in behalf of brotherhood, pleading that they will remember and practice the principles of their religion, without which, our practical-minded scientists are telling us, civilization and the human race are doomed.

A statement for this day issued by the Federal Council of Churches of Christ in America forcefully declares that: "Our American leadership in securing a world order of justice and peace for all peoples will be fatally handicapped so long as we fail to solve the problems of justice in our own country. While we talk of the four freedoms," says the document, "we see lynchings and riots, the rebirth of the Ku Klux Klan. We see the zealous champions of white supremacy attempting to dominate by legal or illegal power, while men and women of Negro and Japanese ancestry, who fought and suffered for democratic freedom, are ostracized, beaten, and in several sections of the country, even killed, as they seek to enjoy some of that freedom."

Those are hard facts to face—hard and depressing facts—but every decent American will heed the call to face them and correct them.

"Creative democratic living is cradled in our homes, in our churches, in our places of work, and in our local neighborhoods and committees," says the Council statement. Yet we have to recognize that it is in these same centers of inspiration that ill-will and hatreds are too often bred. It is doubtless with this unhappy fact in mind that the Federal Council makes specific suggestions for dealing with this situation. We are urged to:

"Take effective measure to oppose movements and agencies which aim to set one race or group against another."

We are urged to: "Seek an economy which will spread abundance of our fields and factories to feed, clothe, and house the many, irrespective of race, creed, or national origin."

We are urged to: "Work to guarantee civil rights and privileges to all."

To: "Respect the dignity of every human being."

Eight years ago, in 1939, fear and hatred had taken hold on millions of people throughout the world, inspired by the satanic leadership of Hitler. This monstrous demagogue had declared that "Judaism and Christianity are the religions of slaves and fools." In our day of rapid communication, this infection of hatred spread over wide areas of democratic America. America was being divided at the most dangerous moment in the world's history by racial and religious prejudice—a time when, if ever, it needed goodwill and unity.

It was at this time that *The Churchman,* disturbed, as were large numbers of thoughtful Americans, by the widespread hatreds, and conscious of its dangerous potential for disaster, decided to make a gesture toward goodwill and understanding which would go beyond the reach of its own columns. It decided to establish *The Churchman* Award, to be given annually to an American who was outstanding in the promotion of goodwill and better understanding among all peoples. Beginning in 1939 that award has been made each year. It has been received by such notable exponents of the best in American democracy as President Franklin D. Roosevelt, Wendell Willkie, William Allen White, Bernard Baruch, and General Dwight D. Eisenhower.

I mention this award because from it stemmed *The Churchman's* Sermon-of-the-Year and Sermon-of-the-Week project, which today is being launched on this station. *The Churchman* believed that it might inspire clergymen throughout the nation to preach specifically on goodwill and better understanding among all our people. The response from clergymen of all denominations in every part of the country has astonished us all. Hundreds of entry blanks have been requested. In one mail a few days ago came requests from places as widely separated as Alaska and Cuba.

Since no sermon can be submitted unless it has been preached to a congregation, it is obvious that millions of church people in all parts of America will hear sermons on subjects that desperately need to be stressed in these anxious and critical times.

1. Brotherhood Denied

WHICH WAY LIES WISDOM? . . .

THE REVEREND EUGENE CARSON BLAKE
Pasadena Presbyterian Church, Pasadena, California
(Second Award)

IF YOU GO TO THE MUSEUM of antiquities in Cairo, Egypt, they will show you the mummy of an ancient Pharaoh whom some scholars identify as the Pharaoh of the Exodus—this man who refused to heed the pleading of Moses and Aaron, who forced the enslaved Jews to make bricks without straw, who persecuted them with grim humor, hardening his heart against their pleas for mercy or justice, this very man who said: "Who is the Lord that I should obey His voice?"

The mummy that they show you there in the museum is not one easy to forget. When you see, within reach of your hand, the very body of the king (with his blondish curly hair) who acted his part in the drama of the ancient peoples of the Bible, your imagination is kindled. You begin to wonder what it was like there in Egypt several thousand of years ago at the time when first in all their history the Egyptians found themselves confronting a race problem in these Hebrews who had lived for several hundreds of years in the land of Goshen, where they had been allowed to settle during a famine by some half-forgotten king and his minister of state, a certain Joseph who was even rumored to have had some Hebrew blood in him. An impossible story, of course, for he was a great Egyptian hero!

This week, as I was thinking about that Egypt of long ago, I let my imagination have free rein and found myself sitting in the dining room of the best hotel in Thebes; Hotel Rameses I. It was a room full of men, apparently some kind of club. Oh yes, there on the wall was a banner on which was inscribed in hieroglyphics: "Thebes Waterwheel Club" and underneath the club's motto:

> "We meet to eat and we can't be beat:
> Every Thursday at 12:15."

Hotep Thomes from down the river, past president of Memphis Waterwheel, was to talk on "The Egyptian Way."

After a good many announcements, one of which interested me especially—a meeting later that same afternoon of the Thebes Realty Association (which I decided to attend) —and after a good deal of joking, the speaker was introduced.

Most of what Hotep said was so general that no exception could be taken to it. He believed in patriotism. He referred very briefly to the problem of the Hebrews who used to live over there in Goshen but had in recent years begun to spread all through the land—there were so many of them and they had such a queer religion; they didn't even respect the Sacred Bulls or Cats of Ammon Ra.

Pharaoh was a fine king, he said, but some of those bureaucrats around him needed cleaning out. He urged them all to be more regular in going to the temple. Hotep Thomes concluded with a stirring recital of the club motto: "We meet to eat and we can't be beat," and sat down.

The president suggested that after such a fine address we all ought to sing a Waterwheel song. So we sang one verse that went something like this:

> "We are the men of the Waterwheel
> All good fellows, not a single heel!
> So let's get together in cold or heat
> For we meet to eat and we can't be beat!"

I found myself walking out into the Egyptian sunshine as the members of Waterwheel all scattered back to their businesses. Later I walked into the offices of the Thebes Chamber of Commerce. Sitting around the table in the conference room were the Board of Directors of the Thebes Realty Association. They didn't notice me as I sat down in an empty chair. (Was I a ghost perhaps or did they all think I belonged? I was dressed just like the others!)

The president (whom I recognized as one of the Waterwheels) was telling them that there was but one item of business that called them together. They had to decide how they were going to deal with this Hebrew problem. It appeared that some of the Hebrews had got enough money to want to buy homes in Thebes outside of the district down by the river where they had lived ever since they came in from Goshen.

The Hebrews were of an alien race. Most of them were poor. One of them had bought a home up in the hill district and there had been quite a fuss about it. The real estate values of the whole district were jeopardized. The president asked for definite suggestions as to what ought to be done. One man said they ought to go to Pharaoh and get a law passed making it illegal for the Hebrews to buy any land in Thebes.

Someone suggested that they approach the Chamber of Commerce board to see what they would do in co-operating to keep the Hebrews from spoiling the residential districts. Then someone remembered that the vice-president of the chamber was Hatshetsup, head of the Rosetta Building Company. He was the man who was bringing all these people into Thebes as brickmakers and laborers on those big public works he was doing. He was so eager to get the workers he didn't care where they lived. "Smart fellow all right. Made forty per cent last year after taxes. Well, we can't buck him!"

The meeting broke up with the president appointing a sub-committee on restrictions.

It was next day that I slipped into the meeting of the Women's Progressive League. The atmosphere was quite different—feminine and progressive. A few knew what was going on in town but most of them had the feeling that their husbands probably knew better. And several women from the hills district spoke against the resolution that was proposed to invite Miriam Amramson into membership in the league even if she was a very fine musician.

"After all, she is a Hebrew, and the sister of that criminal Moses, you remember, the one who killed the overseer."

I didn't stay long at their meeting but slipped out into the street, as did the priest who had opened the meeting with prayer. He was the same one who had been at Waterwheel the day before. He asked if I would like to go with him to their ministerial association meeting that afternoon.

There were a dozen gathered in a little room off a nice temple to Ammon Ra. After devotions, a young fellow made a speech on this same race question. It was a good speech. After recalling a number of passages from their ancient holy books, he argued that they should actually do something about the needs of these Hebrew people. He acknowledged that they were of a different religion from the true one of Ammon Ra but that they were human beings, children of Ammon. He suggested that they should start campaigning for better housing, better jobs, and better education for the Hebrews and the removal of the restrictive laws that had made them very nearly slaves.

He was applauded, but no action was taken. I heard one serious-minded chap saying to another, "We surely ought to do something effective in this but my official board wouldn't stand for it. You know Joe Isis is my chairman." The other nodded his head in sympathetic agreement. Involved in raising money for a new addition to his temple, he knew he couldn't afford to make any enemies just now.

After the meeting, I found myself entering into the public audience chamber of the palace of Pharaoh himself. Two men were standing before him, one of them making an address of petition. "Who are they?" I whispered to the man next to me. "The one who's talking is named Aaron and next to him is his brother, they call him Moses—he's the leader of the Hebrew community." I heard Aaron say: "Thus saith the Lord God of Israel. Let my people go that they may hold a feast unto me in the desert."

He explained that they were troubled about the new restrictive rules that had been laid upon them, the taxes, the work quotas, and the rest. Would not Pharaoh let them have three days holiday to keep a religious feast?

But Pharaoh, his thin lips set in a straight line (was it the one whose mummy I had seen in the Cairo Museum?) his hand not now stiff but gesturing, replied: "Who is the Lord that I should obey his voice?"

He had taken his position. He would show them who ruled this land of Egypt. "I'll take away their straw allotment and insist they make as many bricks as before!"

As I stood and looked at Pharaoh, the reality of the scene faded from before my eyes and as in a prophet's vision I saw the plagues to come, the rebellion, the violence, at last the desperate escape across the opening waters of the Red Sea. And as I looked I saw a mountain top beyond the sea and heard a voice as that of a peal of thunder: "I am the Lord thy God which have brought thee out of the land of Egypt and out of the house of bondage. Thou shalt . . ."

Then the mountain changed and a gentler voice was addressing a small company gathered in the grass on a hillside and he was saying: "Verily I say unto you, unless your righteousness exceeds that of the scribes and Pharisees, ye shall in no wise enter into the Kingdom of God." And he spoke of brotherhood and of the true community which would be his kingdom and concluded: "Whosoever heareth these sayings of mine and doeth them I will liken him unto a wise man who built his house upon a rock."

Wise? Is this wisdom, I asked myself, this obedience to the law of God and this teaching of brotherhood on which to build a community? Or was old Pharaoh right when he said, "Come on, let us deal wisely with them (he was talking about the troublesome racial minority group). Let us deal wisely with them lest they multiply and it come to pass they join also unto our enemies and fight against us."

Which is wisdom? To take counsel of our fears and repress? To say: "Who is the Lord that we should obey His voice?" Or is it wisdom to obey that voice and to work to establish here and everywhere a true community of all the sons of God—a brotherhood?

And once more I was standing in the museum at Cairo beside the mummy of the ancient king, his arm unnaturally outstretched after scores of centuries; no rest, no peace! And when I looked at him and considered the present decay of all the greatness of what had been Egypt, once the center of the power and culture of the world; then I knew where wisdom lay. I knew . . . I knew.

═══◇═══

MODERN PHARISEES . . .

THE REVEREND ELMER NILES HASSEL
Pace Memorial Church, Richmond, Virginia

ONE OF THE GREAT PHILANTHROPISTS of America is a citizen of the world. The Rockefeller Foundation is well known for its globe-encircling efforts to benefit all humanity. When the magnificent Riverside Church of New York City was built some years ago Mr. John D. Rockefeller, Jr., had a large part in the success of the venture and now no denominational name is attached to the church. A few years ago Mr. Rockefeller issued a ringing statement on the urgency of the need for greater unity among the Christian forces of America in order to assure an equitable and lasting peace. All the world was thrilled by the manner in which he and his sons provided a home for the United Nations, the grand and daring venture of this generation to bring the Kingdom of God upon earth. This man believes in the brotherhood of all men under God.

This spirit of universal brotherhood has never been true with a majority of men. Its opposite is all too often the spirit which characterizes most of our churches. Our numerous denominations are the result of a pharisaical spirit which draws itself apart and, like the pharisee of Jesus' parable, declares: "God, I thank thee that I am not like other men." So marked has this spirit been that it has become well known by the name given it in his little book of the same name written by Dr. Peter Ainslie years ago. That fine minister of Baltimore's Christian Temple called it the scandal of Christianity.

There are some values in the various emphases of the several denominations. No one can deny that they have focused attention upon neglected areas of our faith. Yet, it is quite certain that the denominations have more in common than divides them. The things upon which we all agree, about which there is no question at all, are the basic verities without which there is no salvation. The things that divide us are also likely to damn us. And all the while a hopeful, yearning world looks on in scorn and bewilderment as we fumble along our separate ways.

The most scathing denunciations of Jesus were poured out upon the pharisees who were acknowledged to be the most religious of his hearers. They adhered to all the laws and rites of good religion to cleanse the outside while they allowed the cancerous growths of pride and indifference to fill their hearts. It was upon the pharisee of the parable that Jesus heaped his scorn. To the humble publican he extended his mercy. The philosophy of the brotherhood of men was announced as the philosophy of separateness was denounced. But the words of that ancient pharisee depict the spirit of our modern pharisees as we, too, draw ourselves apart and pray: "God, I thank thee that I am not like other men."

Our modern pharisees emphasize peculiarities instead of fundamentals.

The pharisee of the parable expected salvation on the basis that he was different from other men and he recited his differences. He was undeniably religious, but it was a religion based upon peculiarities instead of upon fundamentals. The essentials of religion were forgotten while he focused attention upon the trappings.

Someone has defined a fanatic as one who majors in the minors and thinks he has mastered the whole curriculum. That may pass as the definition of some people and of some denominations. Methodism, Baptism, Catholicism, etc., are made the basis of hope of salvation. It is the familiar error of pursuing religion while the aim of religion—the salvation of souls—is forgotten.

An ancient legend tells of a wonderful flute in the temple of Jerusalem. The purity and beauty of its tone ravished the souls of the believers. For many years it served to bring men into the presence of the most holy God. Then the reverent priests decided that the plain and simple flute should be honored and they had it coated with a beautiful lacework of gold. It was lovely. But the gold had coarsened its tone and it no longer had the power to lift and ennoble the soul. Just so we adorn our simple faith and then lose ourselves in the adornment.

When Roman Catholic people put their trust in the sacraments or the Church, when Jews put their trust in the keeping of the law, when Baptists put their trust in the rite of immersion, when Seventh-Day Adventists put their trust in the day on which to worship, when strict Brethren put their trust in the simplicity of their garb and manner, when Methodists put their trust in their Method of life or of government—in short, when any Christian trusts his performance of religious duty, he will not be saved

and the world will be indifferent. These things are not big
enough to attract lasting allegiance. As someone has remarked
about a brilliant failure: "He had a god who was not big enough."

Our modern pharisees exclude sinners instead of sin.

A second reason for the denunciation of Jesus is that phari-
saism excludes the sinner instead of sin. True enough, the
pharisee was a deeply religious man. Yet, by his emphasis upon
his own superiority he kept the sinner away and allowed sin to
enter. So we set up our barriers, we draw ourselves apart from
humanity, when we ought to pave the way and to be out on the
pavement waiting to welcome the sinner into a haven where he
will find freedom from sin.

Dr. Rufus Jones tells of writing a piece on the text "Come, let
us reason together." He received a letter of complaint from a
gentleman of some education to the effect that reason was left
out of all the religion he knew. The writer declared that he
wanted to go to church to worship, but that when he did he felt
like unscrewing his head and placing it with his hat under the
pew.

In the very same manner we still go through our motions of
religion, each in his own way, while needy souls wonder and
despair of religion. Like the pharisee of the parable we are all
concerned with ourselves and the score of our virtues while right
beside us is someone groping for the way, the truth, and the life.
Like the pharisee we see only the distinctions that exclude the
sinner instead of the justice and the love and the mercy of God
which is our only hope.

It was a preacher in a tenement district talking with a little
Roman Catholic boy. "You'll never get me to change my religion!" declared the boy. Patiently the minister answered: "I
don't want to change your religion; I want your religion to change
you." Just so may our religion change us.

Our modern pharisees engender dissension instead of unity.

A third reason for denouncing the spirit of the pharisee is that
it engenders dissension instead of unity. Today, with the world
looking for unity, with anxious peoples yearning for some expressions of brotherhood, we persist in our competing interests. When
we might become the one great power for unity we continue to be
agents of distraction and dissension. While a world longs for the
one God to which it can give itself, we each set up our cries of
"Here!", "Here!", and our voices are lost in the clamor. No

wonder the world is cool to our claims. We are like the religious Greeks who set up altars to all the gods, but who had no one God big enough to demand their souls.

Some years before the war a representative of a great missionary order landed at the island of Samoa. He was met by four canoes filled with men. Later, at a feast in his honor, the clergyman was twitted by the governor who had been met by only three canoes. An old warrior who had been converted to Christianity long before, heard the conversation and he came to the support of the minister. Said he: "The governor is the honored representative of the United States, a great temporal power. The minister is the representative of God, the eternal power."

When we all learn to represent God rather than our competing ideas, the world will listen and will be converted to Christ. But that will never happen while we emulate the pharisee of the parable and call attention to the little differences that set us apart.

Our modern pharisees elicit condemnation instead of praise.

The pharisee expected to be praised and rewarded for the manner in which he observed the little things of his religion. Instead he was denounced and condemned by the Lord of all of life. How can we escape the same condemnation? Look at our little recitals of creed. Look at our protestations of faith and our demonstrations of loyalty to some tradition or memory. What of the perpetuation of rites whose meaning is now obscure and almost impossible to explain to the present world? Is this religion? Or is it the spirit of the pharisee, deliberate or unwitting, which draws itself apart and so full of its own conceit dares to address the Father of all mankind with a recital of its differences. When all the while the words of Micah roll down the years as surely as the waters roll to the sea: "What doth the Lord require of thee but to do justly, to love mercy, and to walk humbly with thy God."

Ethel Barrymore, the great actress, was asked for the secret of her life and she replied: "You must learn day by day, year by year, to broaden your horizon. The more things you love, the more things you are interested in, the more you enjoy, the more you are indignant about, the more you have left when anything happens. You must learn above all not to waste your soul and energy and brain and strength upon all the little things. I suppose the greatest thing in all the world is loving people and wanting to destroy the sin but not the sinner. And not to forget when life knocks you to your knees—which it always does and always will—well, that's the best position in which to pray, isn't it? On your knees, that's where I learned."

Our modern pharisees cannot save our world, but there is power that can. When we learn brotherhood among men, when we practice the spirit of it in our churches as well as in our lives, the Master will be seen on earth again.

> "The great Christ found a small man and took him along,
> And they traveled together every day.
> And a man said, 'Who are those two big men?'
> And someone said, 'The one on the left is Smith;
> He's got religion. I do not know the one on the
> Right, but they look like brothers."

====◇====

BLIND SPOTS . . .

THE REVEREND LEWIS L. DUNNINGTON
First Methodist Church, Iowa City, Iowa

THE NEW TESTAMENT IS A TEXTBOOK ON BROTHERHOOD. Ask any man if he believes in brotherhood and he will instantly answer in the affirmative. Yes, indeed. We all do. But we do not always *act* as though we did and, after nineteen centuries of Christian teaching along that line, the world is in imminent peril for the lack of it. Why?

Deep within every one of us is the legitimate desire to be considered important and worthful. Both Christianity and democracy proclaim the abiding worth of every human soul regardless of race or creed. The hate-mongers and brotherhood-destroyers appeal to this powerful instinct and, as we listen to their spurious contentions, we accept their falsehoods as truth because the average man simply does not use the critical faculties of his conscious mind to sift and weigh the evidence.

Let us take a brief look at the human mind. Psychologists tell us that the mind is approximately one-tenth conscious and nine-tenths unconscious. With the conscious mind we reason and judge and choose, accepting or rejecting what seems good or bad, desirable or undesirable, as the case may be. And what our reasoned judgment dwells upon gradually sinks into the deep or unconscious mind and becomes a part of us. The unconscious mind accepts *uncritically* whatever the conscious mind dwells upon and proceeds to bring these dominant thoughts into manifestation in the world of body and of affairs.

Mind is, therefore, creative. Every single thought creates. If we train ourselves to think habitually about what is true and good and beautiful, if our mental eye is single to faith and hope and love, these characteristics will come to flavor and dominate the unconscious and result in happy, poised, integrated personalities. The field of human relationships will reflect this inner state of being. On the other hand, if we allow thoughts of discontent, anger, envy, fear, jealousy, and hatred to occupy a large portion of our waking hours, we will become sour, fear-ridden, diseased souls and our human relationships will suffer accordingly. Jesus said, "A good man, out of the treasure he has accumulated in his heart (unconscious mind), *produces* good and a bad man, out of what he has accumulated that is bad, *produces* what is bad."

Millions of people develop "blind spots" in the field of human relations under a kind of self-hypnosis after listening uncritically, over a long period of time, to false propaganda.

Hitler understood this phenomenon very well. Cutting off most outside sources of information, he and his minions took control of German radios, newspapers, and magazines and, over a period of years, poured into millions of receptive German minds a continuous stream of lies that the German people finally came to accept as truth. "The German people are a super-race of pure Aryans; they are destined to rule the world; they are invincible. The Jews are dogs who must be exterminated for it was they who stabbed us in the back and caused us to lose the first World War. It is not immoral for unmarried girls to give themselves to pure Nordic soldiers in order to bear children for the Fatherland." So ran Hitler's propaganda.

I spent the summer of 1939 in Germany gathering material for a series of newspaper articles and I was puzzled and shocked at the unbelievable change that had come over the whole German nation in six short years. They were not using their conscious minds to reason and judge objectively and critically. And I felt that their innate desire to feel worthful and important and to wipe out past failures was the motivating power that was subtly at work producing these dangerous blind spots.

One would naturally think that the sad fate of Germany, Japan, and Italy would make forever impossible any growth of the same brotherhood-destroying tensions in the United States. We have a relatively free press and we like to think that we are fairly intelligent. Yet a man in a certain state can campaign for the office of governor on a hate-filled platform of white supremacy and defeat a decent administration after four years of good government. Misguided people came to feel a bit more important and superior than their black brothers as they cast their votes in favor of racial discrimination. Prostrate Germany, Italy, and Japan were no lesson for the majority of voters in that state. They developed their fatal blind spots just the same.

In the fertile field of religion, nearly three hundred denominations and sects in the United States show how easy it is for most of us to develop blind spots. Let any spellbinder become convinced of some supposed religious "truth", no matter how insignificant it may be, and he will soon have enthusiastic followers who would die for their convictions.

The scientists who worked on the development of the atomic bomb are well nigh panic-stricken today over the blind spots existing in millions of American minds relative to our relations with Russia. I recently met one of them on the street here in Iowa City. He was walking slowly with eyes on the ground and was visibly depressed. "Why the gloom?" I queried. "I have just returned from a trip," he answered, "and I am appalled at the ground swell of sentiment in some places in favor of a war with Russia. Without any apparent realization of what their views involve, many are saying, 'War with the Communists is inevitable so let's use our atomic bombs and get it over with'."

We stood and talked for nearly an hour in the cold February wind and this in brief is what he said: "We can now make atom bombs a hundred times more destructive than the ones we used against Japan. Instead of destroying everything within a four-mile radius, we can probably lay waste an area of four hundred square miles with one bomb. If we were to destroy Russia's great cities, and we certainly could, the stratosphere would be filled with radioactive poison and death that would be blown around the world. The United States would suffer a rain of death that would gradually wipe us out as a nation."

So there we have it! The fate of Russia is inextricably bound up with that of the United States and, therefore, of the whole world. The fate of all humanity now has become one universal concern. The God of the universe is saying, "Think! Think straight, or perish! Rid yourselves of your blind spots or die!"

The situation is nothing short of desperate. We grant at once that the problem is difficult and its solution requires the utmost patience, skill, and courage. But many of the sources of our information on American-Russian relations are in the hands of those whose hatred and fear of Russia is so deep that they choose to give the American people only one side of the picture. These gentlemen seem not to realize that, even if an atomic war could destroy Russia without hurting us, that we cannot kill an idea with a bomb—not even an atomic bomb.

We have left a few years of grace in which to overhaul our educational system and teach our youth not what to think so much as how to think. In all fields, including that of religion, men must be taught to use their God-given critical faculties to ask, "Is this true or is it false?" Harmony in the whole field of social relations waits upon the development of more intelligent evaluations. Jesus surely understood this when, in giving the great commandment of Deuteronomy 6:5 he deliberately added the word "mind"—you are to love God "with all thy heart (unconscious mind), and with all thy soul, and with all thy mind" (Matthew 22:37).

In other words, think! think! think! and become intelligent as well as emotionally conditioned. Then the second part of the great commandment—to love one's neighbor as one's self—will come alive. Then indeed Jesus' teaching on the supremacy of love, the sacredness of human personality, justice, and fair play in all human relationships and the brotherhood of all men will be seen to be, not an idle dream, but the stark realism that will bring to every man the good life that we all so earnestly desire. And then, too, we shall each find the true fulfillment of our instinctive desire to be worthful and important through service to each other and to all mankind.

WHAT DOTH THE LORD REQUIRE? . . .

THE REVEREND WESNER FALLAW

Andover-Newton Theological School, Newton Center, Massachusetts

POLITE MODERN MAN has dismissed the devil—save as a word used as an epithet. And in so doing grave error has been committed. Listen to the high school boy who recently observed: "People pray to God for goodness; it seems just as logical that some people pray to the devil for evil." Nor was this boy speaking merely as a logician. He understands from observing human behavior that men do attune themselves to the spirit of evil—that men do indeed, through communion with satan, manifest in their conduct the wickedness of the devil himself.

And what is the wickedness which actuates the people of our times? Turn to that eighth verse of the sixth chapter of the prophet Micah: "He hath showed thee, O man, what is good, and what doth the Lord require of thee, but to do justly, to love mercy, and to walk humbly with thy God."

Whatsoever issues from our hearts, whatsoever issues in our conduct *in reverse* of the good which God shows us, is evil. Would you test our individual and collective behavior in order to determine conclusively what of it is good and what evil? Then examine carefully these three cardinal aspects of God's requirements. The first is justice; the second is mercy; the third is humility before God. Today justice concerns us.

Society today, indeed the nations of our world appreciate the fact that inseparable from justice is another closely linked goal. What is this thing, inseparable from justice? It is peace. Our deep desire and passionate longing is that enduring peace shall now be won for all peoples of earth. But we know that peace, like every possession, has its price.

What is its price? Let the economist give his answer: Production, trade, jobs, financial security. And the economist is right —partly.

Let the social scientist give his answer: Food, shelter, clothing, and family stability for all. And the social scientist is right—partly.

Let the statesman give his answer: Political freedom, international goodwill, exchange of goods, and a democratic parliament of nations. And the statesman is right—in a measure.

But for the larger answer to the question. What is the price of peace? What is a sure guarantee of human welfare? What is goodness? We must look to the prophet of God. Summarizing Amos, Isaiah, and Hosea, Micah points us to God and says:

He has shown you what is good. Be just. Act justly. If justice rules, peace and all good things and conditions will follow. Yes, justice—nothing less—is the price nations must pay for a durable peace. It is our responsibility as avowed lovers of things religious to dedicate ourselves without reservation to the creation and preservation of justice. And, be it known, prophetic religion holds that nation guilty of sin which permits justice to be trampled by tyrants. Prophetic religion indicts a people who complaisantly turn aside, when justice calls for heroic and sacrificial support. And God himself adjudges that person a sinner, a disciple of the devil, who sits unheeding in his private stronghold of social prestige and material possessions, when justice is being stifled by prejudiced, greedy men. Nor will all the shallow ritual and careful piety of the man engulfed in the pettiness of self-righteousness suffice to save his soul from the stern judgment of a righteous God.

The wretchedness of sin often causes us to pray to God with our lips and at the same time open our hearts to evil. The words of our mouth may be words about justice—but our inner thoughts and outward act may invite injustice. That is our sin. And that is our self-indictment. Look squarely at issues involved here.

Does a man's race, his color, his status classify him in our minds and determine the rights we accord him—or does his quality as a person classify him? Do we judge a man by his character, by his immortal soul, or by whether he is a protagonist of something we dislike? Do we look fearlessly for something of truth in the views of our political and social and economic opponents, or do we fight them wholesale as long as we think we might win—and then try cheap compromise or bribery, after we have lost?

Surely of all places the Church of the living Christ is the place for the souls of men to pass through a refiner's fire.

We look at our times and conditions, searching for justice growing from the ground-roots—knowing that without justice around our doorstep there can be little around the national capitol or around the edifice of the parliament of nations. What do we see here at home? There is of course much that is promising. For example, we see our public schools democratically sup-

ported, many of them democratically admitting children of any
family, admitting all children and classifying them according to
their mental and emotional ability. At least in a large section of
the nation we see the black boy on balance with the white boy.
We see the Nisei child on balance with the Caucasian child. We
see, on occasion, a gifted Negro speaker appearing before our
white congregations; and some churches are actually interracial.

A prominent church has carved in stone, above the columns of
its stately sanctuary, the words: "A House of Worship For All
People." Let us honor the people who have erected this monument in words and stone to the godly fact that all men truly *are*
brother one of another.

But, just how far has the idea of a house of worship for all
people taken vital hold of our communities? Do we dare seek to
translate the symbol into personal and community reality?

Alas, the very church members who have said they welcome
Negroes to their worship have frequently practiced political and
civic discrimination.

We sing the words, "Let freedom ring" most heartily on the
anniversary of the founding of our America, our democracy—
this home for the once enslaved immigrant whose joy is bound-
less at first sight of the guardian Statue of Liberty. American
justice has signified the right of the penniless immigrant, the
Negro and others of minority groups, to rise socially and econom-
ically and culturally as they may. And many have risen. But
unfortunately not enough.

Now, what of our treatment of political and economic opponents?

There are mouths which open in anthems of praise, and later
open again in denouncement of human justice. There are hands
that lay liberal offerings on the church altar, and later put bribes
in the pockets of evil men. There are kindly people, who pray
for a world of peace, and then go out to sow wholesale the seed
of unfair discrimination, race hatred, and gross injustice.

Surely this sort of conduct is what Isaiah had in mind when he
spoke of people departing from their God. This is what the
prophet meant when he described justice as standing afar off,
and truth fallen in the street—lying there entangled in the wreck-
age of the scales of justice.

If you and I dare look unflinchingly at the facts, we shall see
both the flaws in our reasoning about democracy and the sins
embedded in our social conduct. Our spirits are heavy in prayer

for enduring peace. This longing for peace is the first step toward it. But the next and more important step we can only take as we create, establish, and preserve justice. Justice among nations begins with justice springing up around our very doorsteps, and covering our own community, reaching to the national capitols of the world and finally to the parliament of man.

Twenty-seven centuries ago Amos, the Tekoan prophet-shepherd, spoke for God. An adaptation of his message to our times might read:

"I, your God, do not count you a true worshiper if you merely build fine churches and enlarge your budget. I count as ineffectual your music and your nice ritual, unless to these you add —and make of first importance—justice, righteousness, truth. Your residential, restrictive covenants I despise, saith the Lord. Your racial discrimination, your political dishonesty, your economic insolence, your defilement of truth by resorting to such things as coercion and bribery, your cheating on tax returns, all these I abhor.

"What I the Lord demand, in the name of truth and human welfare, is that justice shall roll down as waters, and righteousness as a mighty stream."

That, my friends, is what the Lord requires of us. And that is good. Dare we seek it?

═══ ◆ ═══

JESUS COMES TO OUR TOWN . . .

The Reverend Roy M. Pearson
Hancock Presbyterian Church, Lexington, Mass.
(First Award)

NARRATOR: *The scene is one of the homes in the heart of our town. The date is any day in the present year. The hour is in the evening. Dinner is over, and three men and three women are moving toward the living room talking as they go. They settle down in the comfortable chairs before the fire on the open hearth. Five of them are people of the town itself, the host and hostess and three friends invited in to share the evening's com-*

*radeship. The sixth is a man toward whom all eyes have been
turned for most of the evening. His name is Jesus, the same who
walked the earth in Nazareth and who was hanged upon the
cross at Calvary. By some strange twist of circumstance he had
appeared again within the ways of men, and having come to our
town, he had taken dinner with these people who held high
standing in a church that bore his name.*

*At first the group had been a little tense around the table.
But it was not long before the candlelighted room had rung
with laughter, and then the other five remembered how cheerful
this man had been two thousand years ago, how he went to
wedding parties, talked with friends for hours at a time, and even
got the reputation of being a ne'er-do-well for what he did.
Nobody quite remembered how the stranger set them at their
ease, but now before the open fire their embarrassment was gone,
and when Jesus spoke, they heard him as a friend long known
and loved.*

JESUS: One question I had meant to ask of you at dinner. I
hope it will not seem too dull of me, but I am new here now, and
this has troubled me since first I came to town. You have so
many churches here, about a dozen I should say. Why so many
of them? I hear it said that not every church is crowded on the
Sabbath Day. Could you not give your cause much added
strength by consolidating your forces?

NARRATOR: *There was a little pause. Two guests cleared their
throats and looked the other way. It was the host at last who spoke.*

HOST: Mary, I think you ought to tell Jesus about denominations. As he said himself, he's new here now. He had gone to
heaven, you know, before denominations came about.

HOSTESS: Of course, John. I should have thought of that before.
You see, Jesus, we cannot get together in the churches because it
takes some people so very long to find out what the truth really
is. Take the Baptists, for instance. Can you imagine it? They
still believe in total immersion! Or the Methodists. They go
all the way up to the altar rail to take communion. Or the Episcopalians. They're not satisfied with the Bible—they have to have
their Book of Common Prayer. Anyway, it's probably best to
leave things as they are. Where ignorance is bliss . . . you know.

NARRATOR: *A pause again. Somehow the other four seem loath
to put themselves on record, and the stranger wears a look of
puzzlement. At last he speaks again.*

JESUS: Perhaps I just don't understand. I guess I thought that churches tried to lead the world to know and worship God. I thought they put that effort first and did not care so much to have their own opinions honored as to know how best they might advance God's purpose in the world. There seems to be a fixed belief abroad that my way of life is rather complicated, something only theologians understand. It was not so when I was here before. I had no trouble with the lowly folk. The common people heard me gladly and understood the things I had to say. It was with the learned and the mighty that I had my trouble then. To love God and to love your neighbor—therein lie all of the law and all of the prophets. In these it seemed to me that men might find one mansion large enough for all. It would be good to have one house of God in every town, and not so many different places claiming jurisdiction over what I said and did that when I come back to earth, I scarcely know who my real decendants are.

NARRATOR: *The fire crackled on. Was it the blaze which brought the color to the cheeks of the five who heard the strange man's words, or was it something that he said which made them blush a bit for shame? To all it seemed a time propitious for the changing of the subject. The hostess cast a meaningful glance across at her husband, and hurriedly he spoke again.*

HOST: O, by the way, Jesus, we want you to know how deeply all of us resent the circumstances of your crucifixion. The things those Jews did to you! The way they scorned you, tortured you, killed you! I guess you know how faithfully we Christians have tried to pay them back through all the years for what they did at Calvary. And the colored people, too! The way they try to throw their weight around the country now! You'd think they own it when you hear them talk! Well, we all look forward to the day when this fair land of ours will belong to Americans alone.

NARRATOR: *There was no pause at all this time. There was a look of pain upon the stranger's face, and he answered the host at once.*

JESUS: It hurts me to have you talk that way about the Jews. You do them wrong when you speak as if they were the ones who put me on the cross. I lived among the Jews through all my days. They were my people even as the people of this land are your own. I said that the common people heard me gladly, and who were they but Jews? Peter was a Jew, the head of my little band of twelve, and James and John and all the rest. Paul, too, was a Jew. Take away the help the Jews gave me, and I should have been alone indeed.

Nor is it fair to blame the Jews for that which happened at Jerusalem. No more fair than to say that the Greeks killed Socrates or the Americans killed Abraham Lincoln. Less fair in fact, because the Romans had a large part in doing what was done. And when it comes to all the years that followed, have you ever stopped to think about the things that gentiles did to Jews? They kept them out of their colleges by their quota system. They barred them from their hotels and summer colonies by their policy of "restricted clientele." They drove them out of the professions by refusing to patronize Jewish doctors and lawyers. You talk about the things that Jews have done to gentiles, but I hear it said that five million Jews are dead in Europe now, and gentiles killed them. Anyway, you follow back your Christian faith to me, and I am a Jew, you know.

NARRATOR: *The faces by the fire were now scarlet, but the stranger did not wait to let his words sink home. He went right on as if he had not stopped at all.*

JESUS: The Negroes, too. It grieves me that you think of them as now you do. They tell me that you have two Negro churches here in town, and when I stopped a Negro man to chat with him this afternoon, he mentioned that he had to go twenty miles to get his hair cut because the barbers in the town refused to let him enter. I hear it said that in the larger places the evil done is even greater and that you often find an attitude as bad as that which Hitler had in Germany.

I do not have to prove to you that God made of one blood all peoples; your scientists found out at last what many men knew anyway. Why then make so much of different skins and colors? Are Jews less human than their Christian brethren? Are pain and persecution felt the less when Negroes bear their blows than when a white man is their victim? Is there not one God? And if God is color-blind, is that a fault so large that men should blame God's children for the things their Father did?

NARRATOR: *The sentence ended with a question mark, but no one seemed disposed to be the one to answer. The host got up and put another piece of wood upon the fire. He looked as if he wished that someone would speak. It was the hostess who finally broke the painful silence.*

HOSTESS: Well, Jesus, you always had the reputation of going straight to the heart of things, and you've lived up to that reputation tonight. There are faults enough in all of us, I guess. But anyway, thank God that we are not as bad as some! Our son was in the army, and the things he told us fairly made our hair stand on end! The way they drank and swore and carried on every night! It isn't just the army either. The newspapers are full of it everywhere. What is this country coming to anyway, I often say? O, you won't find perfect people in the churches, Jesus, but when you really get acquainted with them, you'll be a happy man to learn how different they are from the people outside.

NARRATOR: *Jesus smiled a little then, and when they looked at him, they saw a tenderness in his eyes which made him look as if he longed to have them see something yet concealed from them.*

JESUS: I hope so. I hope so more than you might imagine. I had my troubles with the churches in my day. When I tried to preach in one of them, they ran me out of town, and you all know what happened to me when I drove the cheating money-changers out of the temple in Jerusalem. I often wondered why it was I got along so much better with the people outside the church. They called me the friend of publicans and sinners, you know. I spent a lot of time with them. Sometimes I stayed with them because they were sick of soul, and healthy people don't need a doctor half so much as sick people. But I'll be honest with you: Sometimes I stayed with them because I liked them more. They were easier to get along with. They didn't have so many walls of pride to batter down.

I didn't always find that in the people of the churches. O, they were law-abiding folk all right, but deep within their hearts there was something twisted. They were often selfish; they were often proud; and often they puffed themselves up like that strange fish which bloats itself on being pulled from the water.

I shall never forget the day I saw two men in the temple, the one a pharisee and the other a publican. The pharisee was thanking God that he was not as other men were, and the publican was beating his breast and asking God to be merciful to him a sinner. You know, I liked that publican. I think God liked him, too.

NARRATOR: *No one moved before the fire now. They sat with*

eyes fixed fast upon the flames until at last the guests arose. "We really must be going now," they said.

You know how it must have been—the usual commotion of buttoning up their coats and getting rubbers on, the usual barrage of "Good-night," "Had a lovely time," and "Come again, won't you?" And then more quickly than she might have done with someone else, as though to save them all embarrassment, the hostess spoke again.

HOSTESS: Why Jesus, you must be dead tired! What an evening this has been! I hadn't meant to have you bothered with such things at all. Come now, let me show you to your room at once and let you get some rest. We've a busy day ahead tomorrow.

NARRATOR: *I suppose it was not strange that going up the stairs Jesus thought again of something one had said at dinner— that in the restoration of a colonial town in Virginia such exquisite care had been taken that, coming back to earth again today, men of olden time would think the place unchanged, could even find the things they had touched two hundred years before. Within his room at last, he spoke the words he had not wished to say aloud before.*

JESUS: Even so! Behold I go up to Jerusalem, and black against the sky I see the cross I thought I left behind!

2. The Consequences of Denial

NO SURVIVAL WITHOUT CO-OPERATION . . .

THE REVEREND CHARLES G. McCALLISTER
Congregational Church, Talcottville, Connecticut

HYPNOTIZED BY THE SPECTACULAR DISPLAY of our miraculous civilization, man has been spending much of his energy in breathless anticipation of new and more wonderful physical miracles to come. Little time remained for the solution of the vitally important problems—the problems of man himself. How humanity was to establish some form of group, national, and international life sufficiently stable to avoid disaster was pushed aside in order that man might acquire more material possessions. The acts of obtaining have created pointed tension in many areas of human relations. The acts of mankind will eventually determine his characteristics. Under the compulsion of a driving materialism, individuals and groups gave themselves increasingly to the securing of power which determines their desire to dominate, created many distorted philosophies, and perilous conflicts. Drunk as we were with the power of physical coercion, the power of serving the common good became less and less of a factor in life. The disruption of human relations was developing.

43

In the meantime, imbedded deep in the social organism, erupting with increasing violence through the thinning crust of a materialized civilization, disturbances have been rising. Thus, mankind finds itself again passing through a dark and tragic era. History may prove this period to be the blackest and most tragic of all. The violence of the recent war has undermined the illusions which man, proud of his power and possession of things, may have had regarding the solidity and permanence of this civilization. Man bet his right to happiness on the physical conquest of life. Having lost the wager, he anticipates with horror the drastic terms of payment. As from time immemorial, modern man must learn that life outside the Fatherhood of the Eternal is not life, but consuming death.

The church has been making an effort to combat these encroachments upon humanity's right to happiness and eternity. But the intelligent observer must admit that the effort made has not been enough to stop the uneasiness and disaffection, if not the actual and universal demoralization of a civilization. The church has failed to attack with weapons capable of success. There is no conceivable hope of a victory of bows and arrows against modern tanks and planes. The skepticism and atheism of the moment cannot be turned back by sentimental and traditional arguments.

The institutions of the day tend to conform to the characteristics of the civilization in whose matrix the institutions were founded. As man developed his incentive for physical domination, the church often adjusted itself to harmonious relations with these activities. So it has come about that Jesus, girded with a towel, washing his disciples' feet, is not a popular presentation.

What are we to say to those who have been feeling a rising doubt about the dignity and destiny of humanity? How shall we succor those who suffer from the conflict between what they think is their real self, and their spiritual self? What shall we hold out to those who do not believe as yet, but whose whole existence cries out to be convinced about the ultimate value of life?

In the past, we have taught the history of partialism. Each group within the social organism has, in describing historical phenomena, presented the facts in such a way as to make its country right and the enemy's always wrong. "My country right or wrong," and the original concept of the Monroe Doctrine functioning in our time, are ghastly perversions in an age of atomic bombs, bacterial warfare, and supersonic speed. To set forth the right of superiority which establishes a dividing wedge in the world-wide organism of today, is the beginning of catastrophe. When we attempt to create history out of falsehood, the danger is upon us.

A more intelligent study of the historical process may reveal a startling new and fundamental law of nature. In the past man lived successfully by acquisitive and competitive stimuli; today that very activity may be a toxicant with properties which will fatally poison the social organism. Mankind should ask whether the symptoms abroad in the present disrupted civilization might not be the signs of such poisoning. The times and tides of man have moved onward until now we are obligated to recognize that the higher the degree of success of partialism in yesterday's civilization, the more dangerous its projection into the future may be.

There are adequate reasons to set forth the premise that just as man has learned that he must observe certain physical laws or perish, so, in the functioning of our modern social organism, he must recognize and obey the law of universal co-operation. The evolving universe has been growing away from competition toward co-operation. The simple illustration of the evolution of the nervous system is a case in point. Here the entire process has been away from independence toward interdependence. The one-celled amoeba is created with no facilities for co-operative relations. It engulfs its food, digests it, and utilizes the nutriments as a single independent cell. In its complete independence the amoeba is ideally equipped for competition.

On the other hand, we are aware that the efficiency of the human body, a vastly later organism in the scale of time and evolution, is basically the result of the harmonious and co-operative process of specialized cells. One highly adapted colony performs the vital function of pumping blood throughout the body; other groups of cells perform other important duties. Out of the co-operative effort come the magnificent capabilities of the human body. Physical death is the refusal or inability of some specialized cells to perform their co-operative function. When this total co-operation is interrupted, life ends in death. Here we see the possible emergence of a new law of the social order—humanity must co-operate or die. Perhaps we shall learn that all physical life is ultimately dependent upon moral law for its survival.

If the price of human survival is unconditional co-operation, then there must be mobilization for survival. The temper of the times will make this difficult. In the delusion of the present materialism our temperament is such that we rationalize our actions and reject our sins. We prefer the scapegoat to personal and corporate atonement.

Therefore, the real prophets of the day will be those who, unmoved, proclaim this new law governing human destiny. Unless these leaders are produced, the way of civilization will be in grave jeopardy. Mankind must now have that sense of destiny for self and the world which makes no distinction between the self and the world. Recognition must be given to the common destiny of all human life. This will mean that mobilization for survival will require a moral control of life and action not essential in a civilization marked by the rugged individualism of an acquisitive society. Humanity, crystallized in the hardened coat of material values and motivation, will have the gravest difficulties in acknowledging this. The world's supreme danger lies in this area of development. Can man give up his combative and acquisitive drives and accept those controls which will warrant survival?

Even more personal is the question of the institution which proclaims the evangel of the Christian message. Surely any adjustment to partialism which the church has made must be confessed and rejected. Will the church see this need in time? The answers to these questions contain the answer to the immediate destiny of man.

For some this new hope, competition giving way to co-operation, is the one light left in the foreboding darkness. When this aspiration is anticipated as becoming reality, deep calls to deep in the souls of many spiritual pilgrims. To whom shall they turn for leadership and guidance?

In Jesus as a leader, not the accretive theological Christ of history, lives our hope for the universal destiny of humanity. He eternally proclaims that entrance to the Eternal Fatherhood of God is through acts of reverence and respect of personality. If civilization does not follow Jesus at this point, if we will not agree to put the claims of universal humanity before all petty and limited ends of secular living, then nothing can or will save us.

The outmoded theological disputations about Jesus must give way to a personal and complete dedication to his way of personal and social living. No habit, personal or corporate, can go uncriticized. No values can remain unexamined. No institution is too sacred for re-evaluation.

In the slow upward evolution of life, painfully, and often fatally, the human race has learned of and adjusted itself to certain recognized laws of nature. All normal human beings have learned to recognize and respect the universal law of gravitation. In obedience to this law, there was progress for the race and personal security for all members of the race.

Man is now challenged with the responsibility of the moral recognition of an adjustment to another law of nature; universal co-operation for the common good. The acuteness of our world disorder sets forth an extreme urgency. There must be immediate mobilization for survival. It must be total.

Man is under a great compulsion to escape from the possibilities of a new dark age. As he has found that he must conform to physical law or perish, now, he must acknowledge, both by word and deed, that moral law under God is just as invincible. Total mobilization, not for personal but for world good, is the essence of this survival.

Civilization will stand or fall because of the decisions of this day. Nothing less than the whole man in total mobilization for survival in spiritual and ethical actions can be adequate. Anything less than total surrender of all actions to the new law of human co-operation will be contradictory to Jesus' teachings, anything less will be treason to God and lead to the destruction of humanity.

====◇====

WE ARE ALL GUILTY . . .

THE REVEREND HARRY C. MESERVE
First Unitarian Church, Buffalo, New York

ONE OF THE ITEMS ON THE AGENDA for the current meeting of the United Nations is the adoption of a treaty which will provide for the punishment of those individuals or nations which are guilty of the crime of genocide. Genocide is a new word. It means the attempt to exterminate a whole race of people. It is

one of the dubious distinctions of our time that men have be-
haved in such a way as to make the coining of such a word necessary. Since 1933, in the most brutal and calculated effort at
genocide the world has ever known, six million Jews have per-
ished. Try to understand the figure if you can: four-fifths of
the population of New York City, or more than the total population of Norway, Finland, or Denmark. Each one was a human
being—man, woman, or child. They have been deliberately shot,
gassed, beaten, burned, starved, or worked to death, for no crime
save that they happened to be known as Jews. The end is not
yet. The remnant of Europe's Jews, some hundreds of thousands
of them, are still without peace and security, still living behind
barbed wire, still crammed into the foul holds of old ships and
shuttled back and forth across the sea, shut out from the few
havens of safety where they might find a chance for a new life.

There is no tragedy in our time which touches this one in bitterness, no cruelty quite as bestial as that to which they have
been subjected; no indifference quite as callous as that with
which they have been met even by their nominal friends and
allies. Many events in our age will soon be forgotten in the long
sweep of history. But this crime is the blackest mark on the
record of our Christian civilization to date. For this crime was
perpetrated by men in the heartland of Christian civilization,
men with hundreds of years of Christian tradition behind them.
And this crime was observed and all but ignored from 1933 to
1939 by the self-styled guardians of the finest flower of Christian
civilization. I have even heard good Americans say recently that
"after all, Hitler was more than half right about the Jews."

So I say that what has taken place in this tragedy presents a
Christian problem. We are all guilty in some degree. I imagine
that almost all Americans would stoutly deny that they have any
anti-Semitic feelings, except those of the most trivial sort. Our
guilt is subtle and negative; we have not actively participated
in persecution, but we have passively connived in the prejudices
and lies, which when inflamed by the words of demagogues, and
intensified by hard economic and political conditions, have resulted in persecution. The things we have done do not make us
guilty so much as the things we have left undone: the words of
friendliness never spoken, the acts of brotherhood and reconciliation which seemed a little too inconvenient, the effort to
understand, to put ourselves in another's place which we have

never made. Here is our guilt, not as great as that of Goebbels
and Streicher, but too great.

Try to imagine it. You are a Jew. You feel you are an American like everybody else. But as soon as you are aware of life at
all, the drops of water begin to fall, one by one, inexorably. You
read in the paper that some Christian minister has said that you
and your people killed Christ two thousand years ago. You plan
a vacation and look into resort hotels and learn the meaning of
the little phrases "Christians Only" and "Restricted Clientele."
You find that there are places where most people can go and buy
board and room, but where you can't, no matter what you pay.
You find a house you would like to live in, but there is something
called a "restrictive covenant" which provides that the house
cannot be rented or sold to you. You hear about the Jewish communists and the Jewish international bankers. You dig out the
facts to refute these charges, but they are repeated in spite of
facts. You hear it said that you are greedy, money-grubbing,
though you and your people give several times as much per capita
to religious and humanitarian causes as any Christian group.
You read in your paper that thousands of your people are in new
concentration camps in Cyprus after being "liberated" from
Germany, or you read that thousands of your people, in a desperate effort to reach Palestine, have been intercepted by the
British navy, herded on to prison ships and transported back to
Germany and placed in detention camps again. You begin to
wonder what, if anything, the Christian conscience means. You
seek comfort and fellowship with your own people; then, you
discover that you are "clannish," that you "set yourself apart,"
that you do not really care about being a part of the rich varied
pattern of American life. Try to imagine what all these things
would do to you, if you had to bear them day in and day out.

Look at the other side of the shield. This sort of thing is very
bad for Christians. The normal, upper middle class American
today has to confront so many fancied threats to his security and
his superiority that often when the real threats come, he never
sees them. He is off, like Don Quixote, attacking a windmill. He
must "protect his property" by keeping Jews, Negroes, and others
out of his block. He must preserve the purity and sanctity of his
social circle by refusing to recognize certain groups there. He
must beware of them in government, industry, business, politics,
housing, education, recreation, and practically everything he ever

comes in contact with. His horizon becomes narrow. Having excluded Jews, Negroes, orientals, foreigners, to say nothing of various suspect shades of political opinion in his own group, there is almost nobody left for him to associate with except those who are exactly like himself, those who share his own prejudices, fears, and desperate strivings to preserve intact his narrow security and fancied superiority.

The price of anti-Semitism to the one who practices it cannot be over-estimated. It makes him less than Christian, less than democratic, and, too often, as Germany has made plain, less than human. Even in its most trivial forms it corrupts his best faith in the fatherhood of one God and the brotherhood of all men in Him, a faith, incidentally, which the Jewish Jesus passed on to all men out of the rich heritage of the Jewish people. The price which anti-Semitism has cost Christianity in hypocrisy, in corruption, in injustice, and in the blood of millions of innocent folk is too great to be borne any longer. ·

There are things to do about this, things which everyone can do. In the first place, each one of us can cleanse his own life. Those of us who are parents can see that a different attitude reaches our children, that the lies and fears and slanders of anti-Semitism are quickly and emphatically corrected. We can challenge those lies and affirm our faith in a real human family without second-place races and groups, for the spirit of the living God dwells in man with indifference to his race, creed, color, or ancestry. How poor would our science be without the work of Einstein, Steinmetz, Bohr? How many of us and our children might already be dead without the discoveries and work of Berman, Ehrlich, Flexner, Landsteiner, Metchnikoff, Warburg, Wassermann? How much poorer would be our democracy without Brandeis and Cardozo; our philosophy without Spinoza and Bergson; our music without Mendelssohn, Rubinstein, Koussevitsky, Kreisler, Heifetz, to say nothing of Romberg, Kern, Gershwin, and Irving Berlin; our literature without Sholem Asch, Franz Werfel and Stefan Zweig. These names have all become part of what we call "Christian civilization." Because of these and so many more, our lives are richer and happier. In return, what have we given? The worst of us have given the concentration camp, the crematorium. The mildest of us have given restrictive covenants, and quotas, and select clientele, and "Christians Only," and all the rest of the petty meannesses of respectable anti-Semitism. It is time for us to discipline our tongues so that they do not wound with careless words; to discipline our acts so that they do not any longer contribute to the division of the human family into favored and inferior races. In short, we must become Christian, for we can destroy anti-Semitism if we will. Sigmund Livingston, a Jew who certainly has no reason to be optimistic, writes: "One hundred leaders of progressive thought in America, properly organized and backed by the churches and the newspapers, could destroy this monster and render a lasting service to our country and to humanity at large."

On the cultural and educational level we can do much in schools and churches to emphasize the widely varied sources of our civilization and the contributions which have been made by groups like the Jews, the Negroes, the Latin Americans, and so on. It is this variety which gives our civilization its wonderful richness and breadth, and no child should be able to graduate from any school without having gained some appreciation of its importance.

Once we have begun to meet this problem personally and seriously, our society will throb with new life and returning health. For these poisonous racial prejudices, hatreds, and fears are no part of the Christian faith or of the American dream.

I wish we could say to our Jewish neighbours in simple humility: "We Christians are coming to our senses. The old lies and myths are dead and we will neither resurrect them nor live by them again. Forgive us. Help us to make amends for all the old injustices and join with us as brothers in the building of the world we both believe in, and at our best have always longed to see, a world where men walk together without fear, in simple equality, in freedom, and in peace."

Can these things be? Have we the honesty, the humility, the courage, the love to bring them about? That is the Christian problem.

FOR WHOM THE BELL TOLLS . . .

THE REVEREND FRED E. LUCHS
Presbyterian Church, Athens, Ohio

MANY MONTHS AGO, in a popular American weekly, a well-known American humorist bequeathed us this valedictory: "I'm proud that I never set myself up to be my brother's keeper, having been sufficiently occupied by the job of being my own keeper." On first reading many of us said "Amen," but as we thought about it, the thinness of the statement stood out boldly. Your lodge never made that statement. Your service organizations and Women's Federated Clubs never said that. Your fraternity and your sorority never said that they were proud not to be their brother's keeper. Your best community minds never said that. Your boy fighting in the mud of Luzon or the snows of France, seeing a buddy in distress, never said that.

Her mistress tried to stir the ambition of Eliza by telling her she might get herself elected to a position in the Tents of the Sons and Daughters of I Will Arise, if she would only move around with more energy. But honor and acclaim held no lure for Aunt Eliza. "Law, honey," she replied lackadaisically, "I don't want to be no queen mother of nothin'! All I wants is to be a bencher that ain't got no compelments." What a philosophy —to sit on the bench and never be compelled by the great urgencies, never to have a troubled conscience about the countless problems gnawing at the pillars of America! How comfortable to have a duck's-back conscience! That varies but little from the philosophy of the valedictory written by that noted American.

Over against this idea that a man is proud never to set himself up as his brother's keeper is the brotherhood principle implied in the fourth chapter of Genesis. "And the Lord said unto Cain, 'Where is Abel, thy brother?' And he said, 'I know not; am I my brother's keeper?' " It is a turbulent question which troubles the mind of John Doe. The conflict is as ancient as civilization and as recent as your last breath. As Christians, we believe that man is his brother's keeper.

Look at the life and teaching of Jesus. Jesus believed he was his brother's keeper. Listen to him speaking: "The spirit of the Lord is upon me because he hath anointed me to preach the gospel to the poor; he hath sent me to heal the broken-hearted, to preach deliverance to the captives, and recovering of sight to the blind, to set at liberty them that are bruised." Not only his life, but his teachings, carry through this brotherhood philosophy. In this conflict between the "bencher" and the brotherhood philosophy, the Bible gives us no middle ground, no inter-weaving shades of gray. There is the book pulsing with the theme in black and white that man is his brother's keeper.

In the second place, we believe in the brotherhood philosophy because it speeds social progress. See what women have done. Look into the world of science. By this time tomorrow five hundred people will have died of cancer in the United States. Out in Chicago, on the great campus of Chicago University, Maud Slye works with mice. What is the relationship? Maud Slye is experimenting with mice, and thus, slowly, gradually, with snail-like pace, she is creeping up on the answer to the riddle of cancer. No zealot ever led a more consecrated life than does this woman dedicated to a single purpose—to rid mankind of the curse of cancer. Why? Because of this persistent, gnawing feeling that she is her brother's keeper.

Women go to the polls—a privilege which was bitterly fought for by women like Emmeline Pankhurst, who underwent ostracism, disgrace, maulings, and beatings, because she believed that women had the right to vote.

In 1801, a slim twenty-five-year-old youth wandered into Licking County, Ohio, leading a pack horse loaded down with appleseed gathered from cider mills in Pennsylvania. Had the young man gone mad? No. Along the Licking Creek, where the sun is bright and the soil is rich, he planted the apple-seeds. For forty-seven years, until he died at the age of seventy-two, Johnny Appleseed, that is John Chapman, journeyed back to Pennsylvania each year from the midwest for apple-seed, which he planted that we today might reap the result. Johnny Appleseed might have stayed in Pennsylvania, a good, honest, hard-working farmer, taking pride in the fact that he never poked his nose into other people's business, but Ohio today would be poorer.

How have we made our advancements in public school education? By men minding their own business? No. But by a host of educational leaders sacrificing that children might enjoy the privilege of reading and writing. Those men believed that they were their brothers' keepers. Look at one of those fighters for education, Horace Mann. At the age of thirty-nine, he about-faced on a very successful law career in Boston, locked his office door, and as he crossed his Rubicon, made the famous statement, "The next generation is my client." But, as happens in the history of all great social movements, the efforts of Horace Mann were opposed. Allied against him were the religious press, the Tories, the school-masters. Besides these enemies, his health, his poverty, and his wife's death fought against him. He did not live to see many fruits of his efforts that modern education still reaps from his labors. Why are we his debtors? Because he passed on to his pupils those famous words, "Be ashamed to die until you have achieved some victory for humanity." Almost every person here is indebted to Horace Mann, who did *not* say, "I'm proud that I never set myself up to be my brother's keeper."

Look back through the history of social progress. Almost every privilege we hold in our hands we enjoy because our forefathers believed in being brothers' keepers. In our town, if we ever expect to get that recreation center, that ideal scout program, that week-day religious school, that new student union, it will never come from those who smugly mutter, "I'm proud that I never set myself up to be my brother's keeper." It will come from the hard work, the sufferings, and the prayers of men and women and youth who think it is still true that "I am my brother's keeper."

When mountain climbers reach a shelter on their way upward, they find food and dry wood. How did it get there? It was left by some party before them who had provisions to spare. Then before they continue their upward journey, they, too, gather wood and leave it to dry for someone else. And on their descent, if they have more food than they will use, they leave it in a shelter where it may save the lives of some party lost in the snow.

What works in mountain climbing works in life. Life is like mountain climbing. This need to help one another is almost as old as the written record of mankind. In the poetry of ancient Persia, these lines are found:

> "Vex no man's secret soul—if that can be—
> The path of life hath far too many a thorn;
> Help whom thou may'st—for surely unto thee
> Sharp need of help will ere the end be borne."

If you allow the fires of brotherhood to die, you, too, will be frozen.

Germany allowed freedom to slip through its fingers when the various social and religious groups refused to stand against the persecution of the Jews. When our Jewish brethren were persecuted, the Protestants, the Catholics, the Socialists, the liberals were silent. Some may have cheered. Hitler later attacked these silent parties, but he settled with them one at a time. All minority groups lost when the Jews lost. Intolerance travels like an epidemic. Snub a Jew today and you open the doors of snobbery toward others. Discriminate against an American whose parents were born in the Orient and you let loose an intolerance which may eventually affect you. All of us may, in some way, belong to a minority group. If we start persecuting other minority groups, our minority group will finally come under the guillotine. Brother Americans, don't let any of the pillars of democracy totter. If we remove those pillars one by one, the house falls, not only on minority groups and oppressed peoples, but upon ourselves.

You receive the benefits of pasteurized milk, chemically treated drinking water, health service, police protection, educational progress, free speech. All these you will receive because someone said long ago, in spirit: "I must be my brother's keeper so that the people of this town may have these privileges."

Ernest Hemingway's title, *For Whom the Bell Tolls,* comes from the pen of that great religious poet of the early seventeenth century, John Donne. The poet had been thinking of the custom of ringing the church bells on the occasion of the death of a native. Often people came running to find out who had died, to discover for whom the bell was tolling. The minister's answer is one of the finest passages in literature: "No man is an island, entire of itself; every man is a piece of a continent, a part of the mainland; . . . any man's death diminishes me, because I am involved in mankind; and, therefore, never send to know for whom the bell tolls; it tolls for thee."

Whenever you hear the bell toll for the death of justice, brotherhood, religion, tolerance, and democracy, never send to know for whom the bell tolls; it tolls for thee.

3. The Narrow Path

NO TWO WAYS . . .

THE REVEREND LOWELL R. DITZEN
First Presbyterian Church, Utica, New York

ONE OF THE MOST DRAMATIC INCIDENTS in the Old Testament tells of a contest on Mt. Carmel.

There were two forces bidding for the allegiance of a third force on that verdant rise in eastern Palestine, known as Carmel, "the garden of God." One force was the lone prophet of God named Elijah. The meeting on Carmel came about through a proclamation of King Ahab in response to Elijah's challenge for a more righteous character in the nation. Elijah stood alone—representing moral purity, national faith, religious freedom, simplicity, the access of man to God.

Four hundred and fifty priests of Baal composed the second force. The Baal leaders represented fanaticism, cruel and degrading worship, immorality, a despotic and crafty priesthood.

The third element was the people of Israel. They had ignored the laws and commands of Jehovah. They had become worshippers of Baal. The people had found it hard to follow the idealism, the perfectionism, the spirituality of Mosaic religion. They could understand and enjoy the pompous ceremonies, the sensuous worship of this deity.

Elijah tore aside all that was superfluous with his explosive

question, "How long go you tottering between two opinions? If
Jehovah be God, follow him; but if Baal, then follow him." The
question cut like a sword through the flabby compromises of the
people. You can't be loyal to the light of God and the dark desires of man all at the same time. So Elijah spoke, "and the
people answered him not a word."

Were they silent because they were remembering? Were the
great verses of the Torah filtering back through the gates of
memory to shame their actions and stun their speech? "And the
people answered him not a word."

Perhaps they thought they were getting by with their spiritual
inconsistency and moral mediocrity. But Elijah pulled them up
short. "How long go ye tottering between two opinions?" "And
the people answered him not a word."

Carry the strength and clarity of that text from the past to the
present. Let it speak to us on the matter of racial attitudes here
in America. For the issue is as decisive for us today on this score,
as it was for the people of Israel centuries ago on the score of
spiritual delinquency. "Why go ye tottering between the two
sides?"

If the Bible's oft-repeated word that men are one, destined for
a brotherhood of man—if that is God's word, then follow it. If
all men are human beings, children of God, they should be protected, supported, and nurtured as such.

But if Hitler was right that the Jews and the Poles and others
are inferior, then be consistent. Follow that pagan doctrine. Believe it. Practice it. If the all too prevalent thought in too many
Americans that the Negroes or the Asiatics or any new group of
immigrants are somehow a lower order in creation—if that is
right, then follow it. Laugh at them. Sneer at them. But why
stop here? Go further; annoy them, thwart them, exploit them,
torture them, segregate them. And why stop there? Why not kill
them? Be consistent! Stop limping! Why not exterminate them
once and for all? Why not ship all the so-called "undesirable"
or "inferior" peoples (if we could just determine who they were)
to the deserts of Africa? Put them all in a concentration camp
and drop a few bombs on them. At last the nasty problem of the
"undesirables" would be over. Think and act consistently! "If
Baal—then follow him. Stop limping between two sides."

There it is. We can't hold both ideas. The one denies the
other. To say "I believe in honesty," and then to slyly cheat and
defraud, creates an apostasy that chills one into silence. Such a

man is both traitor and coward. To profess allegiance to one
conception, and then engage in acts that deny that allegiance is
indefensible.

We need not dwell long on the facts that support the Christian
contention that mankind is one family. We know them well.
Check them off in quick reminder.

1. Man is the same physiologically. A drop of human plasma
has the same chemical constituency whether it comes from a red,
white, yellow or black man. St. Paul's testimony is verified by
our clinics: we are of one blood.

2. Man is the same psychologically. Shylock and modern stud-
ies of the mind say the same thing of any man: "Hath (he) not
senses, affections, passions? If you tickle him, does he not laugh?
If you poison him, does he not die? And if you wrong him, shall
he not revenge?"

3. There is no superior race. In any pantheon of those who
have done most for human betterment, there will be individuals
representing every race and nation of the world. No group holds
a monopoly on genius.

4. Each man is related to mankind. Mathematics tells the un-
answerable story. Each of us has four grandparents, eight great-
grandparents. If we will go back twenty-two generations each of
us will count more than two billion grandparents. Arithmetic
says the human race is your family. It's literally true that our
kith and kin is mankind.

But now come closer to the results of prejudice and intolerance. What happens when Americans profess allegiance to God
but practice the ritual of Baal in human relationships?

For one thing racial prejudice keeps a man from becoming
American, and keeps America from fulfilling her greatness.

Our Declaration of Independence, the Constitution, the Gettys-
burg Address, and other documents that have guided and nurtured our destiny assume that we can live rationally, that our
communal life may give equality of opportunity to all, and that
freedom and fraternity shall be extended justly to every citizen.

Now, when we belittle a man for his color or his creed we join
the fifth column against America's guiding principle. If we
hinder or bar an individual from participating in the political,
economic, or educational life of the nation, we are acting traitor-
ously to the faith that brought America into being. "American"
is synonymous with tolerance, equity, freedom, justice. We can't
go wobbling between the two and be American.

And when we envision the role of America in the drama of history, we surely see a unique opportunity now for her to guide and influence the world. But these are obstacles. Among the major ones is racial bigotry and ill-will.

As a student a dozen years ago, I was shocked when E. Stanley Jones told how every lynching of a Negro, every published incident of restriction or injustice against an Oriental in America was given top billing in newspapers all over the Orient.

That same chagrin was expressed the other day in a letter from a Reformed clergyman in Holland. Our correspondence was devoted to explaining the current attitudes of our respective peoples. He replied to my last letter:

"I am interested in the reasons you give why Americans have antipathy for Russia: the disregard of the individual's place and dignity, the cynical use of large masses of people in slave labor camps; the totalitarian aggressiveness, the unwillingness to be amenable and co-operative in a given project, etc. I cannot help believing that you Americans take too much for granted. The Russian people make just the same accusations against the American people—your race antagonism, your share-cropper system, your class struggle. In Russia *Grapes of Wrath* is widely read."

Oh, Americans, must it not be said of us in the light of such accusations "the people answered not a word?" For while we have paid tribute to the God under whom this nation is established, we have followed the practice of Baal, and we stand condemned as false Americans.

Secondly, see that racial prejudice dams up the streams of culture and understanding that give breadth of comprehension and sympathy. See how bigotry creates a dull, stolid, unimaginative individual or nation.

America is a composite of all nations. This is her strength. May we glory in it! Let us learn from each tradition and race, and so fit ourselves with the breadth of understanding needed for leadership in our international times.

Then observe, too, that to follow Baal, to practice racial intolerance and hatred, is a sign of weakness. It is not the magnanimous man, never a large man who belittles or tortures his fellows. One schoolboy defined the playground bully as "just a mean, little guy, with big muscles." We had better look at ourselves honestly and ask if we may not be just "mean, little guys— a mean little nation—with big muscles," in the eyes of those who suffer through our racial unfairness.

Let us be on guard lest our strength be perverted into our weakness. Recognition of a heritage may become tainted with narrowness and lead to fearfulness, and eventually deteriorate into jealousy over prerogative, fretfulness, viciousness and cruelty toward others. Be on guard lest the acolyte of Baal, known as Conceit, cloak itself with empty pomposity and usurp the throne of real merit and honest worth!

Can we not put the end of the matter simply? It is to say, "I will believe and act like an American."

How long, America, go you tottering between the two sides? If Baal be God, then follow him. But if not, then, for God's sake —for the sake of his broken world, and for the sake of the thwarted, hopeful lives that daily touch yours and mine, *follow him!*

=====◆=====

THEY PREACH BUT DO NOT PRACTICE . . .

THE REVEREND THOMAS F. OPIE
First Methodist Church, Great Barrington, Massachusetts

MILLIONS OF CHRISTIANS still seem to hold that humanity can be saved by "much belief." Many Christian folk appear to think that they have purchased heaven (for the next world, of course) because they believe in a creed or have submitted to some ecclesiastical ceremonial.

Look at preaching and then at practice. By preaching, I mean all the presentation of creedal concepts, of authoritarian priest-craft, of Articles of Faith, etc. By practicing, I mean all that has to do with social relations—public welfare, race and religious tolerance, community service—all that would make for an introduction of such a fine social, political, religious order, here and now, as would bring in the Kingdom of God. By that I mean all that has to do with the good life—with love, with pure and honest living, identification with the community, with the whole family of mankind.

Christianity has all but been preached to death. Words have

all but superseded deeds, relationships, and daily actions. Non-religious organizations now carry on a large part of the works of mercy and well-being which Jesus indicated should be the responsibility of his followers. Look at the Masons, the Odd Fellows, the Knights of Pythias, the Y.M.C.A., the Y.W.C.A., the Boy Scouts, the Knights of Columbus, the Young Men's Hebrew Association. Look where you will, and you will find that the church, as such, has been too largely content to preach, and has left practice to others.

This preaching has resulted in the division of Jesus' followers into almost three hundred competing camps while individuals and groups and organizations not essentially religious have too often had to look elsewhere for hands and lives that would lift the level of living and make for better human relations. Preaching has put Luther against Wesley, Roger Williams against George Fox, Pope against Protestant. It has too often proved a divisive and disrupting influence. It has driven brother and sister from the family. It has left the atheist and the agnostic no grounds on which to stand—placing such great souls as Voltaire, Ingersoll, Tom Paine, Clarence Darrow, John Dewey, Bertrand Russell, beyond the pale.

Why do preachers overlook the teaching of Jesus in his parable of the Last Judgment? By that parable everybody is judged, not in some far-off Christian court, but every day of his life, whether he be black or white, Roman Catholic or Protestant; Episcopal, Methodist, Presbyterian, Baptist—everybody is judged by his identity with the human brotherhood, by his ministering to the total good, by his contribution in character, service, and means.

Jesus in his parable did not say, "Enter into the joy of thy Lord," because you accepted a creed, castigated the Jews, isolated yourself from the Negro; nor because you had a bishop lay his hands on your head, or confessed your sins to a clergyman; or because you believed in a Presbyterian or a Congregationalist God. He did not say all is well with the soul and body of a man because he set himself up as better, holier, more correct in doctrine than others, or was in conflict with other sects, races, or nations.

Harold E. Stassen has said, "Anyone who kindles the fires of intolerance and hate is building a fire under his own house." He was right. I believe that this matter of bad preaching has kindled more fires of intolerance and of hate, than has anything else in history. Men, women and little children who during every week-day associate in business or pleasure, separate on Sunday. In the name of Christ, each goes to his own sectarian church merely because those churches have been separated by some thin hair of ecclesiastical or theological divergence.

This procedure, as was indicated by Mr. Stassen, keeps burning the flames of hate and intolerance under one's own house.

It is certain that Jesus made the test of fellowship with him a social test—a test of doing, more than of believing or preaching. He identified himself with humanity—"Inasmuch as you did it unto one of these, even one of the least, you did it unto me." (Maybe a needy Jew, maybe a brother Catholic, maybe a lowly Negro, maybe a "heretic," a "pagan," a "heathen"—all within the brotherhood.) And, please note that Jesus makes this practice, this ministering to others, this lack of hate and intolerance, the test of fitness to "go up higher." That is to say, he placed religion's emphasis on practicing brotherhood, not on creed or belief. Note that the "fitness" to go up higher was wrought out of the fires of practicing love, out of the hard experience of sharing what we are and what we have, with others, with any and all others. This was not in the nature of a reward. The development for higher living comes by way of social services. The individual wins his spurs by getting into the battle of life and standing to lose all that he has, in a throw for the common good. That is the test of Jesus. "They practiced—they did not preach."

We have an organization called the United Nations. It has a true religious basis. What shall Christians and other religious people do in regard to this statement in the United Nations preamble? "We, the peoples of the United Nations, determined . . . to reaffirm faith in fundamental human rights, in the dignity and worth of the human person, in the equal rights of men and women, to promote social progress and better standards of life in larger freedom, to practice tolerance and live together in peace with one another as good neighbors, to promote international machinery for the promotion of the economic and social advancement of all peoples . . . have resolved to combine our efforts to accomplish these ends." If I were a pacifist, for example, and believed really in practicing Christian pacifism and good-will, I would make much of a grand assertion of that sort—and I would print millions of copies of that short human document and give them the wings of the morning, to carry them to the ends of the earth. This I would do—practice, rather than preach about and despise the courageous acts of brave men who made this document possible and saved for humanity, at the risk of life and all, the noble things about which the pacifist dreams.

In an address before the Congress, January 6, 1942, the late Franklin D. Roosevelt, spoke this way: "We . . . are not making all this sacrifice to return to the kind of world we had. We are fighting for security . . . progress . . . peace . . . for all men, for all generations. We are fighting to uphold the doctrine that all men are equal in the sight of God. Only total victory can reward the champions of tolerance and decency and freedom and peace." What Christians, Hindus, Jews, Moslems, Catholics, and Protestants would not combine in this way to save humanity from slavery and from savagery? Is it too great a goal to set before you and me and those of all races and creeds—this goal of lifting humanity to the high planes of practicing peace—to establish the Kingdom of God on this earth?

Two doctors were being introduced. "What kind of a doctor are you?" asked one of the other. "Oh, I practice; I don't preach!" was the reply. There is more religion in the Golden Rule than in all the creeds and confessions. There is more religion in Micah's "Do justly, love mercy, walk humbly," than in all the rites and rituals of a thousand pious priests at the altar.

Religion must get outside the four walls of preaching and genuflection, out in the marts and in business, in politics, in every social relation, else we shall never bring the Reign of God into the affairs of men. If worship of Divinity does not inspire service to humanity, it is certainly not the Way of Life that Jesus exemplified.

Following up the story of the Good Samaritan, who did a kindly act for a needy brother, Jesus commanded, "Go and *do* thou likewise." He did not say, "Go and think likewise"—but "Go and *do!*" If what one preaches, what one believes does not impel him to do something to better a bad social order, I care not what ancient religion he holds to nor how completely he accepts a creedal formula; he can hardly expect the approval of God.

As someone once said: "I love you not only for what you are, but what I am when I am with you. I love you not only for what you are making of yourself, but for what you are helping to make of me. I love you for helping me to make of the lumber of my life not a tavern but a temple. I love you because you have done more than any creed to make me happy. You have done it by just being yourself. Perhaps, after all, that is what Love means."

BANKRUPT PROVINCIALISM . . .

The Reverend Leslie J. Tuck
Congregational Church, Belmond, Iowa

THERE ARE TWO KINDS OF PROVINCIALISM that have always been common among the peoples of the world.

One of these is the kind that sees little good in the immediate environment. There are some who feel that no people are quite so disagreeable, none so hard to get along with as those close to home. This sort of attitude may have a very limited usefulness, a certain "nuisance" value, in helping to prevent smugness and self-content.

But it is the other sort to which I want to call your attention this morning. It is the kind of provincialism that sees nothing good away from home. It is likely to be seen in people who live in large or important cities. A lady in Boston once said, in the hearing of your minister, that she would rather live on one cobblestone in Boston than in a palace anywhere else on earth. But it appears also in small communities. It is promoted, in a small way, by our schools and colleges, in fostering athletic rivalry. It appears in sororities, and fraternities, and lodges. It seeks to build prestige by belittling the accomplishments of others. It is sometimes promoted by certain business interests for selfish purposes: buy only what is produced at home, or within the state. It is demonstrated in a false patriotism that enlarges on our own greatness by ridicule, or by belittling the life and achievements of other people; by a refusal to recognize the accomplishments of different peoples. There is an arrogance that assumes a superiority on account of a national name or the color of one's skin.

This particular sort was exaggerated in Jesus' day. His own people were in many ways more advanced than surrounding peoples. Particularly in the field of religion they had achieved far beyond any early people. Their leaders were often inspired; their institutions of religion were sometimes grand and impressive. But many had become self-righteous to the point of self-satisfaction. Their leaders were sometimes proud, even arrogant. They were God's "chosen." Their city was alone the "holy city." In an earlier day there had been but two classifications of people

—Greeks and barbarians; now there were but two others: Jews and Gentiles.

Nathaniel was from Cana, in Galilee; Jesus was from Nazareth. When Philip told Nathaniel about Jesus and about his coming from such a mean city, the rather spontaneous reply of Nathaniel was, "Can any good thing come out of Nazareth?" And this question required no answer: it was an expression of disdain and arrogance.

What has all this to do with us, in this nation and in the modern world? It seems to this minister, it has a good deal to do with America and with the world of our day.

Part of the reason why the world has come to its present pass is to be found in the persistence of this sort of provincialism.

There are those who say that the chief cause of friction between peoples is economic rivalry, the struggle for existence. No one doubts that that sort of strife has been common in the history of many upon the earth. But everywhere in the world in our day the life of man is marred by an exaggerated "group consciousness." The early clash between clan and clan and tribe and tribe has been succeeded by strife between nations. Races are sometimes in open conflict with each other, in America and in the world.

It so happens that this minister was born in Australia. From his earliest years he was confronted with the accepted Australian motto or slogan of "white Australia." It was, and apparently still is, the intention of those good people to keep their continent, comparable in size and natural resources to our own United States, as a white man's paradise. One result is that the population of only seven and a half million is largely concentrated in the southeastern part. The resources remain largely undeveloped, and the people have lived in constant fear of invasion from the massed population of the yellow and black-skinned people of the north. The slogan has confirmed in the hearts of the people the myth of white supremacy.

Does anyone imagine the situation is much different in these United States? Perhaps you know something of the discrimination practiced against our Negro citizens in the armed services during the recent war. It was my experience to serve for a short while as a chaplain in the army during that conflict. I was frequently both embarrassed and ashamed at the treatment accorded Negro soldiers by white, civilian bus drivers. Even if seats were available at the front of the bus, Negroes were often ordered to the rear, even if it meant standing up, in unbearable heat. On one occasion, a two-day gathering was arranged by the National Conference of Christians and Jews, for the purpose of promoting racial and religious understanding among the men of the camp. The high point of the meeting was a banquet of the post chaplains and their wives, honoring the visiting speakers, and having the post commander and other high ranking dignitaries as special guests. It was again with shame and humiliation that I learned the rather simple explanation of the absence of two Negro chaplains and their wives from the banquet—they simply were not invited. And when I wrote a letter to a leading religious weekly, protesting the hypocrisy of holding a conference for the promotion of racial and religious understanding and at the same time excluding intelligent and educated brother ministers on account of their color, I was taken to task, in the name of the Commanding Officer by the Service Command Chaplain, himself a long-time Protestant minister.

For a number of years we have been suffering from an exaggerated nationalism. A famous British religious leader has called nationalism "man's other religion." Our own William Lyon Phelps has remarked with what pride and readiness we send our sons and our daughters off to serve the Caesar of national self-interest, and what reluctance we show in sending them out to serve the Christ in other lands.

Therefore; responsibility is laid upon us who would be Christian to lead the way in breaking up, or breaking down, this sort of provincialism. Jesus saw his own people going the sure way to their own destruction because of its persistence. He heaped scorn on the scribes and pharisees who promoted it. He found in the Syrophoenician woman and in the Roman centurion greater faith than he found in the Israel of his day. He illustrated the true spirit of neighborliness by the famous parable about the "Good Samaritan," and Samaritans were regarded by many of his own people as less than the dogs of the street.

Every one knows the story of the cleansing of the temple. But there is a point to the happening that is almost never mentioned and probably never understood or appreciated. The religion of Israel was a *world religion*. God's rule was known to be universal; *all* men everywhere were his children, therefore, all were supposedly free to worship in his temple. But in recognition of the favored position of the "chosen people," there was a separate Court of the Gentiles. Under these circumstances few gentiles were ever found worshipping in this segregated spot. It was probably this "Court of the Gentiles" that the money changers and sellers of birds and animals had taken over as the scene of their transactions. With shame and humiliation on account of the trickery and the dishonesty, but also with anger over the hypocrisy, the narrow-mindedness, and the callousness of those who practiced this desecration of the temple, the Master cried out: "It is written, 'My house shall be called a house of prayer *for all the nations,* but ye have made it a den of thieves.' "

In the modern world, we have plenty of opportunity to know the folly and the stupidity of this sort of provincialism. We have an acquaintance with the other peoples of the world that has been possible to no other people in history. Madame Chiang has been called the "first lady of the world," because of her charm, her character, and her graciousness. The Negro, George Washington Carver is recognized as one of the foremost scientists in the world; he was also a philosopher and a Christian gentleman. Marian Anderson is a gracious lady, an artist in the truest sense, as well as the possessor of a voice that occurs "once in a hundred years." Albert Schweitzer, the German, is a man of brilliant attainments in the field of New Testament scholarship and organ music, as well as a lowly servant of the Christ and the people of Africa. Kagawa, the Japanese, has been called one of the significant Christian personalities of our time.

There are certain excellent words that have suffered from misuse or overuse. They have sometimes been misinterpreted and often misapplied. One of these is the fine Christian word, conversion. It has usually been associated with emotionalism, or the practice of mass psychology, or a questionable revivalism. But the word in reality calls for a change of mind, and a change of heart—a change in the course or direction. There must be a change of attitude and a change of behavior. In this sense the world of our day, and particularly the so-called Christian world, needs a conversion. Can any good thing come out of Nazareth? Or out of Germany? Or Japan? Or out of Africa? Or, out of Russia? From among our own Negro citizens? Let us look for it, and have "eyes to see" when it appears! Let us encourage it, cultivate it, enlarge on it, share in it. And let us know that in the sight of God all men are of equal value; each has a worthy contribution to make to the ongoing of our civilization and to the cause of humanity upon the earth. We are all together members of the family of man, the family of the Father, God.

4. Brotherhood Affirmed

BROTHERHOOD WEEK . . .

THE HONORABLE WILLIAM O'DWYER, *Mayor of New York*
JUSTICE MEIER STEINBRINK, *Supreme Court of New York*
THE REVEREND THOMAS PARRY JONES, *First Methodist Church,
Sheboygan, Wisconsin*

MAYOR WILLIAM O'DWYER: New York is our town. It's a big town—a lively town—a *great* town! But what makes it great?

Is it the Empire State building? Coney Island? Broadway? Is it the fact that we have the busiest port, the greatest textile industry, the largest publishing center in the world?

Not at all. Magnificent though they may be, these are only miniature reflections of our real greatness. They are the results, not the causes. Our town is a great town because its people are great. Each New Yorker has a measure of greatness in his own right, a greatness that is nurtured by his own individuality, fostered by his own freedom of conscience, and illuminated by his comradeship with all men of good will. Multiply him by eight million neighbors—eight million people who are brothers in the sight of God—and there you have it: the spirit, the glory, the fraternity among men that have made our town a great town.

69

It is men—all kinds of men, from many racial stocks and beholden to many faiths and creeds, and living, by common consent, the tenets of the golden rule—who have made New York not only a center of cultural scientific, economic, and civic progress, but, more significantly, they have made our town a monument, a living, breathing tableau of democracy in action. And that is as it should be—in the greatest town on earth.

Today, on the advent of Brotherhood Week, I join with New Yorkers and with Americans throughout the nation in hailing this year's slogan: "Brotherhood is a pattern for peace." I am very glad to share in this Sermon-of-the-Week broadcast with these good men here today. I believe it will do much to foster goodwill and better understanding among all peoples.

This is the week in which the people of our town will re-dedicate themselves to a principle of lasting brotherhood among men that will resolve our actions not just for this week but for fifty-two weeks of *every* year. There are disruptive and selfish forces who seek a cleavage among us by stirring up conflicts between labor and management, whites and Negroes, native and foreign-born, gentiles and Jews, Protestants and Catholics—that can only result in crumbling our town into the dust. We must never let that happen! But preaching and speech-making are not enough. We must demonstrate in our everyday activities that we offer more than lip service to the loftiest of all American traditions—the God-given fact that all men are created equal.

There is deep significance in the fact that the Statue of Liberty stands in the harbor of our town. For more than a century New York has symbolized a town of brotherhood. Because of that, it has grown and prospered. Our town will continue to grow and prosper so long as all New Yorkers observe that spirit of brotherhood.

JUDGE MEIER STEINBRINK: During the war an anonymous sage made this pointed statement: "It makes no difference whether your ancestors arrived here on the Mayflower or came by steerage: we are all in the same boat now."

That remark is even more pertinent today, for if the shooting is over the peace is far from won.

This new era of civilization that has burst upon us—this age of atomic and supersonic science—has shrunk our world and has

placed humanity at a perilous crossroad. There are two paths
that we must choose from, and each path leads us to a destination
that is diametrically opposed to the other.

Either we rush pellmell downhill on a road paved with ignorance, misunderstanding, and mistrust of one another and find
ourselves deep in a quagmire of conflict and hate that must
destroy us all; or we climb uphill, moving more slowly perhaps,
but sure-footed in the knowledge that we are guided by sign-
posts of faith, understanding, and brotherhood amongst us. This
is the road that leads us to our rightful destiny of a world of free
men, living and laboring in peace and harmony for the greater
glory of all.

The unity among men of goodwill that so dramatically mani-
fested itself in winning a great war must be preserved, and
furthered if we are to win a great peace. On this day that
inaugurates two distinguished observances, National Brotherhood
Week and Bill of Rights Week, let us examine our consciences
and determine if we are, individually, maintaining the heritage
left us by the founding fathers of this great nation. Are we
clear in our understanding that the right of "life, liberty, and
the pursuit of happiness" bears with it the responsibility of
upholding the spirit of brotherhood, which is the basic foundation of our American democracy?

We must be ever alert to crumble false barriers of race and
religion that are created by the evil schemers to divide and
conquer us. We must not only be understanding of one another,
but we must be conscious and grateful of the benefits to our
culture and to our society that we, as individuals, reap from the
unity of brotherhood. When the hatemonger attacks the Catholic, it is not the Catholic alone who is concerned. We are all
in peril. We must recognize that liberty is indivisible.

I hesitate to use the word tolerance this morning. It is a faulty
word. It is not enough that we tolerate one another. To do so
would be to negate God's own commandment that "thou shalt
love thy neighbor as thyself." Our expressions of brotherhood
must be forceful, both in our words and in our deeds.

I commend this program, The Sermon of the Week, as a
praiseworthy example of brotherhood in action . . . of the goodwill among men of all faiths and creeds that is so desperately
needed if we are to travel the right road. Here in America, if

we are to go forward without scuttling the ship of state on which we sail together, it must be in a spirit of fraternity, brotherhood, and co-operation.

THE REV. THOMAS PARRY JONES: Katherine Lee Bates has given to America its most beloved patriotic hymn, and the words of the first stanza should be written on every American heart:

> O beautiful for spacious skies,
> For amber waves of grain,
> For purple mountain majesties
> Above the fruited plain!
> America! America! God shed His grace on Thee
> And crown thy good with Brotherhood
> From sea to shining sea.

No provincialism here—no cheap sentimentalism, or evil gloating. Written in the nineteenth century, it shows the way out of the twentieth century problems.

America's heart is good.

Last May, Robert Johnston, Jr., an eighteen-year-old lad of Downingtown, Pennsylvania, was killed in action fighting the Japanese. On January ninth of this year his parents announced that his $10,000 insurance was to be given to a college to be used as scholarships for Japanese students. Americans are like that. And that is not an isolated case.

The husband of a young woman was a major in the United States Army. One day the news reached her that he had died in a Japanese prison camp. The word circulated rapidly through the community, especially among the members of the Cosmopolitan Club to which she belonged. One member was a Japanese. Some of the saddened woman's friends discussed telephoning the Japanese woman, suggesting that she not attend the meeting of the club scheduled for the next day. The young woman had a better idea. She drove her car to the home of the Japanese woman and took her to the meeting. Jesus might have described this as a twentieth century illustration of the golden rule.

And then there is another American mother who is sending the monthly allotment of her soldier son, killed by Japanese, to Japan, saying, "I want it to be used to educate some Japanese boy to become a Christian minister."

Americans are good—but even our goodness is not enough, says

Katherine Lee Bates. It must be crowned with brotherhood from sea to shining sea. Where shall we start? Is there any more obvious place to start than in our own community? We are Christians and Jews. It would not be sporting to ignore that issue for the less obvious problem of Negroes and whites, since there are few Negroes in this community.

As Christians we have no choice—we are enjoined to love one another. We have the example of Jesus who scorned bigotry and intolerance, and whose immortal story of the good Samaritan makes every person our neighbor to whom we must do good. This picture of God is of one . . .

> Who will not ask thy race
> Nor will He ask thy birth:
> Alone He will demand of thee
> What hast thou done on earth?

At its least objectionable level anti-Semitism is un-American; at its highest level it is anti-Christian. George Washington, in a letter to the Hebrew congregation in Newport, Rhode Island, 1790 wrote: "The citizens of the United States of America have a right to applaud themselves for having given to mankind examples of an enlarged and liberal policy: a policy worthy of imitation. . . . It is now no more that toleration is spoken of as if it were by the indulgence of one class of people that another enjoyed the exercise of their inherent natural rights, for happily, the government of the United States, which gives to bigotry no sanction, to persecution no assistance, requires only that they who live under its protection should demean themselves as good citizens in giving it on all occasions their effectual support. . . ."

And Abraham Lincoln in a speech in Illinois in 1858: "What constitutes the bulwark of our own liberty and independence? It is not our frowning battlements, our bristling sea coasts, our army and our navy. These are not our reliance against tyranny. . . . Our reliance is in the love of liberty which God has planted in us. Our defense is in the spirit which prized liberty as the heritage of all men in all lands everywhere. Destroy this spirit and you have planted the seeds of despotism at your own doors . . . accustomed to trample on the rights of others, you have lost the genius of your own independence, and become the fit subjects of the first cunning tyrant who rises among you.

"Let us discard all this quibbling about this man and the other

man, this race and that race and the other race being inferior,
and therefore, to be placed in an inferior position. Let us discard
all these things, and unite as one people throughout this land
until we shall once more stand up declaring that all men are
created equal."

Anti-Semitism is anti-Christian. Both the Old and New Testaments came from the hands of Jews. Jesus, our Lord, was a Jew
and if it were not for the Jews we would have no Bible.
He who thoughtlessly or deliberately depreciates the personality
of another is acting contrary to the spirit and teaching of
Christianity.

This opening day of Brotherhood Week is a good time for
changed behavior, that we may be worthy of the name Christian
or Jew, and thus crown our good with brotherhood.

═══◆═══

WE ARE HIS CHILDREN . . .

THE REVEREND MATTHEW C. CAVELL
First Presbyterian Church, Evansville, Indiana

> If any man says, "I love God," and hates his brother, he
> is a liar; for he who does not love his brother whom he
> has seen, cannot love God, whom he has not seen. And
> this command we have from Him, that he who loves God
> should love his brother also. I JOHN 4:20-21

IN HIS ACT OF CREATION God invested matter with splendor when
he made man in his own image, and *informed* him with a living
soul.

Thus there is an affinity between God and man such as does
not exist between the Creator and any other of his creatures.

But this splendor with which man was crowned was early imprisoned behind walls of disobedience and wilfulness. Endowed
with freedom, man chose to exploit this God-given privilege to

express an arrogant defiance which added more prison walls around the splendor God had breathed into his being. Robert Browning gives a good description of what happened to man who was created in the image of God:

> "There is an inmost center in us all
> Where truth abides in fulness; and around
> Wall upon wall, the gross flesh hems it in,
> This perfect, clear perception—which is truth;
> A baffling and perverting carnal mesh
> Binds it, and makes all error: and to *know*
> Rather consists in opening out a way
> Whence the imprisoned splendor may escape."

What is this "clear perception," which will bring release to man's imprisoned splendor? Paul, with his keen insight, supplied an answer in his letter to the Romans: "We know that the whole creation has been groaning in travail . . . and . . . we groan inwardly as we wait for adoption as sons. . . ."

This is a graphic description of our plight—the whole creation groans as with birth-pangs to bring forth a more glorious day. Why is the emergence of this day so long delayed? To put it briefly and bluntly, our arrogance has stifled our filial relationship to God and thus that which is uniquely distinctive of man is imprisoned behind walls of his own making.

The release of man's inner splendor is awaiting a greater groaning of the mind than the majority of people are either prepared or willing to undergo. Mental perspiration is as essential to the achievement of man's distinctive splendor as plowing is to the preparation of a field for sowing.

As a man thinketh in his heart, so he is. What thoughts do we nurture? Where does the trickle of ideas lead us? Is it finding its way beneath the underbrush of thought-choking slogans in which business Hitler was the most recent past master? His diseased brain spawned the monstrosity known as Nazism. Nazism was never a philosophy. From its inception it was a deadly virus —against everything: anti-Semitic, anti-Christianity, anti-Slavic, anti-Negro, and anti-civilization. Thank God, a house so bedeviled with antagonisms cannot stand.

On the contrary, sound and positive ideas are like a stream. It is in the very nature of a stream to seek the ocean. This it will do even if it must carve canyons to reach its destiny. Likewise, ideas are basic to all great achievements. Where man has rightly used the function of his mind he has revealed something of the splendor of his being in the contributions of his inventive genius. He has built suspended bridges and skyscrapers; he has put wings to sixty tons of steel and has flown this new Leviathan through space with the ease and grace of an eagle; he has harnessed the ether waves so that his voice is heard instantaneously around the world, and he has brought under control the pestilences which decimated large sections of the population.

But man's most insidious malady, which imprisons his glory, is his failure to emerge with ideas as vital and transforming in the realm of human relations as he has done in the domain of the material. The battle is set and the best defense is a good offense. General Foch once sent this message to Marshal Joffre: "My right has been rolled up; my left has been driven back; my center has been smashed. I have ordered an advance from all directions."

Against all the issues which impede the onward march of brotherhood; all the false ideologies which preach hate, and set man against man, against all the lies about race, we must marshal the reserves of sound ideas which will penetrate the most stubborn resistance.

Furthermore, man's splendor is imprisoned not only by walls of perverted ideas, but also by barriers of an unsound faith.

Edwin Arnold's line, "The way to God is by the road of men," expresses a sentiment which strikes a responsive chord in all who believe in the brotherhood of man and in man's compassion capable of encircling the needs of mankind around the globe. But it does not go far enough. Failure to realize that brotherhood is an empty slogan unless it is infused by the breath of God is our most fatal error.

Brotherhood will continue to be so much gibberish until men recognize the Fatherhood of God. If morality is to make any noticeable difference in men's behavior, it will need to be rooted in a God-centered faith. This is the *first* and great commandment, namely, honor the Lord, thy God, with all thy heart, soul, mind and strength. And the second is "like" the first, but it is so only in relationship to the first—love thy neighbor as thyself.

This is the supreme splendor with which God crowned the family of mankind. It is one family, for there is but one God— "Our Father!" This is the faith which men need desperately to recover today! Then we shall not live behind "iron curtains," nor in fear of the atom bomb. Then it will be truly "One World," which Scripture envisioned twenty centuries before a book, well-known and justly popular, was written about it. The unity of the human race will come by faith, not by fear.

God is awaiting the time when the discords of the races will give way to the harmony which will come when all the notes on the staff of mankind combine to create the symphony of brotherhood.

Sound ideas lead to a sound faith, and the faith which starts in God reaches out in a ministry of reconciliation.

> "Where cross the crowded ways of life
> Where sound the cries of race and clan,
> Above the noise of selfish strife,
> We hear Thy voice, O Son of Man."

The recognition of God, as Father, will make us sensitive to the cries and needs of men. The voice of the Son of Man, who came not to be ministered unto but to minister, will disturb us as long as the tumult of contention and strife abides in our midst. Or, as our text has it, "he who loves God should love his brother also." Unless faith in God drives us to life's crowded highways and to its haunts of wretchedness and need, it becomes an empty creed imprisoning the splendor of brotherhood. The recognition of our kinship to all men is the open road which leads from God to man, and back to God again. This is the road of reconciliation.

Last November, a veteran of the recent war sent a postal card to one of the social agencies in Evansville, Indiana. The card was forwarded to the Interracial Commission of the city because it concerned a colored man. The writer was seeking help to locate a certain Dorphus Murphy. "For your information," the writer said, "he was in the infantry with me during the last international conflict and I would like to ask his forgiveness for an unwarranted wrong he suffered at my hands." While it is not possible to speak with certainty about the man's faith, there is no question about the fact that there was no peace in his soul, that he was conscious of a departed splendor which would not return until he had made peace with one whom he had unjustly injured. It was reconciliation seeking to restore the glory of brotherhood.

In the winter of 1946, the Friends Service Committee sent out an appeal for funds to feed our erstwhile enemy, the Germans, who were starving. Among the many responses there was one from a rabbi. His people had suffered atrocities without parallel in all history at the hands of these same Germans. The letter which accompanied the rabbi's contribution had this to say about the appeal: "I do not wish to delay by a single moment my expression of heartiest approval of your humanitarian appeal. The Nazi monsters have almost exterminated my people not only in Germany but throughout Europe. Their anti-Semitic propaganda has had its repercussions throughout the world. Nevertheless, I still believe in the Fatherhood of God and the brotherhood of men. I still believe that the German children should not suffer for the sins of their misguided fathers. I believe with all my heart that we should rise above the hatreds and prejudices engendered by the war and succor all people who are afflicted and heavy-laden."

The rabbi's faith in God made reconciliation a necessity, and, his readiness to forgive reflected that splendor of faith which makes brotherhood a glowing realization.

Thank God for these glimpses of splendor we catch when man permits the glory God placed within him to shine forth! Said Admiral Nimitz in a communique of March 16, 1946, when enemy resistance on Iwo came to an end: "Among the Americans who served on Iwo Island, uncommon valor was a common virtue." The admiral was reporting on the behavior of all the American soldiers—Negroes, Jews, Roman Catholics, and Protestants; common to all of them was uncommon valor.

In his creation, God breathed into man a living soul whose greatest affinity is with his Maker! The most glorious thing about him, this acme of God's creation, is the recognition of his kinship to all the peoples of the earth. This is his distinctive splendor.

This is God's road opened by the prophets, illuminated by the Christ—the only road to understanding, good will, and a peace that will endure.

THE ROOTS OF THE TREE . . .

THE REVEREND LEE FLETCHER
First Congregational Church, Albany, New York

"Then he showed me the river of the water of life . . .
flowing from the throne of God . . . through the middle
of the street of the city; also, on either side of the river
the tree of life with its twelve kinds of fruit . . . and the
leaves of the trees were for the healing of the nations."

REV. 22: 1, 2.

I AM ASKING A VERY SIMPLE, but, I think, exceedingly important
question today. Most of us possess a belief in a certain set of
values, in what we sometimes call a way of life. From whence
did this set of values, this way of life come? Is it something that
we have thought out for ourselves, the fruit of our own wisdom
of understanding of life? Why do we believe in a free type of
society instead of an authoritarian type, democracy instead of
communism? Here we are living in what we call a free country,
worshiping in a free church, planning our own lives, the bene-
ficiaries of a free democratic civilization. Our question is simply,
from whence does all this come?

The figure of speech used in the text in this highly pictorial
final book of the Bible suggests a clue. It is the figure of growth.
The tree sinks its roots into the earth. Without that rootage
there would be no fruitage. The water, the soil, the sun, and rain
produce the leaves that will be for the healing of the nations.
But it is that life-giving substratum that makes it all possible.
The answer to our question lies in that kind of approach. Our
civilization cannot be explained, nor indeed can it be maintained
apart from the Christian ideals and principles that lie beneath it.
This is the soil that nourishes our way of life. There was a free
church before there was a free state. Before we had a constitution the ideals of this free land were being preached with no
uncertain accent from the leading pulpits of the nation.

Our chief danger, then, would appear to be in this area—that
the source of our idealism might dry up, and so our tree of life
die and its leaves wither. We speak rather glibly of our way of

life. There is no future for our way of life apart from these roots, apart from those basic spiritual principles and ideals that alone can maintain it.

These roots are not hard to discover. One cannot read his New Testament without becoming aware of them.

Take as an example our ideal of the rights of minorities. One of the reasons for entering World War Two was that we were fighting to protect the rights of minorities—fighting to make impossible the kind of wholesale destruction that was visited upon the Jews of Germany, for instance. We were fighting to make it possible for small nations to maintain their own chosen types of government, to make the little peoples of earth as secure in their rights as the people possessing that power. As you will recall, we talked much about the rights of minorities. It was a Christian civilization, coming to grips with a pagan civilization; a philosophy of life that believed in world brotherhood instead of this horrible, ruthless philosophy that rode roughshod over everyone and everything in its path.

The story is familiar enough. And most people responded wholeheartedly to that kind of appeal. Why? Not because it was something we thought out by ourselves. Not because it was the product of our own wisdom. Rather, here was a way of looking at things that rooted deeply, that was a part of the priceless spiritual heritage of the ages.

I suggested a moment ago that all we need to do to discover the roots of these highest, these most hopeful ideals of our civilization, is to read again our New Testaments. This way of looking at things began to take hold of men powerfully after a certain Teacher stood up and told a story. A lawyer had asked him a question: Who is my neighbor? In response to that question Jesus gave us what is probably his most universally known parable, the Parable of the Good Samaritan. That parable challenges us at many points. For one thing, it turns the question the lawyer asked around. "Who is my neighbor?", he asked, but when Jesus had concluded it became clear that that was not the important question. The central question was: "Whose neighbor am I?" This is not merely playing with words. The implications of these two questions are quite different. When a man sits down with his own conscience and asks that, he is asking a pretty searching question. As a child of God, whose neighbor am I? "God has created of one blood all nations of men to dwell on the face of the earth." Where, then, shall I draw the line?

Moreover, note that Jesus' selection of a hero adds even greater scope to the implications of the parable. We have something more here than charity being doled out by a member of a superior race to a member of a minority race. The hero is a member of the minority race. The implication is plain. Here is a spirit that knows no limits of race, of nationality, of custom; that asks no question save one—"How can I be of help?"

So, as we look at this simple parable, we can begin to see some of the roots of our concern for oppressed peoples, underprivileged minorities. It stems from Christian love.

Christians, then, by a kind of logical necessity, must take their stand at this point. It would not be a cause for rejoicing if some prejudiced group in our community were to destroy a Jewish synagogue, a Protestant or Catholic church, or to foment a race riot. No, that would be a breakdown of community and we should all lose. This is not to say, of course, that we should surrender all of our Christian convictions in a lazy kind of easy-going tolerance that uncritically accepts everything. There is nothing in this story to indicate that Jesus accepted all the beliefs of the Good Samaritan. As a matter of fact, the Samaritans had many beliefs that were not accepted by surrounding neighbors. However, this did not prevent the operation of Christian love. So, if we are to have a Christian world, what must we do? We must sink our roots deeply into this spiritual reservoir from which men have drawn their highest inspiration across the centuries. We shall not have a brotherly world where the rights of minorities and majorities are secure if we cut ourselves off from this unfailing source of supply.

Or consider another thing about which we talk a great deal—the right of individuals, the sacredness of human personality. When men are brutalized, dehumanized, made mere cogs in an economic or military machine without any regard for their rights as persons, we cry out in protest. This is not the way men were meant to live. To look upon men in terms of their capacity to help or hinder someone or some groups in the struggle for power seems to us to cheapen human life in a way that is intolerable. That is one of the reasons we so strongly believe in the free type of state as over against the police state. We believe in the rights and the dignity of the individual

But let us ask ourselves once more this same question: From whence does this belief come? Is it the product of our own social conscience, our own superior wisdom? The answer is quite apparent. "How much better is a man than a sheep?" asked Jesus. "And they were bringing children to him that he might touch them; and the disciples rebuked them. But when Jesus saw it he was indignant and said to them: "Let the children come to me and do not hinder them; for to such belongs the kingdom of God." No one ever before had quite seen the worth of a little child. A leper came to him and Jesus reached out his hand and touched him, because he was aware of the humanity of the leper. So he said: "The very hairs of your head are numbered." Every one counts. Publicans, sinners, outcasts—he received them all, and summarized the inner purpose of his ministry in these words: "The Son of Man came to seek and save that which is lost." Every man counted so much in the sight of God that no life was to be allowed to go on the rocks if it could be prevented.

So whenever we decry anything that cheapens or brutalizes life, it means that the Christian spirit within us is rising up and finding expression in our own attitudes, our own moral and spiritual ideals. This is the source. And if we ever do come to the place where every individual is looked upon as a child of God, it will be because we sink our lives into these eternal principles of our faith. We must never forget the roots of the tree.

We are thinking about democracy's roots in spiritual principles. We have many slogans to express our central convictions. Take for example the phrase, "with liberty and justice for all." We believe that no civilization deserves to live that does not provide justice. Governments exist that every man might enjoy equality before the law. We are rightfully outraged by the fake trials of dictator states, where the fate of the prisoner is already determined even before he enters the court room. Where there is no justice, there is no security for anyone. Our forefathers were very particular in their insistence upon the right of trial by jury because of this sense of justice. I have heard lawyers speak of the Supreme Court as an agency that exists not simply to try the big cases, but as a guarantor of the rights of the last and least citizen.

This word justice is a big word. And if we should even approximate it in the nation and the world most of the bitterness, the divisiveness that now mar the relationships of men and nations would disappear. It is one of the final goals toward which we must strive. Even if we are not just, ourselves, most of us would be ready to admit that we can never have a decent way of life here upon earth without justice for all.

But where does this come from? Let us go back to a Man
preaching from the seaside, and listen to his ringing words:
"Judge not, that you be not judged. For with the judgment you
pronounce you will be judged, and the measure you give will be
the measure you get. Why do you see the speck that is in your
brother's eye but do not notice the log that is in your own eye?
Or how can you say to your brother, let me take the speck out
of your eye, when there is a log in your own eye? You hypocrite,
first take the log out of your own eye, and then you will see
clearly to take the speck out of your brother's eye." There is the
seed of justice, the breakdown of those prejudices and blind
spots that keep us from seeing clearly. And when one day men
possess his spirit there will be justice in our own hearts and in
all the world. That is the way it will come. That is the root of it.

One can dip down almost anywhere into the best in our common life and find these roots. We are afraid of some of the
world's leaders today because we are afraid of what power may do
to them. Power is a dangerous thing, especially in the hands
of men who exercise it irresponsibly. When this nation was
founded, our forefathers said that tyrannical use of power by
individual leaders or political organizations was wrong. Government was to be for the people. Service was to be the motivation
of leadership. That was to be the test of the real value of men
in public life. That spirit would change the world if it could be
made universally operative.

But where did this spirit of service come from? What is the
source of this ideal? The answer is in words that have been
heard so many times all over the Christian world that they may
seem almost trite. And yet can they be repeated too many times?
Salome and her two sons came to Jesus and asked that they be
given a place of favoritism in his kingdom. Positions of special
privilege would be handed out one day, so Salome thought, and
she wanted to be perfectly sure that her sons would be in on the
ground floor. You will recall Jesus' answer: "You know that
the rulers of the gentiles lord it over them, and their great ones
exercise authority over them. Not so shall it be among you; but
whoever would be great among you shall be your servant, even as
the Son of Man came not to be served but to serve and give his
life as a ransom for many.

"And on either side of the river the tree of life with its twelve
kinds of fruit and the leaves of the tree were for the healing of
the nations." This is the source of our idealism and our hope.

This is the bedrock on which our culture and civilization must rest. Without it there is no hope. The motto on the statehouse in Nebraska puts it this way: "Eyes and ears are poor witnesses when the soul is barbarous." Pray God that we may sink our lives in increasing numbers into this creative Christian soil until we shall at last achieve here in this embittered and confused world "one kingdom uniting all mankind in service and love."

======◇======

NO RESPECTER OF PERSONS . . .

THE REVEREND F. HOWARD CALLAHAN
Church of St. Paul and St. Andrew, New York, New York

TEN MEN ARE TRAMPING STEADILY NORTHWARD along the eastern shore of the Mediterranean Sea. The coastal road stretches more than forty sandy miles from Joppa to Caesarea. It is a good two days' journey for foot travelers, and the men are weary. First in the little procession, a Roman soldier and Apostle Peter walk side by side. Then come a half-dozen Jewish friends of Peter. Two servants, under the command of the soldier, bring up the rear, perhaps with a donkey or two to carry the baggage.

Take a good look at Peter! He is in the midst of an experience which will be epochal not only for him, but for all Christians who come after him in the long history of the church. This journey from Joppa to Caesarea is an important adventure. It will take Peter and his Jewish companions into the house of Cornelius, the Roman centurion. They will associate with gentiles, eat with them, live in their home, join with them in prayer and worship, and with them witness the benediction of God upon such unorthodox association and fellowship.

This journey is far more important than Peter can realize that day. He knows that he is being led to break through the racial exclusiveness and religious prejudice which would limit the Christian fellowship to members of the Jewish community. He is being led toward a great conviction by the logic of events. Years later, the New Testament will record that conviction in these words: "Peter opened his mouth and said: Truly I perceive that God is no respecter of persons, but in every nation any one who fears him and does what is right is acceptable to Him." But Peter could not understand the full meaning of his own conviction that day. Nor could he foresee that his little procession of ten men up the Mediterranean coast to a single household of gentiles in Caesarea was to continue until it became the mighty march of Christianity around the whole earth, over all continents, and to all peoples. Important indeed was this journey, for it was a journey of the mind, a journey into fellowship.

The great adventures of men always involve journeys of the mind. And greatest of all are the adventures which lead across barriers of prejudice and into wider areas of human association. Usually there are definite steps or stages in such pilgrimages of the spirit. They are clearly discernible in this story of Peter and Cornelius.

To begin with, there is vision. You will recall that Peter had a vision while he was praying on the housetop. A great sheet was lowered from the heavens in which were all kinds of animals, both "clean" and "unclean" according to the standards of Jewish ceremonial and dietary law. The voice of God seemed to say to him: "Your prejudices are wrong. What God has made clean, you must not hold in contempt." And, when at that very moment the servants of Cornelius came knocking at the gate with the unconventional but urgent message from a Roman and a gentile inviting him to come to Caesarea, Peter began to understand his vision. Though it must have meant a wrench to his deep-rooted religious pride, and though it took an effort to restrain a kind of revulsion which was rooted in his habitual emotional reactions, he invited these gentiles into the house, lodged them that night, and consented to accompany them back to Caesarea the next day. Peter's horizon had been widened. Certainly, the many half-remembered teachings of the Master were bearing fruit in the mind of his disciple. Vision came to Peter, and vision of such a meaning as set him forth on a journey of the spirit.

Then there is action. In every adventuring spiritual journey, there comes the time for thinking to turn into doing. With Peter, the opportunity to put his vision into practice in his conduct was immediate. He chose to act positively. He began at once to associate with these fellow human beings who had come to his gate, and every act of association led him further along the pathway into fellowship. By his invitation they came into his house and sat with him at the evening meal. By his hospitality, they were given lodging for the night. The next morning he began the two days of physical travel which led, hour by hour, along the coastal highway toward Caesarea, but step by step and hour by hour his mind also was journeying along the spiritual road into deeper acquaintance and understanding.

Finally, there is general acceptance and approval. In this story of Peter at Caesarea we read that Peter preached with such power in the house of Cornelius that "the Holy Spirit fell on all who heard the word." When, some time later, he went back to Jerusalem to tell the story to the leaders of the Apostolic Church, the evidence he presented won their reluctant approval. And now, across the years, we can see clearly that this episode was a step of the utmost significance in opening the way for Christianity to become a world religion. Peter's willingness to put his vision into action helped to break the bonds of narrow thinking which would have made of the Christian fellowship a cult within Judaism. He helped to push open the door through which Paul set out upon his missionary journeys over the Mediterranean world.

Many illustrations of this sequence of vision, action, recognition may be found in the long history of man's spiritual adventuring. Columbus finds his mind seized by the compulsion of a great and daring dream; he labors through a lifetime to put his vision into adventurous actions; then the recognition of the world lifts him to unique and undying fame. The name of Louis Pasteur may be allowed to stand for a vast multitude of lonely scientists who have had born within their minds a vision of new truth; who have labored, suffered, and many times died in their efforts to implement their vision; and whose names the slow and stubborn world has finally inscribed upon its roll of honor.

Today, vision seems to have far out-distanced action. The world in which we are living has seen the rise of leaders who have in many lands united in the dream of world-wide peace. Many peoples share the vision. But they seem unable to find paths of fellowship. Too often, on the actual frontiers where people meet, there are friction and antagonism and the actual threat of acts of aggression and war. The plain people of the world want peace, but they do not find the ways which lead to peace, Wendell Willkie's "One World" remains a dream.

Can Christianity lead the way to peace in such a day as this? I believe that it can. I believe that the plain and simple story of the Christian gospel contains the world's best hope of finding the ways which will lead men into that fellowship upon which peace can be built. And I think one may find sound reasons for such a belief.

To begin with, the source-book of Christian faith is permeated with ideas of free and equal fellowship among men. When men want to teach racial exclusiveness, or class pride, or special privilege of any sort, they steer clear of the New Testament. Totalitarians and autocrats of every kind find the words of Jesus uncomfortable. On the other hand, whenever men will simply read the New Testament together, they will find themselves drawn toward each other. When we seek to walk in imagination beside the Master along the roads of Galilee, we find that we are walking roads of fellowship where pharisee and publican, prince and outcast, rich man and beggar may freely join the company. The New Testament is a book of fellowship.

In the second place, the Christian faith has worked whenever it has been fairly tried. Sometimes the religious wars and sectarian persecutions which blacken the story of the Christian Church have been pointed to as the failures of Christianity. They should be called the failures of men who have sadly departed from Christianity. The whole story of foreign missions is filled with demonstrations of the power of Christian faith to bring men out of literal savagery into Christian fellowship, as many of our returned soldiers have witnessed after their experiences in the Orient and among the scattered islands of the South Pacific.

Wherever the Christian faith has gone, there has come to life in the minds of men the vision, in some sort, of the unity of all mankind. Whenever men have tried seriously to live that faith, they have found themselves on roads of fellowship and journeying toward brotherhood; and where men have lived in Christian brotherhood, there has been the witness of divine favor. The vision is the same through the years. For Apostle Peter, at the beginning of the Christian history, it was voiced in his half-startled confession, "I perceive that God is no respecter of persons." For Wendell Willkie it was a slogan, "One World!" For the poet Gilbert K. Chesterton, it becomes a dream of the house whose door is ever open to all men:

> "To an open house in the evening
> Home shall men come,
> To an older place than Eden
> And a taller town than Rome.
> To the end of the way of the wandering star,
> To the things that cannot be and that are,
> To the place where God was homeless
> And all men are at home."

===◇===

THOU SHALT LOVE THY NEIGHBOR AS THYSELF . . .

The Reverend Frederick Keller Stamm
First Congregational Church, Chicago, Illinois

ALL THE ARGUMENTS IN SUPPORT of the superiority of one group of people over another fade away in the presence of Jesus of Nazareth. Abraham Lincoln found it difficult to define democracy, but he had no difficulty in coming to the point of declaring the basis upon which democracy had to operate, when he said, "As I would not be a slave, so I would not be a master. This expresses my idea of democracy. Whatever differs from this, to the extent of the difference, is no democracy." Just as Lincoln cut through to the core of democracy, so Jesus cut through to the core of religion when he said, "Thou shalt love the Lord thy God with all thy heart, and with all thy soul, and with all thy mind . . . and . . . thou shalt love thy neighbor as thyself. On these two commandments hang all the law and the prophets." That is more than a code of ethics. It brings God and man together, and that's religion. "Whatever differs from this, to the extent of the difference, is no religion."

There can be only one solution to the race problem, and that is a regeneration of the Christ spirit in the hearts of people who make up the body of the church. Our amoral expediencies during the last war poisoned man to the bone. What he needs is to be made clean. There are some things that do not need more discussion, and the attitude that devolves upon a Christian toward every man regardless of creed or color, is one of them. It is as simple as this: God is no respecter of persons. The color of a man's skin does not guarantee him a place in the Kingdom of God. Only by the grace of God working through man will racial prejudice be dissolved.

The whole world has gotten itself into a frame of mind where it imagines that the great menace to goodness comes from the outside. So we shout ourselves hoarse against the rising tide of other economic systems, and set ourselves against them by becoming "tough," and threatening them with the power of military might. It hasn't dawned upon our darkened minds that evil has within itself the germs of its own destruction, or that the only way you can successfully combat an idea is by producing a better idea.

When the rising tide of color laps at the shores of our comfortable homes and ecclesiastical clubs, the only thing we know to do is to cry, "Unclean! Unclean!" We retreat, close our churches, or move them out into fine residential sections and blame the Negro for pushing us out. It never seems to dawn upon people of those churches that they didn't have sufficient religious vitality within their own ranks to lighten the darkness in the midst of a great city with the burning lamp of the good news of God.

Segregation or nonsegregation, the question of whether Negroes shall join white churches, the matter of social equality, or the ever present query, "Would you like to have your daughter marry a Negro?" all belong to the periphery of the problem. Jesus declared that this is a moral universe, and that things work out well when we work *with* the laws of the moral universe, and badly when we work *against* them.

The first thing that will lead us to the place where Jesus stood when he declared, "Thou shalt love the Lord thy God . . . and thy neighbor as thyself," is a deep sense of childlikeness. Wordsworth was not simply romancing when he cried: "Heaven lies about us in our infancy!" To the child there is "nothing common or unclean." He is born to love, and marvel, and to such belongs the Kingdom of Heaven. And if Jesus is right when he says that the realm of God is dependent upon adults having the heart of a little child, then most of us have paid a terrible price for growing up. We've lost a simple faith, the art of seeing God, an at-homeness with the good, and the spiritual uses of love. We've made a world of hate, jealousy, revenge, and racial tension, into which we have insisted on fitting the child. We have not yet acquired a simple trust in God and our fellows.

Great issues demand great men, and great men are made out of the stuff of humility. A mother in Princeton, New Jersey, was worried by the absence of her ten-year-old-girl. The child explained, "I had trouble with my homework in arithmetic. People said that at Number 112 there lives a very big mathematician who is also a good man. I went and asked him if he would help me. He was very willing and explained everything very well."

In distress, the mother went to Einstein to apologize for her daughter's boldness. She was told, "You don't have to worry. I certainly learned more from the child than she from me."

One can hardly conceive of that sort of childlikeness in all grown-ups having any difficulty over the color of any other man's skin.

"In Germantown, Pennsylvania," says Mr. E. B. White, a writer for the *New Yorker,* "there are two schools, one predominantly white, one predominantly colored. The gangs of little boys from the two schools often play together. One day they invented a new game called Race Riot, but when they got assembled to play it they discovered that there were more white boys than colored boys. Clearly the thing was out of balance and unfair . . . what to do? Like a flash the children had the answer. The proper number of white boys promptly volunteered to play colored, and the race riot proceeded with even numbers in perfect equality. Adults, we feel, would have the devil's own time with a situation like that."

We've fallen into the habit of talking about a complex world and complex problems as over against a simple world and simple problems of other days. I would be the last to deny that we are living amidst a tangled maze of affairs. But I'd also like to be among those who assert that much of the difficulty in the world is the result of man's own selfishness, stupidity, ambition, greed, and intricate mechanical ingenuity. If he would get his thinking straight and his religion pitched on the plane where Jesus walked and talked, most of the problems would be seen as simple of solution. Problems of any kind never look so complex and formidable when the mind of Jesus is sought.

There is a very little letter of only twenty-five short paragraphs nestling within the covers of the New Testament, without which our religion would be as odorless as the woods would be without violets. It was written out of the little damp prison underneath the Capitoline Hill in Rome to a prosperous citizen, Philemon, in Colossæ. He had become a Christian under the preaching of Paul, and was the leader of the little church in his house. He had slaves, for neither he nor anyone else in that day knew any better. One day, a slave by the name of Onesimus stole some valuable articles from his master and made off with them. In due time he found his way into the city of Rome, and eventually to Paul in prison.

Here was a dilemma—how to get two widely separated men as to wealth, position, color, and social status, together. Paul approached the problem from the only angle such a man as he—who had come out of great tribulation—could use. He said to Philemon: Take him back. You are a man and a Christian. Onesimus is a man and a Christian. I am a man and a Christian. We three can do much by way of straightening out the tangled relationships between men. In your house you have a little beloved community of believers. You gather about the Communion table and break the bread and drink the wine, symbols of the death of our Common Friend. He didn't die for you and me alone, but for Onesimus also. He didn't promise forgiveness to people who exclude other people. That Supper is not a mere ritual. It means that men belong together. Take him back. Take him back not as a slave, but as a brother. I can't force you to do this. Let it be a natural, spontaneous outburst of your love for God and man. Let me see a demonstration of Christian love, a thing that will make its way down through the ages.

It was an appeal to the Christ spirit in Philemon. And that's the appeal I should like to send out across this nation—to little homes nestling in the hills, to homes along the avenue, to church people, and non-church people.

I can't force you to stand on this height, but by the same token you can't light the path over which every man has the right to

walk toward the development of his fullest powers, if the light
that is in you be darkened.

Then once more. There can be no *barriers which religion does
not insist upon breaking down.* For long years before the an-
nouncement of the birth of Jesus, religion was at a low ebb. He
broke the traditions of the elders, crossed boundaries which no
other man dared cross, and took up his abode in the hearts of a
Samaritan woman, a Roman Centurion, a hated tax-gatherer, a
Sidonian mother, and an obscure visitor to the city of Jerusalem
on the day of the Crucifixion. All he saw as he moved about from
place to place were men. He couldn't wait until the religious
leaders of the day caught up with him.

And now here stands the Christian man and woman in the
wake of a great war, and with human values shuffled as they've
never been shuffled before, I can hardly imagine the way out to
be, "Let us hope that gradually and with due and careful regard
to vested interests, and provided the majority will not object,
and when prejudices are less acute, we can bring about changes
in our attitude toward the Negro." I imagine Jesus would turn
his back on that way. No advance in human relations is made by
that process. It is the living breath of Christian goodwill we
need today. Nothing else will heal the divisions between class
and class, and man and man.

It is a very dark night through which the world is passing just
now. But in spite of it, I still believe in the dawn against the
darkness. Hilaire Belloc tells how once he and a friend were
climbing by night in the Pyrenean Mountains. Suddenly a terrific storm burst upon them. "This," exclaimed his friend, "feels
like the end of the world." "Not so," replied Belloc, "this is how
the dawn comes in the Pyrenees." And may it not be true that
all this nightmare of a degenerate prejudice is only the prelude
to the coming of the dawn and the rising of the Day Star in our
hearts?

═══◆═══

ALL ARE ONE . . .

THE REVEREND CLARENCE E. LEMMON
First Christian Church, Columbia, Missouri

> "And he made of one every nation of men to dwell on
> all of the face of the earth." ACTS 17:26

THIS TEXT WAS DRAWN FROM THE ADDRESS which the Apostle Paul
made from the Areopagus in Athens. Here in this center of
Grecian learning, Paul is presenting his own faith. In the midst
of the evidence of many gods he is speaking for the one God
"who made the world and all things therein." And as the creator
of the world he made man, and he made him for fellowship and
not for enmity—for "he made *of one* every nation of men to dwell
on all of the face of the earth." This learned Jew, speaking to
learned Greeks, proposes a world united in fellowship on the
basis of belief in one God. This ideal has always been the hope
and dream of our Christian faith.

There are three things today that re-enforce the necessity for
the fellowship of mankind.

The first is in our circumstances. In the days of Paul it was
quite a journey from Jerusalem to Athens, much farther in point
of time than it is today from Washington to Moscow. Modern
man faces a shrinking world. Within the last twenty years this
world has contracted in terms of travel and communication into
a single community. The nature of this world community is
such that the alternative to fellowship is anarchy and war.

The second necessity for fellowship is in our fears. Terrible
new weapons of destruction have been invented and the alternative to fellowship is not merely an old type of war with its
devastation, but a new type of war which means extinction. The
issue is now fellowship or death.

The third necessity is in our gospel. The New Testament has
not been repealed. If we are Christians we cannot permit our
prejudices and divisions to be held with an easy conscience. We
cannot put up barriers against other men and at the same time
call ourselves Christians.

As we approach this mid-point of the twentieth century we must recognize the fact that we are facing a crisis in fellowship. The war has demoralized the whole world and left us in a state of suspicion, fear, and hatred. There is not an ugly word in the English vocabulary denoting human disparity, division, or belligerency, that cannot be read in our daily headlines. This postwar bitterness and division is to be found in every nation, whether defeated or victor. Desperately needing fellowship, we find ourselves in a juncture of history when nearly every fact is arrayed against our Christian hope of a united world.

As we examine this social situation we find five forces that tend to destroy our fellowship. The first is our prejudice of race. While we are anthropologically and biologically one, we do have differences of color. The pigment of our skins varies, and this difference boils up into racial prejudice. The second dividing force is class consciousness. Our industrial order tends to separate men into various interests. We become owners or capitalists or workers representing labor. This class consciousness becomes rooted in economic dogma. There is a third cleavage which we call nationalism. We develop patriotisms, loyalties, and national devotions. These patriotisms are held as an exclusive passion and create divisions of the human race that are bitter and fearful. All of these tend to find expression in ideologies that are worldwide, such as capitalism and socialism, democracy and communism. It is upon these ideologies that we divide with the most vehemence.

It is well to notice that these divisions are irrational. They will not stand intellectual probing and do not constitute a reasonable ground for a break in fellowship. For example, in America we have five million people of Jewish descent, forty million of Scottish and English descent, nineteen million of German descent, and fifteen million Negroes. Let us look at the normal racial prejudices of middle-class Americans. I judge that our prejudices, if we have them, are directed toward the Jew and the Negro. An examination of intelligence, made ten years ago, among thousands of high school pupils in a mid-western state, showed that the students of Jewish parentage ranked first, that those of old line American parentage ranked seventh, and that the Negroes ranked sixteenth out of the seventeen examined. It would seem that we are prejudiced against the Jew because of his superiority (so-called) and against the Negro because of his inferiority (so-

called). This seems illogical and capricious. We know too that
if we were to go out onto the street and choose three persons at
random, the intelligence of the individual Negro might be first
and the Jew last. It would seem that the reason for this prejudice
is because we refuse them fellowship. On the other hand, two
terrible wars in the last thirty years have involved the German
nation as our enemy. We have millions of Americans of pure
German blood and we do not hold them in prejudice; we have
extended to them our fellowship. When fellowship is given,
prejudice tends to disappear.

This being true, we should notice the nature of fellowship.
There are two elements of fellowship which should be stressed.
In the first place, fellowship is not a perfectionist concept. It
is not a Utopian dream. It is probably altogether too much to
hope that we will attain the unity of mankind in the foreseeable
future. It is not too much to hope that we may have the healing
fellowship of men of many nations, creeds, and races within the
foreseeable future. Fellowship is a means, not an end. It is the
bridge which we build across the chasms of our divisions. Men
can find fellowship even through disagreement. They can find
fellowship even if they cannot attain perfection.

Jesus used fellowship as a means. His disciples were not perfect men and they often disagreed. But standing together they
were able to survive the disappointment of the cross and plant
the church. Sometimes Jesus was criticized because he ate with
publicans and sinners. It did not mean that Jesus agreed with
the ideals of the publicans who were for the most part greedy
and predatory. It did not mean that he approved their way of
life. It meant that he would promote unity and righteousness
by means of fellowship.

What this world so badly needs is to increase the use of this
great "means" which we call fellowship. Exchange students of
many nationalities in our universities and colleges, representatives
of many trades in many countries, statesmen moving about across
the world on errands of understanding, missionaries doing their
work in many fields and at home on furloughs, all tend to dis-
sipate our prejudices. These lines of fellowship must be held if
we are to have unity and peace.

In the second place, fellowship recognizes diversity and difference. There is a finer unity in diversity than in sameness. Our

nation has one of the oldest continuous national governments
in the world, and is the oldest and most powerful democracy.
And yet it is made up of diversity. We have a diversity of racial
heritage, of resources and climate; diversities of religion and
creeds, diversities as marked as those of Europe. Yet we have
been able to bring these diversities into one unity of government
and fellowship. Even our communities have diversities of race
and creed, of economic stature, of culture and heritage. Yet there
is an over-all fellowship of street and shop, of fraternity and
church, of school and government. And to increase our unity we
must increase and multiply the means of fellowship.

Because of the healing influence of fellowship, Christian people
should support the United Nations as a great hope. For a period
the old League of Nations held the world together. It was too
bad that our nation did not join. It was ominous when Japan
withdrew her fellowship in 1932; it was threatening when Germany withdrew in 1933; it was critical when Italy withdrew in
1937; and it was calamitous when Russia was expelled in 1939.
All of these breaks in fellowship were harbingers of war that
was soon to come. If we can keep the nations together in the
fellowship of the United Nations there is hope for peace, for
without fellowship there can be no peace.

This concept of fellowship and unity is not a marginal item
of our Christian faith. It is central and absolute. To limit our
fellowship with our fellow men is to engage in the major heresy
of Christendom. Let us note three accents of this truth in our
Christian heritage and practice:

This idea of the oneness of mankind is central in our theology.
We are told, not only in the text but in the creation story, that
God is one and that he is the creator of all men. Implied in this
act of creation, in this cosmic process out of which mankind was
evolved, is his unity. To discriminate against a fellow man is to
discriminate against God, and to go counter to his central purpose in the act of creation. If, as Paul says, we are "made of one"
then our divisions are not only against men but against God. If
we believe that God is the creator of all life we must accept all
men as fellows and brethren.

This sense of fellowship is central in the teaching of Jesus. He
lived and died as an expression of his love for mankind. To the
great commandments he added the new commandment that we

love one another. This word love cannot quite be translated into our language. It means goodwill in the active sense of energetic fellowship. If we are true to him we will build a bridge of goodwill which will surmount our disposition toward prejudice of our fellowmen. We cannot have barriers against our fellows and be true to his spirit.

We must face this matter of our Christian fellowship with open minds and active consciences. If we are doubtful we must rehabilitate our convictions in the ancient truths. If we are timid or afraid we need to learn the lessons of fellowship in the practices of the church. If we are sinful or rebellious at this point may we seek forgiveness in the spirit of penitence and prayer. We are called upon in our generation to make living testimony to the truth so long ago uttered on the Athenian hill by one of God's noblest prophets that "he made of one every nation of men to dwell on all the face of the earth."

═══◆═══

NEGROES ARE GOD'S CHILDREN, TOO . . .

THE REVEREND SAM NADER
First Methodist Church, Jennings, Louisiana

> "Have we not all one father? hath not one God created us?" . . . MALACHI 2:10

ALL RELIGION IS IN THAT SENTENCE; all philosophy, all the history of man, all the beauty and pathos of human life.

Race prejudice is the most dangerous foe of western civilization and Christianity. Our world is rapidly being turned into a wilderness of ruthless savages because of intolerance, injustice, arrogance, vengeance, greed, and persecution. Humanity has already passed the crossroads of life and death; and, the basic problem which confronts all of us is: "Will it be love—and life, or hate—and death?"

The ringing proclamation, "There is neither Greek nor Jew
. . . Barbarian, Scythian, bond nor free; but Christ is all, and in
all," was the preamble of the Magna Charta of the early Christian Church. Paul was willing to cut through all the artificial
boundaries which men had erected in their selfishness and for
their benefit. It is no wonder the early Christians were able to
make progress and conquer a heathen world!

There are several observations which I desire to make before
we consider the main question of the morning. First, *race prejudice is not an inherited characteristic; it is developed.* We were
all born with capacities for good and bad, and with the ability
to love and hate. It stands to reason then that whatever race
prejudice we might have is a characteristic which we ourselves
have developed, either from background or through environment. Many of us grew up having Negro playmates. We knew
no differences until someone placed differences there!

Second, *there is no such thing as a biologically inferior or
superior race.* Historians have shown us that all races sprang in
the beginning from a single stock, which originated either in
Africa or Central Asia, and that all represent a natural differen-
tiation on the basis of simple heredity and environmental influence. Well might we ask ourselves if a tenor voice is superior
to that of a bass? There are inferiors and superiors in all races.
I never feel my heart beat without thinking of the Negro doctor,
Samuel Williams, who performed the first operation; I never
hear of blood poisoning without remembering that a Japanese,
Kitasato, isolated the bacillus of tetanus; I never think of atomic
power without admiring the Jewish mathematician, Albert Einstein, who worked out the formula of the secret of the atom; I
never give a blood transfusion without thanking Landsteiner,
an Austrian; I never see the X-ray machine without recalling
Madame Curie and her faithful husband, who worked so dili-
gently to give to the world the secret of radium; I never learn
of typhoid fever without being grateful to a Russian, Metchnikoff. Since we are thinking primarily of the Negro this morning, I would like to say that when I read poetry, I think of
Countee Cullen, Langston Hughes, and Paul Lawrence Dunbar;
and that when I hear music, I recall Roland Hayes, Marian
Anderson, Paul Robeson, and Dorothy Maynor.

Third, *the race problem is not an insoluble problem!* The differences we have are those we make. Race superiority is neither

true American nor Christian. Dr. John Haynes Holmes tells us that the white man's "whole life is determined by the Negro— his personal habits, his local customs, his public policies, the very lay-out of his city, the very architecture of its buildings." As long as we try to hold the Negro down, we keep ourselves down. As long as we try to show that "he's inferior" and will always be, we reveal our inferiority. Washington Carver stated this truth when he said that he couldn't hold a man in the ditch without having to stay in the ditch himself. When we have solved this "race" problem, we shall have solved the major problems that man faces.

I think we should avoid extremes in this question of race. There is one group which *holds that there is one superior race and that all other races must be subject to that race.* This was the Nazi and Japanese philosophy. It meant and can mean nothing short of hatred, strife, and endless wars.

Lillian Smith, in her book, *Strange Fruit,* shows what happens to the white man when he assumes an attitude of superiority toward the Negro. In her portrayal of the semi-paralyzed white idiot who was warped, twisted, and deformed, she gives us a sign and symbol of what prejudice does to the so-called superior race.

Paul was right when he said, "God hath made of one blood all nations of men for to dwell on the face of the earth."

There is another group which *would deny all God-created racial differences.* This group demands that we close our eyes to all the sociological consequences of those differences. In nature animals of a kind live together, and even within a species they have a tendency to group. For example, mallards and teal fly in different flocks.

Denying these differences can never be the solution to racial tension, for all races have a racial integrity that they desire to maintain.

Now, there is a third group, which I think has a better solution for this problem. This group *recognizes all the God-created racial differences, but positively denies the inherent supremacy of any race.* It urges all races to practice brotherhood and the Golden Rule in their relations with each other. It believes that the real salvation of any race is within itself. The stress is placed upon each race treating the other with justice, mercy, and righteousness.

Just what would this mean in our relation to the Negro here in the South? It means that *he must have justice in his political and*

civil life. Negroes are more apt to be convicted in the courts than
are the whites against whom the same evidence might be produced. Mistreatment and abuse are all too common. Pick up
your local newspaper; on the front page you read about the lynching of a Negro here in the South, while in the middle or back
section of the news you read of a wonderful talk that has been
made on brotherhood. Thomas Jefferson admonished in his
First Inaugural Address: "All, too, will bear in mind this sacred
principle, that though the will of the majority is in all cases to
prevail, that will to be rightful must be reasonable; that the
minority possess their equal rights, which equal law must protect, and to violate would be oppression." The Negro, who is in
the minority, wants political and social equality.

It means that *he must not be discriminated against in the industrial and labor worlds.* He wants security and freedom. We
are told that two-thirds of all Negro wage earners are found in
two of the lowest paid occupations, farming and domestic service.
A study of agricultural incomes before the war revealed that
the national income average was $528; for the South this figure
fell below $200 per year. The average per capital wealth of the
southern states in 1943 was $1,785 as against $3,609 for the rest
of America. In the field of domestic service in which approximately two million Negroes work, the average annual income
fluctuated between $125 and $300 per year. Their economic plight
will cripple the entire South.

It means that *he must have equal opportunity in the field of
education.* In very few towns and cities in America are the Negro
schools what they ought to be. The inequalities in per capita
expenditure, equipment, building, school term, teachers' salaries,
and curricula, are well known. The most spectacular illustration
of this is in Mississippi, where the money expended for white
children in 1943 was roughly nine times as great as that expended
for Negroes, although the Negroes form forty-nine per cent of
the population.

It means that *he is no longer to be treated as a serf in the field
of agriculture.* The share-cropping system of southern agriculture has held millions of Negroes in virtual economic slavery.
Eighty per cent of all Negro farm operators are tenants. He does
the same amount of work, if not more, as a white person, and yet
he receives less pay for his services. The Civil War was fought
to rid America of slavery in any form; let's make Lincoln's dream
a reality!

It means that *the most careful considerations should be given to his social welfare and health.* The health of the entire South is being jeopardized by this problem. There is one hospital bed for every 150 whites in our nation. There is one bed for each 2,000 Negroes, though the illness rate among the Negro is greater. Thomas Carlyle has told us the story of an impoverished widow who went to her neighbors for help. They refused. She became sick and died. She infected the whole neighborhood with typhus fever. Seventeen members of the community died. They were her brothers even though they had denied it.

If our visitor from Mars, of whom we have spoken so frequently, would come to our planet and ask us to name two of the greatest teachings in our world, we would state explicitly, "Love God and love your neighbor." He would listen to our explanations, look up the definition of brotherhood in the dictionary, search almost in vain for the genuine conditions of this phrase at work, return to his planet bewildered and confused, and then state with pathos, "There can never be peace on earth until there is goodwill among men."

There is only one answer to atomic and biological warfare: *Brotherhood!*

> Tear down the walls! God made of one
> All men who live upon the earth;
> He is our Father, we his sons,
> Whatever be our human birth.
> Tear down the walls that separate
> And breed estrangement, pride, and hate.
> The poor, the oppressed, the rich, the great
> Are brothers in one human state.

5. That They All May Be One

REMOVING BARRIERS . . .

THE REVEREND ARCHIBALD MURCHISON
New Hempstead Presbyterian Church, New Hempstead, New York

"STICKS AND STONES," says the childhood rhyme, "can break my bones, but names can never hurt me." It sounds true enough, but is it really? Now, let's see.

Suppose one of your neighbors does something you do not like. Let's say he's a red-head; his grandparents were born in Ruritania; and he is cowardly and grasping. He deserves the censure of any decent citizen. But should you decide, from this one man's behavior, that all red-heads are cowardly, or that all Americans of Ruritanian descent are grasping?

"Of course not," you say. "That would be foolish and unfair." And so it would, indeed. But how many of us forget this! How many of us tend to label whole groups of people with the faults or misdeeds of a few. This kind of name-calling can hurt.

Anyone who defames another's religion or color or ancestry reveals his own spiritual poverty—his own pitiful ignorance. But the hurt he inflicts upon an innocent person is only the beginning. Abuse a fellow-American simply because he is a Negro, a Protestant, Jew, or Catholic—or because he was born in Mexico, Italy or Ireland—and all of us suffer.

103

For America's founders built this nation upon Christ's ideal of individual worth and human fellowship. Just as he stood up for the humble and oppressed of the ancient world, so did America stand for the stricken of modern times, saying to each newcomer, "You are not like a cow or a sheep, part of a herd. You are a unique being, with special talents of your own; virtues, faults and desires; a personality of your own. Here in America you are welcome, not because of your race, which you share with millions of others, nor because of your birthplace, where other millions were also born, but for your own God-given qualities of mind and spirit, not to be found in any other individual on earth."

That is America's guarantee to her people! Freedom to exercise individual conscience, freedom to develop individual skills, freedom to cast off whatever shackles of race and class keep men from joining in brotherhood. America long ago released the spirit of fraternity, through democracy that became the source of our strength as a nation.

Now, in the atomic age, Christ's great commandment, "Love thy neighbor," offers us the only way to peace. Yet to love one's neighbor truly, one must know him well. It is, therefore, cause for serious concern when we are isolated from the rest of the community—whether in the scholar's ivory tower, the self-sufficient family circle, or in an ostrich-like attitude toward other peoples.

Not long ago, a group of mothers in New York were discussing this danger. They felt their children were not getting sufficient opportunity to mingle with boys and girls of other races and creeds. Over a cup of coffee, these mothers reasoned that, if we are ever to have lasting peace in the world, we must foster a spirit of brotherhood even among the smallest children in the neighborhood. There was no nursery school in their district organized for this purpose; so these mothers decided to start a school of their own.

This school, which now has an enrollment of two hundred, puts democracy into action. It does not merely *admit* children of all backgrounds; it holds its doors wide open to them. Children of many racial and national strains—Chinese, Negro, Filipino, Mexican and white; children of different faiths—Protestant, Catholic and Jewish—all study and play together under one roof, and accept one another as individuals. Prejudice is unknown to them. The offensive labels which adults, in ignorance or malice, sometimes apply to whole groups mean nothing to these boys and girls. To them, little Angelo or Saul or Manuel are welcome playmates, not looked upon with hostile eyes as representatives of unfamiliar racial or religious entities. Learning to live happily together as friends, these children have first-hand experience of the Brotherhood of Man under God.

Such experience brings lasting benefits to every community, large or small. In every church school, public school or American home, children can discover the contributions of other people to the spiritual and material wealth of our nation. They can learn how courageous men and women from all lands came to America and, with strong hands and willing hearts, built a great civilization; how the full energies of all Americans are needed today to keep that civilization flourishing.

Let our children's eyes be opened to the dignity of every human soul. Teach them respect for the individual members of any race and the essential equality of all races. Fill their hearts with a deep love of God and an understanding of how others worship this same God, whether in church or mosque or synagogue.

These are the concepts behind the many new programs of intercultural education in our public schools and community organizations. They are, in fact, the basic principles of Christian living, brought into the class-room, the club, and the town hall, to nourish the roots of good citizenship.

In many communities, the practice of realistic brotherhood has brought startling changes. One of the finest examples was a tough slum area—the stockyards district of Chicago, known as "Packingtown." It began about six years ago, when the people of Packingtown decided to do something about the discord between various racial, religious and nationality groups in their section. They got together and set up the Back-of-the-Yards Neighborhood Council—an experiment in community co-operation. It has worked with incredible success.

This Council finds no problem too big or too small. It concerns itself with leaking roofs and school lunches, as well as juvenile delinquency and race prejudice. And today, it's "one world" back of the yards. It doesn't matter what a man's race, religion, or nationality is. The whole community works things out *together*.

As one citizen of Packingtown put it: "It's easy when you get to know one another as human beings." Another said: "If every city would do as we do, the world would be on the road to peace."

In another town, it was war and its aftermath that brought the Golden Rule back. In Phoenixville, Pennsylvania, before the war, the community was sharply divided. The descendants of the early settlers kept to their side of town, rarely mixing with people from the north side of the tracks, whom they considered "foreigners." Americans of thirteen different national backgrounds had settled in Phoenixville as early as the 1870s. But even their children and grandchildren, born and bred in town, were looked upon as "foreign" by snobbish fellow-citizens on the south side.

All that was changed when the Valley Forge General Hospital went up nearby to care for many of our badly wounded soldiers. Getting together to help blinded and crippled boys learn to live again, the people of Phoenixville rediscovered the meaning of brotherhood—and Phoenixville became *one* town. The ice barrier between the north and south sides melted under the influence of these casualties—young men from every part of the country, of every race, religion and ancestry, who had sacrificed so much to keep America, and Phoenixville, free.

An old-timer described it this way: "Poor folks, rich folks, blue bloods, foreign stock—they were all one when it came to doing something for those boys, and before we knew it, our town was all made over. It wasn't a miracle, or anything like that, but it had some part of a miracle in it."

Packingtown and Phoenixville are only two of many American communities where the "miracle" of brotherhood and true understanding is being wrought.

In these times, evil men are among us, seeking to divide us for their own vicious ends. They would have us blame our postwar difficulties on one another—on Americans whose skin color, form of worship or ancestry happens to be different from their own.

Here is the answer—clear and simple—that true Christians and decent Americans are giving to these hate-mongers and warmongers. We shall not turn on our brothers in a time of stress. For we have found that in unity and good-will there is strength—to carry through adversity, and to build the foundations of a better world.

The mothers who started the school in New York, the slumdwellers of Packingtown, the townsfolk of Phoenixville—all of them feel the relationship between brotherhood on the block and peace across the globe. Long ago the truth was known and given to us. We shall come closer to lasting peace with every step that takes us closer to our neighbors.

EXPERIENCE AND BELIEF . . .

THE REVEREND HERMAN F. REISSIG
The American Committee for the World Council of Churches
(Third Award)

MOST OF US HAVE ASKED OURSELVES why it is that people of equal intelligence and sincerity and with similar backgrounds are often so far apart in their views on religion, politics, and other important matters. You and I consider a question, and the right answer seems as clear as anything could be. Our next-door neighbor, who is an intelligent and responsible person, doesn't see it that way at all. We sometimes begin a statement of our personal opinion by saying, "Every reasonable person will agree. . . ." Then we are surprised, and often a little offended, to discover that an acquaintance, who is not unreasonable, has come to the exactly opposite conclusion.

Why, for example do not all persons who have access to the same facts either believe or disbelieve in God? In the same business office or in the same pew in church sit two people. They live in the same town, read the same newspaper, see the same moving pictures, eat about the same kind of food. Both think of themselves as fairly intelligent and decent citizens. Now—supposing that they are Christians and belong to the white race— ask them to talk about Jews or Negroes or some other minority group. So completely do they disagree that you think they must be talking about totally different subjects. They simply cannot see each other's point of view. Perhaps the most vivid illustration of this strange clash of opinion is in a national election campaign. How difficult it is for one group of intelligent and loyal Americans to understand how another group of intelligent and loyal Americans can support "that man" or "those people!" The political leader whose activities have made headlines and who spoke the other day on the radio appeals to me. I like him. I trust him. My neighbor around the corner can't stand the sight of his face or the sound of his name. How do you explain this?

The instinctive response of most of us is to decide that the person who disagrees with us, on a matter where we feel strongly, is not as bright as he might be. There must be *something* wrong with him, or he would agree with us! The epithets begin to fly,

"Ignorant!" "Narrow-minded!" "Selfish!" "Un-American!" "Reactionary!" "Radical!" This, of course, is the cheap way to dismiss an opponent.

There is a better and truer way to handle our religious, racial, and political differences. We commonly insist that our beliefs are the result of thinking. "I have thought it all through," we say to ourselves, "reasoned it all out, and I simply cannot see it." That is what we like to think. Alas for our pride! The fact is that personal experience, voluntary or involuntary, does much of our thinking for us. Our early home environments; the religious influences, or the absence of it, in our youth; association with a person whom we admired or disliked; the kind of work we do; the pain or pleasure life has given us; the deep, driving ambitions inside us—these are the things which, mainly, shape our thinking and determine our points of view. One does not have to ask a psychologist about this, though the psychologists have been wonderfully helpful in opening our eyes to the fact. Cool reason? Nonsense, say the psychologists. "Every time you try to make up your mind on a question of importance to you, your experiences, your interests, your open or secret ambitions come crowding in, and, without your being aware of it, they pull and push and deflect and twist—until it's almost impossible for you to say what part of your thinking is rational and what part is emotional."

The same set of facts, approximately the same degree of intellectual ability, no difference that one can measure in the matter of sincerity, *but wide differences in personal experience!* And, *therefore,* wide differences of opinion!

The simplest and, perhaps, the most conclusive illustration can be seen in the way some of us think about a problem in the middle of the day and the way we see the same problem late at night. When our energies are running strong the problem seems easy to handle. But by midnight, when we are tired—"No!" we decide, "It's too much for me. There's no way out." The objective facts have not changed. *We* have changed.

The author of the Book of Ecclesiastes was a disillusioned man. Listen to him: "I have seen all the works that are done under the sun; and, behold, all is vanity and a striving after wind. . . . For all man's days are but sorrow, and his travail is grief; no, even in the night his heart taketh no rest." Now do you suppose that this man dipped his pen in liquid reason and wrote that "all is vanity and a striving after wind?" No, his own particular ex-

perience was in that melancholy refrain. He gives himself away
in another part of his book. He was a rich man and, he tells us,
he had the wish and the means to satisfy every whim, "I builded
me houses . . . I made me gardens and parks . . . I bought men-
servants and women-servants. I gat me also men-singers and
women-singers, and the delights of the sons of men." After that
he decided life is a striving after wind! A program of self-indul-
gence like that is enough to make a cynic of anyone!

The effervescent optimism of a man like Robert Browning also
roots back in personal experience. Browning possessed a magnificent physique. He had such health that he hardly knew the
meaning of physical fatigue. No wonder he could sing,

> How good is man's life, the mere living!
> How fit to employ
> All the heart and the soul and the senses
> Forever in joy!

You see what all this means! When we say to another, "That's
your opinion! Now let me give you *my* opinion!" We could
more accurately say, "That's your *experience!* Now let me tell
you *my* experience!" You can question another person's logic.
You cannot so easily question his experience. You can condemn
a deliberate distortion of the facts. But if a man says, "Thus and
so happened to me. This I saw. This I was taught," you still do
not have to agree, but you can hardly put him down as a hypocrite or a rascal and put yourself up on high as his superior.

Walk down the street or into almost any place where people
congregate. You will pick up opinions like this: Church people
are mostly hypocrites. Negroes are, as a race, inferior to white
people. Roman Catholics go to church out of fear. Protestants
don't believe anything. Jews are greedy. Foreigners are trying
to run this country. Lawyers are a bad lot. Doctors are heartless
fee-collectors. Clergymen are soft-headed idealists. New Yorkers
think the rest of the country doesn't exist. Midwesterners are
isolationists. Is it too much to say that almost always such wholesale judgments grow out of one or two, or a few, personal experiences? Otherwise, how can you account for the fact that other
persons of equal intelligence do not believe any of these things?

You say to me, "Labor leaders are irresponsible agitators. They
care for nothing except their own power and profit." I reply,
"I'm sorry it seems that way to you. It does not seem that way to

me. I know a few labor leaders. They are kind husbands, thoughtful fathers, delightful friends, and about as unselfish and conscientious and patriotic as the general run of us. That's my experience." If another asserts that employers and bankers care only about lining their own pockets, I reply, "Most of the employers and bankers I know are not like that at all. They have about the same virtues and vices as the rest of us. I don't know the whole truth but one thing I do know: on the basis of my experience you can't put together employers or labor leaders or any other group of individuals and pin the same label on them all."

If you don't know Roman Catholics in whose religion fear plays a very small part and Protestants who are as settled in their faith as any Roman Catholic and Jews who make you ashamed of your own greediness and people of foreign extraction who would be the glory of any country and Negroes who make many a white man feel he's been wasting his life, then you are unfortunate. Your experience is mighty limited. Better go out and widen it!

My neighbor down the street—I can't accept his religion; his politics seem to me badly mistaken; maybe he is a member of another race and I don't like some of his attitudes. But if I had his *experience!* That's what I must keep on saying to myself. Probably I'll still disagree with him. But I won't call him names. I won't get angry because he does not see what I think I see. For some of his experiences, which I have not had, I may learn to give thanks. Some of them I shall regret. And he will respond to my experiences in the same way. And we shall learn from each other. And live together like friends and neighbors.

I have not used the words "humility" and "penitence" and "forgiveness." But we've been talking about them all the way through this sermon. When you and I understand that our opinions and convictions are not so much the product of superior thinking as the fruit of personal experience, over much of which we have had little control, we lose some of the self-conceit and complacency which make differences of opinion a cause of bitterness. We begin to be a little humble. For the extremely limited character of our experience and for those things in us that make it difficult to think straight we begin to feel penitent. As for my neighbor, who in my judgment holds such lamentable opinions, if I cannot agree with him, I must at least forgive him—seeing that he, like myself, lives a limited life and is as incapable as I of completely objective and disinterested thinking. Which is to say, to put it in religious words, that both of us need to pray, "God, be merciful to me, a sinner!"

Tolerance won't do the trick. Tolerance, as Gilbert Chesterton said, is too often the virtue of people who don't believe anything. I am *not* going to be genially tolerant of religious and political ideas which I believe to be gravely mistaken. But a little honesty and a little Christianity teach me to hold my opinions in humility, with a prayer of penitence always in the back of my mind. And they teach me also to forgive my neighbor, as God, in His mercy, forgives me.

This is the road to peace and brotherhood.

=====◆=====

MUSICIANS OF GOODWILL . . .

THE REVEREND GARY BOUSMAN
Plymouth Church (Baptist), Milwaukee, Wisconsin

ACCORDING TO ONE OF GRIMM'S FAIRY TALES, a donkey, a dog, a cat, and a rooster started out on a journey. One evening they stopped at what appeared to be a deserted farmhouse. On close examination they discovered that there was a light in the house and a band of robbers were eating their supper.

Now it happened that the four animals were very hungry. They wanted the food that the robbers were eating but they were in doubt as to how to get it. Surely no one of them was strong enough to fight a band of robbers.

So they held a council. They considered various means and finally decided on a plan.

Accordingly, the donkey put his front feet on the window sill. Then the dog climbed on the back of the donkey and the cat climbed on the dog's back. Finally, the rooster perched himself on the cat's head.

At a given signal all the animals began to make music in their own ways. The donkey brayed, the dog barked, the cat mewed, and the rooster crowed. The robbers, never having heard such a sound before, ran out of the house and into the forest. Thereupon the four animals (or four musicians, as the author calls them) went into the house and had a feast.

Now this may be a very simple way to begin a sermon. Yet when we look at our world it becomes clear that robbers are feasting on the things that hold the world together. They are devouring the understanding of nations and destroying the hope of peace.

As in the fairy tale, where no one of the animals could frighten away the robbers, so in our case, no one of us can wipe out prejudice. And like the story there is no one method by which we may destroy international, racial, and religious hatred. But like the four musicians, working together persistently, we may hope to get rid of those attitudes that lead to suspicion, distrust, and strife.

I don't think it is necessary to elaborate on the fact that prejudice is always with us. It lifts its hideous head in daily conversation. When it can get enough of its kind together it rides with the Klan or dons a brown shirt.

I could spend so much time telling you about the dangers of prejudice, my real aim is to tell about the four musicians of goodwill. I want to suggest four ways that we may overcome the attitudes that divide us. Collectively they may lead us into paths of peace.

The first musician of goodwill is that of adequate personality. Much of our prejudice comes from frustration. All of us are confused at times but when confusion becomes a major problem in a person's life, then that person often begins to act in a way that is harmful to the rest of us. And how often that behavior takes the shape of an animosity toward other people. A nation of frustrated people will soon follow a frustrated leader, and I don't have to tell you what happens from that point on.

Or, look at the case of religion. One suspects that the "holier than thou" attitude of certain religious groups could not endure if it were not for the fact that such an attitude provides a haven for the sense of failure and frustration. I did not say that all people who belong to the so-called narrow religious sects are frustrated individuals. The fact is that all religious people, conserva-

tive or liberal, inclusive or exclusive, Protestant, Catholic, or
Jewish, must ever be on guard lest they become ensnared by the attitude that they are better than others because they are different.

Do you remember what Jesus told his disciples about worship?
He said, "If you are offering your gift at the altar, and there remember that your brother has something against you, leave your
gift before the altar and go; first be reconciled to your brother,
then come and offer your gift."

So that is worship—cleansing our souls of animosity and coming before the altar of God knowing that we have no grievance
against any man.

The second musician of goodwill requires that we develop an
intelligent sense of values. This ties in closely with what I have
just been talking about. Frustration develops not only from
warped personality, it also comes from wanting the wrong things.

Our problem is one of re-education. We have got to be sure
that people can find satisfaction and security in the simpler
things of life. It is not a matter of a car in every garage. It is
much more a matter of helping people find happiness in the
everyday pursuits of life.

Hitler used to say that the war was a struggle between the
"have-nots" and the "haves." But how would Hitler explain the
pacifism of the Scandinavian countries, or of Switzerland, or for
that matter, scores of "have not" nations? Some of the most peaceful people in the world have very little of material goods.

The Bible does not say that money is the root of all evil. It
says that "the *love* of money is the root of all evil." The tenth
commandment, "Thou shalt not covet," is not simply a theological formula. It has social and practical implications. Covetousness leads to animosity, to strife, and war.

You often wonder how people can say such unpleasant things
about one another. You may wonder how people can join the
Ku Klux Klan or some of the fascist or communist organizations
in our country. You may wonder how people can build up such
prejudice against the people of other races and other religions.

Here again there is no one explanation, but at least a part of
the answer is to be found in a comparison with steam in a boiler.
If the steam cannot find its way out through the cylinder or safety
valve, it will break the boiler. So animosity is often energy going
out in the wrong direction. But we can get along together if we

can discover a set of values that brings happiness in the every-day pursuits of life.

The third musician of goodwill requires that we have a greater sense of responsibility for wiping out prejudice and working for peace. If during the next ten years we could spend half as much energy building for peace as we spent fighting the last war, we may expect to live in a world of peace.

Here again our problem is one of re-education. Why not teach more people that all heroes do not wear uniforms? Why not give more credit to those who day by day labor for the cause of peace? Why not teach people that wars begin long before armies start marching?

Let us mark this well: fascism does not require great leader-ship. It does not have a hard time getting enough recruits. But fascism's greatest enemies are the people who will not become a part of its narrow racial and religious policies.

If fascism should ever become the American way, it will happen because too many of us give up our day-by-day vigilance against anti-Semitism, anti-Catholicism, anti-Protestantism, or any form of racialism.

This means, so far as you and I are concerned, that we must do all in our power to root out those weeds that strangle the flowers of freedom and tolerance. In daily conversation, in the press, in politics, in business, yes, even in our churches, every word of bigotry must be given the "no vacancy" sign. We cannot sleep while our Master sweats blood in Gethsemane.

The fourth and last musician of goodwill is a faith that with the help of God, and through our own efforts, we can have peace.

To say that evil will ultimately triumph, that human nature is essentially bad, and that we must have war is to deny the funda-mentals of Christianity. It is the antithesis of goodwill.

Here are two philosophies that have always been in conflict. One says that man is animal and if he does not plunder he will be plundered. The other says that man is the child of God and man therefore must believe in the ultimate triumph of good. One philosophy says, "eat, drink, and be merry for tomorrow you die." The other says "live your best today and tomorrow the world will be better because of what you have done."

I ask you, which of these philosophies is the best for all con-cerned? The shortsighted, materialistic philosophy of cynicism, or the long range faith of Christianity? Which is the most practical? Well, here is the answer that Jesus would give: "Love your enemies, bless them that curse you, do good to them that hate you, and pray for them which despitefully use you and persecute you."

There is much more that could be said. But here are the four musicians of goodwill. First, a society of parents, teachers and friends who work together for the development of adequate personality. Secondly, a workable philosophy of values for all people. Third, a greater sense of responsibility for wiping out prejudice in our communities. Finally, a conviction that God's way is the only way that men can live together.

═══◆═══

WORLD BROTHERHOOD BEGINS
IN OUR NEIGHBORHOOD . . .

THE REVEREND ALFRED W. PRICE
St. Stephens Episcopal Church, Philadelphia, Pennsylvania

"GOD GRANT THAT NOT ONLY the love of liberty but a thorough knowledge of the rights of man may pervade all the nations of the earth. . . ."

So wrote the great American philosopher and statesman, Benjamin Franklin. He spoke at the end of a long, fruitful life, a life of service to his fellowmen and the cause of freedom. His words ring down the centuries, calling us to action today.

Franklin witnessed and took part in the creation of a new, free nation. We are witnessing and, in our own way, taking part in the creation of a free new world. We want to do everything in our power to guarantee peace for all the generations to come. So we talk, work, and plan. Out of the multitude of efforts of sincerely idealistic citizens throughout the land come many proposals covering many subjects. Various though they are in content, they all have one aim: to establish harmony among men. And most of them are based, in principle if not always in words, on the Christian ideal of brotherhood.

The greatest challenge to the concept of brotherhood is posed by modern war itself. For the first time in history, the destruction of the entire human race is possible. Jet-propelled planes, rockets and atom bombs, chemical and germ warfare make universal slaughter a horrifying possibility. Unless we learn to live at peace with one another, guaranteeing freedom to men and nations, we may become the pitiful victims of our own scientific ingenuity.

One of the most important sections of the United Nations Charter calls for the establishment, on a world scale, of the basic human rights and fundamental freedom to which all men are entitled. These "articles of faith," as they may be called, would be guaranteed to all citizens by their governments. Problems and issues concerning the protection of these rights and freedoms would be dealt with by an international Human Rights Commission. Thus, every man would be protected on a world scale against the inroads of tyranny.

This is a new and inspiring idea. It puts on a global level our relationships with our fellowmen, from the people next door to the people at the other end of the earth. It makes each of us, in a sense, responsible for our brothers. In its very scope lies its strength, for only by the broadcast action can we hope to rid ourselves of the menace of war.

The burden of responsibility for this action must of necessity rest with our peace-makers. They are the only ones who can effectively carry out international programs for the relief of physical distress, the rebuilding of shattered homes, the restoration of citizenship, and so on. But part of the burden also rests with us, particularly in the protection of civil liberties, such as rights of freedom of religion and freedom of expression. Men must be free to speak and write as their conscience dictates—else how can we know the truth? When censorship stifles freedom of conscience *anywhere,* liberty *everywhere* faces a threat. In recent years we saw how truth was throttled, how race hatred and religious bigotry were aroused by deliberate propaganda; we saw the next step—the deliberate breakdown of brotherhood, first within Germany, and then wherever the Nazis trod. We saw the world-wide tragedy that followed the destruction of human rights.

These rights are rooted in the dignity of every person, no matter what his nationality, race, color or creed; and it is only just, therefore, that they should now claim recognition in the treaties of nations. In the final analysis, however, they are based on the fundamentals of Christianity—and as such, depend for their ultimate protection on the day-to-day co-operation of ordinary men and women.

It was Franklin D. Roosevelt who said: "The structure of world peace cannot be the work of one man, or one party, or one nation. . . . It can be a peace—and it will be a peace—based on the sound and just principles of the Atlantic Charter, on the conception of the dignity of the human being, and on the guarantees of tolerance and freedom of religious worship."

Yet pronouncements, resolutions, and provisions in charters cannot extend full human rights to everyone. It takes more than codes of law to safeguard liberty. It takes people, working with their minds and hearts.

Our minds have always been ahead of our hearts. That's why we live today in a world that is truly a mechanical wonder. But where is our progress in man-to-man relationships? History proves over and over again that suspicion, greed, and hatred lead only to war, suffering, and death. Yet, we are only just learning what the prophets of religion have been teaching for centuries: that goodness, mercy, and love are the only pathways to peace. The United Nations Charter now says it bluntly: we must "practice tolerance and live together in peace with one another as good neighbors . . . promoting and encouraging respect for human rights and for fundamental freedoms for all without distinction as to race, sex, language or religion." Now we have to do it, every last one of us.

And we can no longer afford to move slowly. The atom bomb is here—to stay. Civilization may not be—unless we buckle down and face our individual responsibilities—with our minds and our hearts. This is no time to relax, to become indifferent or callous. Any man who does so forfeits everything we have sacrificed and suffered for—everything so many among us have died for.

With greater energy than ever before, therefore, we must set the pattern of our victory over the forces of evil. Not only must we outline—we must fill in the plan for our future. In all our thinking, we must consider mankind as a whole—not as Christian or Jew, black or white, native-born or foreign-born, rich or poor. The time is long past when we could limit our horizons. The time is long past when we could plead ignorance in the face of suffering endured by our fellowmen. The time is long past when we could shirk our responsibility toward our fellow human beings. From now on, we look out on all our brothers, and seek their welfare as our own.

Moreover, our responsibility goes beyond the mere support of civil liberties, as they are set out on the statute books. It is no longer enough merely to guarantee a man safety of person while denying him a job because of his race or creed. It is not enough to allow him to worship God as he sees fit, if he is shunned because of his religion. It is not enough to say all men are brothers under the skin, and then to bar some from college, from apartment house or restaurant because their skin is brown. Human rights have come to mean more than freedom to live unharmed. They are a claim upon society; for a job and security; for education and opportunity; for happiness and the right to live in a world at peace.

The next time you wonder what you, yourself, can do to make the United Nations Charter a real implement for world peace, look around your own community. See whether any of your neighbors are being denied their rights because of racial or religious prejudices. See whether your town needs civic improvements to raise the standard of living—improvements like slum clearance, better housing, better fair employment practices, better public recreation facilities. Then speak to the man and woman next door about it. Form a committee in which every group in town is represented: white and colored; Christian and Jew; native-born and foreign-born. Get together on projects to benefit the whole community—and you will be amazed at what you are able to accomplish.

Recently, people living in a certain district of Brooklyn formed themselves into an interracial, interfaith committee to raise funds to build homes with special equipment for two young veterans, one a Roman Catholic boy, the other Jewish. Both boys, as the result of war wounds, will never move again except in wheelchairs, but now they will have their chance to live useful, happy lives— thanks to brotherhood in their neighborhood.

There are similar examples of co-operation in towns and villages all over America, and wherever you find it, there you will find the faith and the spirit which can move mountains; which can make "human rights and fundamental freedoms" real to every man and woman the world over.

Long, long ago, Jesus showed men the way. "Love thy neighbor," he said. But mankind was short-sighted and heedless. He knew then what we are just beginning to understand: that we are all neighbors on this earth. Children of God, each of us is our brother's keeper, as he is ours.

This was the faith which inspired our United Nations Charter. This is the faith we must carry into our personal lives. So we shall hasten the day when all men, of every nation, race and creed, will stand together in a world blessed by peace and goodwill.

══ ◆ ══

UT OMNES UNUM SINT . . .

THE REVEREND CARL ALBERT SEAWARD
*Christ Church and the Barnard Memorial School (Unitarian),
    Dorchester, Massachusetts*

MARCUS AURELIUS, Roman Emperor and Stoic philosopher, suggested this: "Begin the morning by saying to thyself, I shall meet with the busybody, the ungrateful, arrogant, deceitful, envious, unsocial." The attitude to take toward those who do not act as nobly as we would have them or who have not become by God's ordaining members of our particular race, or who have not secured the refinement of social class which is our gift of inheritance or reward for achievement, is to be and remain convinced that men of all classes, races, and religion exist for the sake of one another. If others trespass upon our ideals and comfort let us not despise and hate but do as Marcus Aurelius suggested: "Teach them, then, or bear with them."

If, actually, we get underneath what we see as offensive in the nature of other individuals and movements we will discover no necessity for having a charitable tolerance. The trouble is in our superficial observation. People and things are not actually as bad as they appear on the surface. It has taken time for the white race to discover that the souls of George Washington Carver, Booker T. Washington and Mahatma Gandhi were as white in purity and humanitarian ideals as ours. In numerous instances intolerance has built up in us pseudo-attitudes without good authority for prejudice towards the peoples of the world of whom we are suspicious and distrustful. "The fault of others," said Buddha, "is easily perceived, but that of one's self is difficult to perceive; a man winnows his neighbor's faults like chaff; but his own faults he hides, as a cheat hides the bad die from the player. If a man looks after the faults of others and is always inclined to be offended, his own passions will grow and he is far from the destruction of passions." If, as Buddha indicates, one capitalizes on the weaknesses and faults of others one can build up a case of passionate prejudice. That is done by the hate-mongers and bigots whose lashing tongue persecution forces social classes, races, and religious groups to organize, defend themselves, and retaliate. At times that attains to such proportion as to create race beatings and race riots. There is arrogancy in liberalism and prejudice in Catholic circles. My answer to both is Paul's, who wrote: "By the favor that God has shown me, I would tell every one of you not to think too highly of himself by the degree of faith God has allowed him. For just as there are many parts united in our human bodies, and the parts do not all have the same function, so, many as we are, we form one body through union with Christ, and we are individually parts of one another."

When we fall short by using ill will and retaliation we are forgetful of Paul's instruction, which was but the echo of Jesus': "Bless your persecutors; bless them, do not curse them. . . . Live in harmony with one another." To do that is not easy, but it is Christian! It is difficult to brush off theological or sectarian insults but it ought to be done. Buddha suggested, "Let him overcome . . . the liar with truth!" Let Christians do it!

A reckless intolerance does not breed goodwill! This does not imply that man must tolerate all manner of abuses in order to establish goodwill. Yet, man must tolerate the ignorance, misunderstandings, and weaknesses long enough to get down into the lives of those who offend him in order that he may teach and give enlightenment. Others do not learn any good from us if we antagonize or persecute them. But it is absurd to carry what we wrongly call religious idealism or tolerance so far that we remain complacently tolerant of all manner of men, philosophies, and environments. We should seek to improve conditions by sympathetic and understanding love rather than by hate, retaliation, and open war—whether that be relative to one's immediate neighbor or to Russia!

We must not merely condemn the evil ones and cast them to the void. We must do more than tolerate. We must go beyond forbearance to enlightenment and reformation, fostered by genuine education and a spirit of goodwill!

If we are to have goodwill in the world we must accept the right of others to be different from us. We need to go farther and seek to understand why those different from us in social class, race, religious belief, and other ideologies are what they are. Right living is a matter of choice; it is not being forced to live according to a strait-jacket pattern created by those who think others ought to measure up to their standards or ideals for living. That holds whether one professes to be Jew, Catholic, Protestant, or the so-called heathen or unchurched. Who am I to say that Gandhi and his theory of life of non-resistance is wrong or that Robert Frost's poetry is superior to the ideas in Rabidranath Tagore's poems? The Indian starts from where he is, with the Oriental slant on things and ideas, and we, born in industrial western civilization, lack his mystic touch with the universe. Buddha, dwelling on the concept of perfect happiness and eternal peace, certainly puts himself into closer communion with the Soul of the Universe than does the profiteer contemplating his almighty dollar. Perhaps those professing views and ways unlike our own are far nearer the eternal truths and design for living than are we. At least, we ought to be tolerant enough of other systems of religion, forms of government, social customs, and plans of education to be willing to study them and find out! It is ignorance, more than any other factor, which gives rise to suspicion and prejudice, and the resulting injustice in our social order.

Who am I to say that because others are not of my household of faith, of my family, of my country, I am a favored son of the universe?

In Voltaire's spirit, we should sacrifice and defend the principle, "I may not agree with what you say but I will defend your right to say it." It is a fair appraisal to say that, theoretically, most Christians agree with Voltaire in granting free speech, a free press, and freedom of worship. It is a different matter when it comes to personality differences, racial characteristics, social classes, and individual religious beliefs. In cases where there is no thought of ill will toward minority groups and other religious sects too few go beyond tolerance to the practice of goodwill in acts of harmony and friendship. The illustration I now give is an exception. Recently a unique wedding took place in a church in New England. The first Negro member of this predominantly white church was married there to a man from Jamaica by a pastor of a Negro church. The bridesmaid was a Chinese girl, a white man served among the ushers, and a choir including Chinese girls from the Christian Chinese Fellowship provided music. That is goodwill in action. Contrast this demonstration of the brotherhood of man with the ignorant prejudice of a bystander at the Boston Athletic Association Marathon race who was disgusted because a Korean won the race. What the bystander didn't understand was that ability is worthy of recognition regardless of nation, race, or creed. The Korean's achievement is proof that physical ability knows no geographical boundaries. Furthermore, as Ralph Waldo Emerson pointed out long ago, mental and moral abilities know no geographical stipulation.

What we assume to tolerate in color, creed, and social class as a necessary evil is actually an essential good. I am sure it is, or the Creator would not have ordered it that way. We ought to more than tolerate those with whom we differ—more than merely "put up" with them. Can we not find foreigners, Catholics, Jews, Protestants, the rich, the poor—all those different from us—to be fascinating, stimulating, and instructing persons who, because of their acute differences from us, can broaden our minds and spirit?

The Christian philosophy of today, like that of Jesus, extols the supreme worth of every human being. Everyone can be an ambassador of goodwill, every day and every hour of the day on the street, at the places of employment, in every recreational center—in short, in every human contact.

What can we do to exercise goodwill toward those who are different from us? Take the Christian attitude Branch Rickey, president of the Brooklyn Club of the National League, has taken. He had heard Methodist preaching for years and took it to heart. He has broken baseball's color bar. Despite the jabs of the ignorant about the "pious" Mr. Rickey, *The Christian Century* magazine says of him, "But don't forget that it was Branch Rickey, the much derided churchman, who took the first, decisive step. Perhaps Mr. Rickey's religion is not such a humbug after all."

Facing all the evils of ill will squarely and bravely by demonstrating goodwill can bring more freedom, justice, and love to all. It can create that better world of friendship and peace which we should all desire for itself, but which we must have if life is to continue in the age of the atom bomb.

6. Am I My Brother's Keeper?

WHAT IS THAT TO ME? . . .

THE REVEREND W. ELLIS DAVIES
First Unitarian Church, Orange, New Jersey

> "Nought shelters thee who wilt not shelter me." Francis
> Thompson, in "The Hound of Heaven."

EVEN FOR THOSE OF US who are not yet quite old enough to begin life at forty, the world in which we live is vastly changed from that into which we were born. I well remember the mellow, safe feeling of my own earliest years in a little place in England named Orrell Park.

There was the chapel at the corner where the tram stopped, the library where you could borrow anything from *A Pilgrim's Progress* to *Ivanhoe*, the Orrell Park *Kinema* where you could invade the wild and garish world of Chicago gangsterdom, the electric railway station from which you could get to the city in a fifth of the time it took the tram car, and Mrs. Clark's inimitable sweet shop—all within a few hedgerows of each other, and all surrounded by detached and semi-detached little houses with sunflowers in the back.

After a quiet, yet adventurous, evening with Sherlock Holmes

you could put down your book from the little library, yawn, and
go to bed. Tomorrow would be another day for Orrell Park.

Of course, one was occasionally made aware of people at great
distances from Orrell Park with whom God had less concern.

But now, what is this? Hitler defies Great Britain! And it all
starts from some little, out-of-the-way, insignificant country that
one had hardly heard of before. One knew neither how to spell
nor pronounce the name of it—Czechoslovakia! That the enduring security of Orrell Park should be threatened by events in a
land of which one knew nothing. Absurd! Yet, Hitler, had defied
England. Chamberlain had invented a policy which might yet
guarantee the safety of Orrell Park. But that was a close call!
They were even digging trenches in Hyde Park!

Poland is invaded! Poland falls in less than three weeks. War.
England is at war! *ORRELL PARK is at war!* The serenity, the
tranquility have gone. A few months and—Norway, Holland,
Belgium! But there's the Maginot line. The war is still a long
way from Orrell Park. "He maketh me to lie down in green pas-
tures. He leadeth me beside the still waters. . . . Surely goodness
and mercy shall follow me all the days of my life and . . ." But,
Dunkirk! Hitler threatens he'll be in Piccadilly Circus. Piccadilly
Circus. Good heavens, that's almost in Orrell Park!

The air blitz!

Nights in the damp cold of corrugated iron shelters. Houses
blown out of existence in one's own street. The dining room
windows have been shattered. That one was close! The air-raid
shelter shook.

There came the morning when Orrell Park was not there.
Where was the God who had always taken care of Orrell Park?

In the end it became clear that the people of Orrell Park were
under an illusion. It appeared finally that they were not selected
to be the special recipients of divine mercy. Incredible as it was,
they were destined to share in the suffering of the peoples of
China, Ethiopia, Spain, and Czechoslovakia. At last the vicar of
Orrell Park was in a position to convince his people that there
could be no dependable tranquility for Orrell Park until the
oppressed of Europe and Asia had been led beside the still waters.

I well remember those days back in 1931 when the first rum-
blings of World War II emerged from China. I was among those
who began to organize a boycott against Japan. I sought the
co-operation of a certain lady whom we shall call Mrs. W. She

told me that I was a fool to be concerned with the woes of a bunch of yellow pagans who had no more sense than to procreate like rabbits, and who, anyway, lived far off on the other side of the world.

I tried again to persuade Mrs. W. that aggression was her affair when Mussolini invaded Ethiopia. But our efforts were fruitless, for Mrs. W. told us that we were crazy to worry about a "lot of black cannibals who'd pay you for your pains by cooking you for dinner."

Even the Franco rebellion in 1936 failed to disturb Mrs. W.'s placid faith in peace for America.

So came Munich when Mr. Chamberlain expressed with precision the sentiments of Mrs. W. He spoke of the Czechoslovak people as "a people of whom we know nothing." But Munich was followed by the entrance into Prague. The pressure of the English people forced Chamberlain to make pacts with Rumania and Poland. Poland was invaded, and Mrs. W.'s precious England was at war. Mrs. W. like myself, had come from England and many of her relatives lived there. Mrs. W. wanted England to be saved. There must always be an England. But she did not want her sons to risk their lives at war. What a dilemma!

But see, now! Hitler himself came to the rescue. He made the colossal blunder of attacking Russia and bringing the Red army into the war. Mrs. W. was overjoyed. Her faith was restored. There was, after all, a God in his heaven protecting the righteous. Now, she exclaimed, the Germans and Russians who were equally hideous, would fight each other, exhaust each other, wipe each other out, and by the will of God, England would be saved without the U. S. having to come to her rescue. Evil would be self-destructive and goodness would prevail.

But, like millions of Americans, Mrs. W. had forgotten that she had failed to try to halt the Japanese invasion of Manchuria. She forgot that she refused to use her influence as a citizen of a democracy to prevent American magnates from shipping oil and scrap-iron to Japan.

And so came Pearl Harbor!

If before the war you had asked Mrs. W. for the location of Guadalcanal she would no doubt have told you it was one of those confusing Latin-American countries. Now, however, she could tell you exactly where to find Guadalcanal. Her youngest son lies buried there.

For what should the W. stand in the name of Mrs. W.? It should

stand for Mrs. What-is-that-to-me. She, with her spouse, exists
in the millions. She became her brother's keeper even to the
point of giving up the life of her youngest son.

History has roared at us—at the people of Orrell Park and the
people of Brooklyn and Kalamazoo, that there can be no security
for anyone anywhere now until all men everywhere have been
made secure.

Never again will American boys go out to meet a war and
keep it away from American shores. On the wings of atomic
power any war of the future will do to America what it did to
Orrell Park. Only worse!

There is no security in America. Security is to be found only
in one world. We shall have to end the artificial divisions which
have repeatedly excused greedy, imperialistic exploitation.

The burning question of our times is the question of what we
have learned from the story of World War II. Have we learned
that man cannot survive at the expense of his neighbor? Have
we learned that there are no scapegoats left? That the exploitation of race prejudice is suicidal? Have we learned that, whether
we like it or not, history holds us responsible for the welfare of
the dismayed Jews of Europe and Palestine, of the persecuted
patriots of Greece, of the freedom-loving fighters of Indonesia,
of the famished, tyrant-ridden peasants of China? Have we
learned that our own safety depends on their safety? Or does
history have to scream this lesson at us with atomic bombs and
deadly bacteria to teach us only when it is too late?

If our newspapers are any criterion it would appear that the
lessons of World War II have, if they were ever learned, already
been for the most part forgotten. We talk as though we were
offering, not only political, but spiritual leadership to the world.

And the Great Power to which we address ourselves is the one
great power which has made race prejudice a crime. Let us not
deceive ourselves. We are not going to win the colored Indians,
Chinese, Africans or Indonesians to our way of life by talking
about democracy and waving atom bombs over the world. I covet
for America the opportunity of giving spiritual leadership. But
I am plagued by the question as to whether we can learn only by
experience—which experience, being suicidal, would end the
chance of our ever learning.

The truth is that all too many Americans have been made over
into the image of the Nazi enemy the allies have so recently van-

quished. They have the same dread illusion which moulded the destiny of Mrs. What-is-that-to-me. They think they can injure others without being injured themselves; they think they can survive at the expense of others.

And so, for these, life's untutored, these who do not know that to save themselves, others they must save, there is no peace in the world today; there is no peace for the race-hater with his strident clamor after war; no peace in the distraught souls of depraved men who, to hold back the clock of time, would let their fellows be destroyed; no peace for those whose passions ride the crest of a mob wave.

There is no peace save for the pure in heart; for those who will neither sell nor be sold; who will neither buy nor be bought. One needs not the hermit's cave of the early Christian; neither the high-walled monastery of the timid ascetic. To meet the cruel onslaught of the mob-crazed, psycho-sick meek armies of today's depraved, the race-haters, the prophet-baiters, one needs no retreat, no sword, no cannon and no armor. One needs only that fortress in the soul which, built out of purity, cannot be assailed.

But to be pure in heart? What is this? It is to know that you have never led the children of men astray; it is to know deep within your own being that without self-love, and without a greed for self-salvation, you have tried to save your fellow-men. It is to know that your brother's pain has been your pain and to have learned that this is not a thing from which to run away. To be pure in heart is to have felt and known the joys and sorrows that should make the whole world one.

For such moral rectitude and spiritual tranquility alone is life worth living; to be alive without this purity of heart is to be spiritually dead, yet emotionally distraught, to share the fate of unsaved modern man, to be torn by tensions yet to be dead in spirit.

To be free, free from the clamoring passions of a disordered sick self which mutilates the members of the body of which it too is a member, so to be free, to be pure in heart, is to see, but not alone to see, but to feel the beauty of a single blade of grass, to embrace the universe in one unfolding bud, to sense the grandeur of your creation in the everlasting rolling hills, to feel your own heart pulsating in the throbbing tides that pound the shores. It is to be one with the universe, one with creation, one with the great reality of life which forever is, one with that which is unsullied, unspoiled, to be pure in the embrace of eternal purity. So to be is to find the fulfilment of life's greatest promise, the promise of life at its divine best on earth. Ultimately and finally to embrace this divine heritage is to have learned that "nought shelters thee who wilt not shelter me."

====◆====

THE RESPONSIBILITY IS YOURS . . .

THE REVEREND REX H. KNOWLES
Cochran Memorial Church (Presbyterian), Oneida Castle, New York

> "Speaking of the things pertaining to the kingdom of God: And, being assembled together with them. . . ."
>   ACTS 1:3

WE HAVE TODAY all kinds of speaking about Christianity, and about the kingdom of God. Everyone seems to be speaking of peace and hope and brotherhood; but more assembling needs to be done, more lodging, more mingling, more sharing. More of us must bear in mind what other people have to bear in their hearts. More of us must feel the lashes that cut into the souls of other people.

It has been said that America's number one problem is learning to live together. After all the practice we have had, we ought to know how. We thought we knew, in fact, but we don't. And the rest of the world well knows that we don't.

In America, the home of the free, there are more walls keeping people in or holding people out than in almost any other nation. After more than one hundred and fifty years of living in an atmosphere supposedly charged with liberty and equality, we have come to the conclusion, it would seem, that while all men are created equal, some are created more equal than others. I say, here in America there are more walls than in almost any other part of the world.

Now, we can keep these walls, or we can tear them down. I just mention in passing that there are two methods of meeting the problem of living together. We can keep the walls, or we can tear them down. You must choose for yourself. But I cannot call you Christian if you choose to keep the walls standing.

Do you really believe that God hath made of one blood all peoples on the earth? If you do not, if you make a few exceptions to that word "all," then I cannot call you Christian.

Do you really believe that in Christ there is neither Jew nor Greek, bond nor free? If you do not, if there is some group against which you must confess to some feeling, then I cannot call you Christian.

Do you merely speak the words concerning the kingdom of God—or just listen to them? Or are you willing and able to assemble together with, lodge with, eat with your brothers?

If we would be Christians, we have a job on our hands. We are told that we must love God with heart, soul, strength, and mind, and love our neighbor as ourselves. Our job is, then, to remember whose we are, and to remember who our neighbors are —one by one. Real Christian living always starts there.

The individual counts supremely in God's world. No matter how small his contribution may be, that contribution counts supremely. It is the quality of the individual life that shall decide for us whether we can really hope for a good new world. Nothing is more important in this universe for the future of peace and brotherhood than your living as a Christian individual. And though I can tell you that, and though I can plead with you, I cannot do that living for you. Christianity's power to change the world lies finally in the strength of the individual Christian. God, or Christ, will not do the work for us. We must do it for ourselves. Too long have we been speaking about the things concerning the Kingdom of God—now we must do something about it.

Is there hunger in the world? Then let's do something about it. Is there distrust of other peoples? Then let's do something about it. Is there need for more love among neighbors right here in our own community? Then let's do something about it.

Many of you have asked what you could do for the church. Here is your answer. Do something about these problems. Do something about public health, about international co-operation, about race relations. Do something about this great problem of

living together, of brotherhood—for it is here that the issues of
the church are at stake today. It is here that the ultimate test of
religion's reality is faced. For religion is not only speaking of
the things concerning the kingdom of God, it is also being assembled together with your brothers.

Yes, I know that Christianity does start with the knowledge
and love of God. But I also know that it does not stop there.
Yes, I know that Christianity does start with the needs of the
individual soul. But I also know it cannot stop there. One man
has said that Christianity is a triangular religion consisting of
God, the soul, and my brother. Leave out the brother and the
love of God becomes an unreal thing. Leave out the brother and
the needs of the individual can never be met, for as John Donne
has said, "No man is an island, entire of itself . . . any man's
death diminishes me, because I am involved in Mankind."

However we look at it, we cannot avoid the issue. The number
one problem of America is the problem of living together. And
on the issue of brotherhood, the church will find new glory or
fall, for surely the New Testament tells us that no organization
can long stand on the dry arid wastes of suspicion and pride.
And the issue of brotherhood will be solved not by preachers,
but by laymen. It will be solved, not in churches, but in shops
and movies, buses and businesses, schools and streets and homes.
It will be solved not by anyone else, but by you.

Not long ago one of my friends said to me, speaking of a common acquaintance of ours, "You're a minister. You have to like
her. But I don't." It made me feel as though I were being hired
by a church to do all the Christlike living for the community; as
though no one else had any real responsibility to translate the
gospel into terms of daily living; as though I had been brought
to the community to preach to the people, to pray for the people,
and to love their neighbors so they didn't have to do.

I assure you, the problem is yours. People can cook for you,
clean for you, and build for you—but no one can love your brother
for you. You must do that yourself. And if you do not, I fear
I cannot call you Christian.

Well, how do you stack up in this ultimate test of Christian
living—brotherhood? How do you react to the difference in an
idea, to the form of a name, to the accent of a voice, to the color
of a skin? Abraham Lincoln, a poor white man; Charles Steinmetz, unwanted immigrant; Toyohika Kagawa, son of a Japanese

dancing girl; George Washington Carver, southern Negro. Or
perhaps you would rather think of a Jewish peasant girl, known
only as Mary, who brought untold blessings to the world. How
do you react to the sound of a name, or the color of a skin, or the
slant of an eye?

I am not wise enough to define democracy, but what I know of
democracy tells me that we cannot judge a person by his race,
color, or station in life. I know enough of democracy to know
that a man is of value because he is a man, not because he is a
white man. And I know that worth in a democracy is based not
on superficial facial differences, but on the contribution one
makes to society. It is the strength of democracy that it can count
on the many contributions of many hands.

We were in danger two years ago, because there was a chance
that we might lose in a fight against the totalitarian regimes of
the world. We are in danger today that having defeated them
we may become like them.

We have won the battle against the dictators of intolerance,
so the lights have gone on again all over the world. But of what
use are the lights all over the world, if they do not light up our
hearts? Intolerance, like chicken pox, has a way of spreading.
And it is spreading today. If you have been affected by its con-
tagion, you must throw off the disease. If you have not yet caught
it, you must avoid it as you would the black plague. It is a dread
disease. It cannot be fought with laws. It cannot be cured at
conferences. It must be combated by you, in your own mind.
And now. For intolerance is not merely un-American and un-
Christian; it is inhuman.

O, I know full well that we all believe in brotherhood—but
brotherhood must be a part not merely of our creeds, but of our
deeds as well. It is not enough to study other people and talk
about them. We must do something.

A somewhat disheveled member of an audience at a church
discussion meeting on brotherhood angrily interrupted the
speaker, shouting "Brotherhood has been preached for the last
2,000 years and look at the state of the world." "Yes," flashed back
the speaker, "and water has been in the world for a great deal
longer than 2,000 years, and look at the state of your face. Brotherhood, like water, has to be applied." As a minister, I shall try
to do my best to apply it. I shall try to build the church, breaking
down the barriers of denomination, creed, race, and nation. But

what I do shall not be the final test. The final test will be with you—where you live and work. The final test will be what *you do*.

Will you do more than speak concerning the things of the Kingdom? Are you willing to assemble together with them, dispelling the mist of prejudice? If you will not, if you continue to see your neighbors through the mist of prejudice, then the church will inevitably fail in its great task of brotherhood.

A traveler once related a strange experience he had in crossing a mountain. "One morning," said he, "when the mist hung upon the hills, I was going along my road when I saw an object at a distance, which I took for a monster. When I came nearer to it, I saw it was a man. When I came close up to him, I found it was my brother."

====◇====

I DON'T WANT TO BE LIKE JUDAS . . .

The Reverend Ralph H. Read
The Wyoming Congregational Church, Millburn, New Jersey

"Two beings only have ever known the secret of Judas: Christ and the traitor himself." Thus spoke Papini. And only God and America will know why if our land ever betrays its age-old love of human freedom. America stands today like a potential Judas among the nations of the world. All peoples are wondering whether we too will sell our cherished heritage for a few pieces of silver.

Let it be said to begin with that the problem of Judas is the problem of history. It was not even new in the time of Judas. It is the problem of how to be true to an ideal when the going is difficult. Almost anyone can be a good sailor on calm seas. The faithful mariner is able to weather a storm. Judas betrayed his Lord amidst darkened skies and a gathering wind. To know Judas is to understand ourselves. Oh thou aristocrat among Judeans, better hadst thou loved Christ more and thyself less!

Because Judas' problem is universal in character, it should be

studied by America this Fourth of July weekend, 1947. Once
a year on Independence Day our people love to call to mind the
greatness of their national heritage. These United States may
well pause to consider their glorious tradition of personal liberty.
We should never forget the price in blood and tears, in struggle
and privation, which we have paid for freedom. We need to be
reminded in order that we may be vigilant. Eternal vigilance is
always the condition for holding the personal and spiritual
values we dare not lose.

Judas Iscariot has become a synonym for betrayal. The name
has an evil sound. But Judas was no demon. Like many a man
today he was simply weak. Or perhaps he was strong and merely
fell from a pinnacle built by his greatest temptation. We do not
know. In any event, let us ask what are the lessons his experience
has to teach? *In the first place Judas suffered from an unhealthy
sense of superiority.*

He was the only Judean among the twelve disciples. It is
thought he felt himself to be the aristocrat among the twelve.
That is always a dangerous feeling. The Judeans bore themselves arrogantly toward the Galileans. A Judean in Galilee has
been likened to an Englishman among the Irish. Lecky said that
English blunders with the Irish were due to a conviction that
they were dealing with an inferior people. Some say it was Judas'
Judean resentment of Galilee that stirred him to treason when
he came to feel that Jesus had failed by his own Judean standards. It is so easy to betray an ideal by holding it falsely.

Jesus' earthly ministry was nearing its end. Judas was now
among his own people, probably sharing their skepticism about
Jesus' future. We may believe he was being influenced by those
who regarded Jesus with scorn and distrust. He listened to the
critics who pitied the Master for being an "impractical dreamer"
—as they called him. They thought Christ's was a withered mission, a daring plan which had failed. What chance could he
ever have in the great metropolis of Jerusalem, this rock of a
town which attracted millions of pilgrims and tourists at the
time of the great feast? It was the contempt of a haughty people
who believed themselves to be superior. For contempt Judas
sold for a bit of miserly silver the Saviour he loved. We know
he loved him. Was his love not proven by the depth of his
remorse? But his prejudice had blinded his eyes. He had for-
saken his dearest friend. What was there left for him to do but

take his own life in payment? It was the retribution that falls
upon all contempt. Those who despise others end by despising
themselves.

America has been called the "land of the free and home of the
brave." Would to God it may always be so! But we betray that
ideal when we have contempt for the foreigner. A few thousand
gentiles and Jews whom we call displaced persons rot in concentration camps in Europe. The nations fight to keep them from
their shores. These are the men and women who loved liberty
enough to oppose Hitler. Now that Hitler is destroyed no one
wants to give them shelter. We fear we may be hurt by these
foreigners coming to our shores. As if a small handful of
wretched, broken refugees would pollute the blood stream of our
national life! What are we afraid of anyhow? In the name of
the compassionate Saviour we serve we should let them in. It
is our great chance to show the world a better way. And these
are days when only example counts. The world has had plenty
of sermons from those who have themselves suffered but little.

In the name of him who said, "Inasmuch as ye have done it
unto one of the least of these my brethren, ye have done it unto
me," we should admit a fair share of these troubled folk. What
are we afraid of? Why can't we give the cup of cold water when
it is most needed? Why do we not bind the bleeding wounds
of this bruised man by the world's wayside who has been beaten
and plundered? Is this land of the free no longer free? Is there
no more refuge from life's turmoil in the great melting pot that
was once so open and friendly? Are we the victims of our own
fears? Will we, like Judas, betray our ideals at the point of our
own national prejudice? Will our treason to the right prevent
us from being "good Samaritans?" Will we be untrue to the
love the Master has planted in each of our hearts? These are
questions America should ask as she nears this occasion in her
national life.

In the second place, Judas betrayed Jesus because of his disappointment over the prospects of material power and gain which
Jesus' cause offered.

Judas had pined for a regal kingdom. He now cringed before
the shadows of Christ's cross. He would manage a small bank
account if there were prospects of a bigger one. As treasurer
of the firm he would keep the books providing there was something in it for him. His courage was high as long as he envisioned

an empire. Would not his Lord establish a kingdom and reign
in power? That was his dream. But it was a dream of a dreamer
who could not face the possibility of defeat and a felon's cross.
So one dark night this chagrined and disillusioned dreamer of
power and wealth slipped quietly away from his friends gathered
in an upper room, took his way up a ravine and down a rocky
highway to the city. His dream of power crushed, his hopes for
the future shattered, Judas bargained for the Prince of the World
and lost. For thirty little pieces of silver he thought to find
him a better security and position. It was an ugly gamble and
a sinful betrayal of the Christly ideal.

We are told that "power corrupts and absolute power corrupts
absolutely." Just as Judas was corrupted by his innate love of
power so also America stands in danger of being corrupted. We
once struggled for a minor place among the family of nations.
The Boston Tea Party symbolized only potential strength. For
the most part it was a pitiful protest against taxation without
representation, against being ruled without any voice in the
parliaments that did the ruling. The Tea Party became famous
because it was such a strong gesture upon the part of an otherwise weak people. Even the Declaration of Independence did
not make us a powerful nation, for our chief power was built
up at a later date.

Today the situation has changed. We now hold a power beyond the wildest dreams of our imagination. We have fought
for the right to be free in some of the bloodiest conflicts known
to man. How shall we treat that freedom so costly purchased?
How shall we use our new-bought power? We cannot, like Judas,
expect to hold it by dreams of empire or greed for profit. Money
will not buy either the kind of land or world in which we wish
to live. It will not make our children and their children's
children secure. To suppose it will is to betray the land we love.
From the Christian perspective it is also to betray the Christ
we love.

The final lesson we must learn from Judas is that there is a
better way.

Judas discovered this fact, but too late. His remorseful and
untimely death suggests he saw his mistake. But there could be
no washing the blood of a just man from his traitorous hands.
If he ever saw the light it was too late. We like to think that
perhaps in the end he perceived that love is stronger than hate,

that co-operation is better than competition, mutual aid more blessed than cunning and deceit.

One wishes, and prays, that America will discover these same truths before the night of another war descends upon her. It could prevent that war from coming.

If there was a Satan in Judas that drove him to treason, there are evils in every man and nation that must be conquered and put down. America and her citizenry must never be too proud to admit sin and failure. There are evils within our own borders for which we must repent, if we are to be loyal to Christ.

In his little book, *Beyond This Darkness,* in his chapter, "That These Dead Shall Not Have Died in Vain," Roger Shinn tells of how a few months after the war, General Stillwell flew from Washington to California. "He was carrying a Distinguished Service Cross. He went to the porch of a little farmhouse and gave to the Japanese-American family there the decoration, won in Italy by a soldier from that family. He had been a sergeant who had led his squad in the attack on the enemy. When the enemy drove the squad back, he stayed to cover them and to die. As his family accepted the decoration, they remembered how six months before a band of Americans had tried to terrorize them into leaving their farm."

Honesty compels us to admit there is a Judas in every man. Every man must fight to conquer his own weak and treasonable self that his larger self may be born. And a nation of reborn men and women can give birth to a new world. It is a way of grace, repentence, and forgiveness. It is a better way. God grant America will follow it. It is the way of Christ.

7. The Church and Brotherhood

ALL ARE ONE . . .

THE REVEREND ALSON J. SMITH
Roxbury Methodist Church, Stamford, Connecticut

"... but God hath showed me that I should not call any
man common or unclean." ACTS 10:28

PETER, WHO WAS SOMETHING OF A SNOB, had just undergone a
rather striking bit of education in the field of race relations. He
had gone to sleep—"fallen into a trance," the New Testament says
—and in his ensuing dream his Lord had shown him all the
created creatures of earth and had bidden him kill and eat. But
Peter had refused, saying: "Not so, Lord: for I have never eaten
anything that is common or unclean." Whereupon the Almighty
delivers a sharp reprimand: "What God hath cleansed, that call
not thou common." Peter, being what we would call today "educable," quickly got the point.

The Christian Church, unfortunately, has not been nearly as
"educable" as Peter on the subject of racial snobbishness. The
theory is equality, but the practice is segregation—at least in the

United States. The colored girl who had her baby on the sidewalk in front of the Methodist Hospital in Washington two years ago last January because the admitting authorities did not like the color of her skin—the young Methodist minister in Marysville, Michigan, who was removed from his pulpit by the Bishop because he preached a sermon against the pattern of segregation and discrimination in the community—the official Methodist paper that refuses to print pictures showing white and colored Methodists together—these are all symptoms of a cancerous lesion within the body of our own fellowship.

Recently I received a letter from a good woman who was living on a ranch out in Nevada. She was a retired missionary of the Methodist Church with thirty years of Christian service in China and the Argentine behind her. She wrote in a bitter vein about the Church's attempt to Christianize the non-white peoples in foreign lands while clinging to discriminatory practices at home. "The Church," she said, "is a necklace of rocks around God's neck." And she concluded with a statement from Dean Inge: "The best thing that can be said for the church is that it has made a mess of telling the world about God."

Such barbed words tear the flesh of all of us who love the Church of Christ. I do not think that they are altogether true, but insofar as they *are* true it is because we have ignored God's admonition to Peter not to call "common" that which *he* has cleansed.

As we ponder on the presence of the virus of racism within the very life tissue of the household of faith itself, we ought to do some deep and basic thinking about the function of the church. What's our job? What are we here for anyway?

Because those are basic questions, there are a great variety of answers. Let me suggest two that I think are fundamental.

Our job—to put it as simply as possible—is deliverance. The Christian Church is on this earth to deliver men and women from the physical bondage of oppression and tyranny, and from the more subtle spiritual bondage of superstition and error. There will be general agreement with this latter goal, and rather considerable disagreement as to the former. But the life of the body is no less important than the life of the mind and spirit—indeed, the new science of psychosomatic medicine shows us that they cannot be separated. Body, Mind, Spirit—all are *one* person, one indivisible child of God. And, said Jesus, "I am come that ye might have *life*"—the bread and meat as well as the bread from heaven and the meat that perisheth not.

The function of true religion as a deliverer from bondage is rooted in that great body of ethical and moral principle that we call "the Judeo-Christian tradition." The long search of the Hebrew peoples for God—the search that culminates in the noble words of the Shema, "Behold, O Israel, the Lord our God is *one* God"—is inseparable from their equally long search for freedom from physical bondage—the bondage of Egypt and Assyria and Babylon and Rome. And it is out of the quest for physical freedom that the profound ethical and moral insights developed—and out of oppression came some of the most poignant and moving music that we know. Hear the poet of Israel beside the alien stream:

"By the waters of Babylon sat we down and wept,
  For we remembered Zion;
  We hanged our harps on the willows in the midst thereof,
  And there they that took us captive demanded of us a song,
  And they that wasted us demanded of us mirth, saying
  'Sing us one of the songs of Zion.'
  O, how shall we sing the Lord's song in a strange land?"

Yet, the children of Israel *did* sing the Lord's song in a strange land, they have been singing it ever since—in the streets of New York no less than in the ghettoes of Warsaw and the horrible gas chambers of Maidanek—the Lord's song of justice and righteousness. How many of us who so glibly sneer the word "Jew!" remember that out of Judaism have come the high ethical values by which we no less than they live, and that only out of Judaism could such values have come?

And it was to his religion, too, that the Negro slave in America looked for deliverance from bondage; it was in the midst of oppression that he yearned for the sweet chariot, swinging low, and complained that "he couldn't hear nobody pray," and that "sometimes he felt like a motherless child."

"Justice!" cries the Almighty through his prophet, "I must have justice!" And the achievement of justice for all men—Jew and gentile, white and black, Protestant and Catholic—is and forever must be a primary goal of a religion the Founder of which enjoined brotherliness upon all men as the fundamental law of life.

We are here, then, to deliver the oppressed from their oppressors, to set the captive free, to proclaim the coming of God's kingdom of love and righteousness among men.

But men are bound not only by other men but by ignorance, by fear, by prejudice, by tradition. It is more difficult to free a man from an obsessive idea than to free him from jail. There is no writ of habeas corpus to deliver the mind obsessed with fears and hatreds of "Kikes" and "Niggers" and "Hunkies" and "Greasers." It is in the mind and heart that the cruelties of the hand are conceived. Jesus, as much as any modern psychiatrist, had this sense of the inwardness of life.

And so the second aspect of our function is a combination of *education* and *analysis*. While we fight oppression, discrimination, hatred and injustice externally to deliver men from present physical bondage, we look beyond the deed to the motive of the oppressor, and as good Christian analysts we probe the subconscious depths where lurks the demon and we seek to exorcise him, not only for our own good and the good of the oppressed, but also for the good of the oppressor—who, we ought not to forget, is also a child of God.

Yes, that is our function—to deliver men from physical and spiritual bondage. In Jesus' words, "to make men free." And whom he makes free are free indeed.

Before we can exercise this function, however, we must repent —we within the church—for our heretical ignoring of God's admonition to Peter: "What I have cleansed, call not thou common." We must repent for having—in deeds if not in words— shouted "common, common" at the Jew, the Negro, the Italian, the Chinese. We must repent and we must bring forth fruits meet for repentance not only in the organizational life but in the whole spirit of the church. "Why call ye me Lord, Lord, and do not the things which I say?" How easy it is for us—some of us— to sing piously about

> "The little black baby who rolls in the sand
> In a land far over the sea"

and how hard it is—for some of us—to treat that little black baby with Christian decency when he leaves the land far over the sea and wants to make his home in our neighborhood? How easy it is for us to exalt the Child of Israel who once fled through the Red Sea to escape from bondage, and how hard it is for us—some of us—to permit that modern Child of Israel to spend his vacation beside *our* sea or in *our* mountains?

The truth is, we have not learned to love one another as Christ hath loved us. Although it sounds trite to say it today, it is only as we learn to love one another in the sense in which Jesus used that word "love"—to build goodwill and better understanding among all peoples—that we even begin to exercise our function as Christians.

What are we trying to do? Simply this—we are trying to create an atmosphere in which the love of God can work in all its creative, healing power. Work to relieve the oppressions of the body. Work to relieve the oppressions of mind and spirit.

In *Death Comes for the Archbishop,* Willa Cather tells about the air of New Mexico. Her Archbishop, after a lifetime of service in Santa Fe, had gone back to his native Clermont-Ferrand in France to retire. But he could not stay in France; he had been too long in the new world, and so he came back to Santa Fe. He cannot quite figure out why he had to come back until one morning he suddenly notices the light, dry air: "That air would disappear from the whole earth in time, perhaps; but long after his day. He did not know just when it had become so necessary to him, but he had come back to die in exile for the sake of it. Something soft and wild and free, something that whispered to the ear on the pillow, lightened the heart, softly, softly picked the lock, slid the bolts, and released the prisoned spirit of man into the wind, into the blue and gold, into the morning, into the morning!"

That is what we are trying to do—to pick the lock of ignorance, to slide the bolts of prejudice and bigotry, and to release the prisoned spirit of man into the wind, into the blue and gold, into the morning!

God grant that it may be so.

═══◆═══

THE LIVING CHURCH . . .

THE REVEREND D. WILMOT GATESON
The Church of The Saviour, Philadelphia, Pennsylvania

"For the time has come for judgment to begin with the household of God." 1 PETER, IV: 17a

THERE ARE MANY BLOTS on the escutcheon of the human family, and "bars sinister" deface God's emblazonry. Even the shield of the land of the free and the home of the brave is splotchy: we are not all free; we are not all brave; we are divided; not all one body we. Racial scorn and religious animosity were not the least among the many evils against which our brave men gave or risked their lives in the old world, and now those noxious infections of the soul are becoming epidemic among us. Would-be dictators seek to line race against race, religion against religion, class against class, with lying propaganda; and gullible disciples of these rabble-rousers are taken in by their inflammatory attacks and insidious innuendoes. Calumnies are printed and distributed; whispering campaigns are carried on in the unrecorded grapevine of suspicion; houses of God are defiled, children of God are taunted and attacked, civil rights are denied, social amenities are refused, unfair employment practices are used. Even otherwise honorable and kindly citizens have in them prejudice and hate against some of their fellow-citizens. It is not a pretty picture. The time has come for something to be done about it.

Can the churches of God help effectively in this crisis? Are they doing their mightiest to promote amity in our diverse religious and race relations? Are they watching their own actions and reactions, and guarding their own tongues with a golden bridle? Are they watching for opportunities to correct false reports and vicious remarks, and to spread good will? The best legislators of the government are watching, through commissions and bureaus; committees of voluntary citizens are watching; some individuals are watching. Can this hymn be honestly sung by the Church as a whole?

> Lord, her watch Thy Church is keeping;
> When shall earth Thy rule obey?
> When shall end the night of weeping?
> When shall break the promised day?

The ideal Church of God is ever watching—the Church as God ordained it to be—praying and bidding us to love all men and do good to them. But the churches on earth, the household of God, are made up of fallible souls, some saintly, more faulty. We sinners do not always love the Lord our God with all our being, and our neighbors as ourselves. It may be that much of the harm can be laid at the churches' doors. Among all the efforts that are being made to improve social relations, the churches, their clergy and members together, need to examine themselves as bodies, to see if they are fulfilling the requirements of brotherhood. "If any man say, I love God, and hateth his brother, he is a liar." There are too many members of the Church of God on earth who disdain, if not despise, many of their fellows of other races, creeds, and colors. The tensions are nearing the breaking point. The churches cannot control the whole population, but they ought to control themselves. This is one suggestion, one approach, too seldom considered: that the churches apply painstaking social self-scrutiny, and correct their faults, their own faults, their own most grievous faults; "For the time has come for judgment to begin with the household of God."

One mistake of the historic churches, Jewish and Christian alike, has been that they did not insist on obedience to the prophetic utterances in the requirements of discipleship. It is easier to observe ceremonial acts than to curb instinct and change our ways, to follow a ritual than to follow after righteousness. In the ancient Jewish church, pious zealots were strict about wearing phylacteries (amulets) keeping fasts and festivals, heeding regulations about the Sabbath, ceremonial washings, even to paying tithes (ten per cent; that's a lot!), and giving all kinds of special offerings; but they were not strict about being just and merciful to people. They were exclusive: they considered the uncircumcised outside the pale; they were the chosen people, they had no dealings with the Samaritans, for example. Why did they not hold sacred the obligations laid on them by the prophets? These were the social zeal of Amos, who fought for the poor against their exploiters, the forgiveness and reconciliation exemplified by Hosea, the warnings of Micah against false prophets and against all kinds of oppression, the universal and incisive righteousness demanded by Isaiah who ranked Egypt and Assyria, all nations in effect, as among God's people.

The primitive Christian Church was on fire with the spirit of Jesus, and free from formalism; it was a way of life, patterned after Jesus, was *The Way;* the disciples were "men of the Way." But all too soon their successors began to debate about dogmas and doctrines to the detriment of pure religion and undefiled. Why did creeds rather than conduct, beliefs more than behaviour, become the criteria of church membership? This is not to say that sound doctrine is unnecessary; the right idea of God is requisite to the right idea of good, but it is not a substitute for it. These things ought to have been done, and not to leave the other undone. The Sermon on the Mount at the beginning of Jesus' ministry was its keynote, and is the constitution of the Kingdom of God; the Beatitudes are its bill of rights and good citizenship in the Kingdom. In a sense the Sermon on the Mount is autobiographical, for Jesus lived it; in his subsequent teaching he illustrated it over and over with parables, such as The Good Samaritan, and with example, such as his talking with the Samaritan woman at the well of Sychar. If only the Sermon on the Mount had had at least equal stress with the creeds all these two thousand years, we should have a different world today. Then, to have become and remained a Christian would have meant such qualifications as these: purity and integrity of thought and spirit as well as act; non-retaliation for injuries, with forgiveness and reconciliation; love for enemies as well as friends; an inward reality of devotion with no display in giving, fasting, and praying; absence of criticism and censoriousness of others but strictness with ourselves; no money madness or anxiety about material things which make us both greedy and often dishonest— taking advantage of others. The Golden Rule would have been the law of Christian lands. People ought to read the Sermon on the Mount often and regularly. It has only one hundred and eleven verses, and can be read slowly in eleven minutes, meditatively in fifteen or more. At first reading it seems to turn things upside down; the second and subsequent readings set things right side up. All religions of the world can accept it. It contains wise sayings of the old rabbis, and incidentally is along the line of the Eightfold Path laid down by Buddha. The Lord's Prayer, given in it, was one expression that all delegates could agree to say together at the International Congress of the World Fellowship of Faiths. What a world of justice, right-dealing, and brotherhood, we might be living in today, if the Sermon on the Mount had been a requisite for joining and retaining membership in the Church! We cannot change the past, but we can take heed for the present and the future. For this neglect, in both the Jewish and Christian churches, "the time has come for judgment to begin with the household of God."

Love for the one God is the great article in the Jewish Creed, and love for neighbor the heart of their social law, called by St. James, "the royal law." In Christianity love is the real orthodoxy, hate the real heresy. Love is the highest virtue; lack of it excludes from the Kingdom of God, and ought to put one on probation in the Church. Love is not blind: both of its eyes are open; it sees both the good and the bad in people. We can love even if we do not like, be benevolent and beneficent. Lovelessness is more than half blind; it sees the faults in others but not their virtues, and does not see its own faults. Love is not critical of others, but is critical of self. The humble and right-thinking person makes the best of his neighbor, and is severe with his own shortcomings. In the Sermon on the Mount Jesus used an old proverb of the rabbis to illustrate this: "Why beholdest thou the mote that is in thy brother's eye, but considerest not the beam that is in thine own eye?" Such an attitude is not only critical, it is hypocritical. It is said that idiots have not the faculty of self-criticism; yet it appears to be a general human failing. It applies to whole racial, religious, and color groups as well as to individuals. The Rabbis and Jesus might say in effect to their followers today: "Look to yourselves; each social cluster of you discern the things that are unfair and annoying to others, things that are characteristic and common among you, and strive to change them; stop telling others what to do for you, and do all that you can for yourselves and for your own kind; set your own spiritual house in order, your own social family; cast the huge beam of hate and error out of your own vision and way of life, and then you will be able to see clearly how to right the wrong you suffer and make others suffer; as much as lieth in you, live peaceably with all men, and they will treat you respectfully; make yourselves desirable and you will be desired." There is a verse of a hymn that expresses what ought to be the motive in every congregation, within every racial stock:

> Help us to help each other up,
> Help us ourselves to prove,
> Increase our faith, confirm our hope,
> And stablish us in love.

All this is not criticizing the ideal Church, neither the Israel of God nor the Body of Christ, but the household of God, of which you and I are members. Nor is it laying blame on one race or religion more than another. Name-calling is only one evidence of the ill-feeling within all groups; all of them have epithets for the others, even for their own kind; insults are symptomatic of a more deep-seated disease. There is need for social self-criticism within each body, aiming at internal reform. This is not the whole solution: legislation will still be needed to safeguard the civil rights of all equally; voluntary organizations must still join hands to foster co-operative brotherhood; each individual must cultivate patience, understanding, and loving-kindness. But surely the churches should lead toward that brighter day, happier among ourselves, more blessed in the eyes of God. There is no time to be lost, "for the time has come for judgment to begin with the household of God."

8. He Whom a Dream Had Possessed

THE DREAMER COMETH . . .

THE REVEREND HARRY TAYLOR
Grace Community Congregational Church, Jennings Lodge, Oregon

IT WAS JOSEPH'S BROTHERS who said, "Behold this dreamer cometh, come now therefore, and let us slay him." (Genesis 37:19, 20.)

One can understand the jealousy of Joseph's brethren. He was a very positive young man at the time. In no way did he try to conciliate. He was young, he was gifted, and his father saw genius in him and did not try to hide his belief.

At seventeen some mystic intuition of his life and destiny must have been his, causing him to believe that God had a special work for him to perform. All down history our dreamers and prophets seem to have had an awareness of their destiny and mission. There is the classic example of Abraham Lincoln in the slave mart in New Orleans, burning with indignation as he saw human beings being bartered like cattle, saying: "If ever I get a chance to hit this thing, I'll hit it hard!"

"This dreamer cometh. Come now, therefore, and let us slay him." Why, then, is this instinct so common among us? Why so often do we force our dreamers and prophets and seers to drink the hemlock, or endure the martyr's fires, or agonize upon a cross? Can it be because there is that in us which resents the

147

goodness that we ourselves dare not try? Can it be that these brothers of Joseph were aware of some fineness in him, some exceptional ability, that they could not emulate? You remember the martyrdom of Stephen and how the mob acted before they slew him?

"They gnashed on him with their teeth."

For the dreamer routs us out of our snug burrows and well-oiled grooves to attempt adventures that we would follow but dare not.

"The dreamer cometh!" Has he not come to you, many times, and has it not been your deep regret that you have turned him from your door? Perhaps you can remember a night when you walked out under the starry sky, and the moon looked like a silver ball suspended in a vault of blue. You looked up at that broad dome of mystery, that fathomless ocean of space, and you remembered your dreams—your forgotten, your neglected dreams —and a poignant regret pierced your heart. Perhaps you remembered how the cares of this world, and the deceitfulness of riches, killed the dream.

"The dreamer cometh!" It comes to you in so many unexpected places and for fleeting moments your ladder reaches heaven. But you are afraid of that which is high. You don't want to climb into that rarefied atmosphere and be alone. You had rather be one of many others; you had rather buy and sell and jostle with the crowd in Vanity Fair. Most of us would.

"And there shall be one fold, and one shepherd!" A dream, you say. But now a dream that must come true or we perish. We need stern old Thomas Carlyle in days like these, to wake us up and show us the edge of the precipice to which our "realists" have brought us. "The case is pressing, and one of the most complicated in the world. God's message never came to a thicker-skinned people; never had God's message to pierce through thicker integuments, into heavier ears. It is Fact, speaking once more, in miraculous thunder voice, from out of the center of the world; how unknown its message to the deaf and foolish many; how distinct, undeniable, terrible and yet beneficent, to the hearing few: 'Behold, ye shall grow wiser, or ye shall die! Truer to nature's fact, or inane chimera will swallow you. In whirlwinds of fire you and your mammonism, your dilettantisms, your philosophies and aristocracies, shall disappear!' Such is God's message to us, once more, in these modern days." So wrote Carlyle.

After the first World War our land and our world was filled
with hard-faced men who would stand no nonsense. You will
remember that these hard-faced men scuttled the dream and kept
on scuttling it. And then the second World War came, swift
and sure. And if the same old breed of hard-faced men and
"realists" have their way today then swift and sure the third and
final global conflict will be upon us.

"Will they kill the dream once again?" you ask. I am not sure
that they will. For there are limits even to human stupidity and
folly. The patient cannot always be hypnotized to bring about
his own destruction. There are signs everywhere that the
"dreamers" may be heard in these dread days.

"Armies and navies," says Victor Hugo, "are helpless against
the power of an idea whose moment has struck." Some of us
seem to sense from afar off the first faint signs that men are
beginning to realize on a global scale that the words of the
Prophets of Israel and the gospel of the Man of Nazareth are the
most practical of practical politics. There is growing realization
of our deadly peril and the simple way out.

That has been the trouble all down the ages: the dream has
been too simple. The Sermon on the Mount has been so simple
and yet so sublime that men have turned to devious ways instead.
And now the sophistries and mammon reasoning of the hard-
faced men of profit and power have worn a little thin. The man
in the street feels a little uncomfortable when he hears them.

Men are not quite so ready to slay the dreamer as they were
of yore. Deep down in the consciousness of millions resides the
feeling that perhaps the dreamer has been right all along and
the "Lords and Rulers" wrong.

> "The dreamer dies, but never dies the dream!
> Though Sin may call the whirlwind to his aid,
> Enlist men's passions, trick their hearts with hate,
> Still shall the vision live! Say nevermore
> That dreams are fragile things, what else endures
> In all this breaking world, save only dreams."

Now is the time in history to believe in this dream. Over all
lands a winged hope is flying. You have your part to play in
making the dream come true.

"The dreamer dies, but never dies the dream!" Again and yet
again the tyrant says to himself, "I will make an end of this
dreamer and his dream forever!" But hardly have the martyr

fires died out than some other dreamer, in some other place, takes up the dream and carries it one step forward.

Be careful then to cherish your dreams of the true and the good and the beautiful. Keep your little candle alight no matter what the cost. Let no gust of sordid gain, or fear of the multitude quench that God-given spark bequeathed to you that others may see the Master walking again on human feet.

In the margin of our Bible, pertaining to our text, instead of "Behold this dreamer cometh" we read "Behold, this Master of Dreams cometh."

"The Master of Dreams." Who but the living Christ? The cruel Roman rulers nailed him on a cross and thought that they had done with him forever. But 'tis his spirit that is touching the hearts of men everywhere. Long years ago in Palestine Jesus dreamed a dream and visioned an ideal. And since that day—though they slew the dreamer—that dream of his has spread from shore to shore. It is the sanest, the truest, the most inspiring, of all the dreams of seer or prophet. He bids you and me be true to his dream.

These are times when a great fear grips the hearts of millions. They have lost both hope and certainty; they are swept hither and yon by the vast eddies and storms that have the world in their grip.

I want you to believe that this dream of a world of goodwill and understanding is the surest thing in this age of dread. There is no other way. Millions upon millions, in places we would never suspect, are holding fast to this dream and bearing witness to it in humble ways. Through them race hatred is due to wither and die; through them the spirit of goodwill is spreading slowly but surely.

You may take part in this master dream of the Master Dreamer. Every day you slay an evil thought you add a brick to that kingdom. Every time you erase from your heart racial pride or national arrogance and make wider the borders of your affection and concern for others, you bring nearer the dream.

Teach your child to despise none because of his color, to hate none because of his race, and Christ's dream becomes incarnate in you.

Here we are in this year of Our Lord 1947. The way is dark. Men of power and cunning seem to be in the seats of the mighty. What can we do, you and I? We can live as far as we are concerned just as if this dream of the Master were right here in our midst. For is not that exactly what he said? "The Kingdom of Heaven is among you." Right where you are is the place to begin. Only in this humble fashion shall at long last the kingdom come in all its fullness.

═══◇═══

MAKING THE AMERICAN DREAM COME TRUE . . .

THE REVEREND ORVA LEE ICE
Calvary Baptist Church, Minneapolis, Minnesota

THERE ARE DREAMS AND DREAMS. There are dreams that are "the children of an idle brain, begot of nothing but vain fantasy." There are dreams that live on "after brick and steel and stone are gone." Dreams that come true!

> "Only the dream is real. There is no plan
>   Transcending even a rose's timid glory,
>   A cricket's summer song. The ways of man
>   Are stupors of the flesh, and transitory.
>   There is no truth but dreams, yet man must spend
>   His gift of quiet days in storm and stress,
> Unheeding that a single breath will end
>   With one swift stroke the hoax of worldliness.
>
>   Only the dream will last. Some distant day
>   The wheels will falter, and the silent sun
>   Will see the last beam leveled to decay,
>   And all man's futile clangor spent and done.
>   Yet after brick and steel and stone are gone,
>   And flesh and blood are dust, the dream lives on."
>   —Anderson M. Scruggs

The dream that is real, the dream that will last, is the ideal that has yet to be realized. "Man is not man as yet," sang Browning.

"When all mankind alike is perfected, equal, in full-blown powers—then, not till then, I say, begins man's general infancy."

This dream, this ideal, is indomitable; it is dynamic. It
"comes, comes, ever comes." The dreamer may be dispatched,
crucified, but the dream lives on. Nothing can withstand the
power of a great idea that is in process of being realized. What
ought to be, could be; what could be, must be; what must be,
will be.

This is the way the American dream has come inexorably down
through the long years. It is an old dream, inching down the
hills of time with glacial slowness, but nonetheless, irresistible.
Too old to be numbered with the centuries, it must have first
been in the heart of the eternal. Down history one can trace its
coming, for its steps are large and wide.

The everlasting dream was in the teachings of Jesus. In him
there was neither Jew nor Greek, bond nor free, rich nor poor.
Men were all of one blood. He fawned upon no special privilege
or position.

On June 15, 1215, at Runnymede, came the Magna Charta.

Then the Mayflower marked the coming, ever coming of the
dream. The Bill of Rights became a way mark, and yet we are
over one hundred and fifty years from 1791. In the fullness of
time came Roger Williams, Tom Paine, and Thomas Jefferson,
holding that this truth was self-evident—that all men are created
free and equal and endowed by their Creator with certain inalienable rights, and the American Dream came to birth.

What of this dream, its heritage, its destiny?

The American Dream was born of God. It is of no human
invention. There is no need to cite authority for this. Things
are true not because someone said them, not because they are
found in holy scripture. Truth is truth and needs no shoring up
of halos or mortal decorations. Empirically it has worked out
in the human experience. So is it with the American Dream.
Men are endowed with certain inalienable rights to which "the
laws of nature and of nature's God entitle them."

Cicero recognized this: "Of all these things which learned men
dispute, there is none more important than clearly to understand
that we are born for justice, and that right is founded not in
opinion but in nature. There is indeed a true law, right reason,
agreeing with Nature and diffused among all—unchanging, everlasting."

The laws of man's nature are superior to all artificial and arbitrary laws set up by man, and will in the end obtain while all that contradicts them will perish. We have seen this come true in the institutions of child sacrifice, divine rights of kings, and human slavery. The eternal stars fought against those evils. Governments that have been built upon these institutions have fallen into decay.

The American Dream will come true; if not in America, then somewhere else. Eternity will break out on some other shore, for this dream was born of God.

The American Dream is destined for all. This liberty is no manna to be kept and hoarded by one nation or people. Said Blackstone, "Man, considered as a creature, must necessarily be subject to the laws of his Creator. This law of nature, being co-eval with mankind, and dictated by God himself, is of course superior in obligation to any other. It is binding over all the globe, in all countries, and at all times; no human laws are of any validity if contrary to this, and such of them as are valid derive all their force and all their authority from this original."

As well try to imprison the sunshine in your small fist as to try to keep the American Dream for one race, one people. "America for Americans" must crash like Dagon on its face before this ideal that is "binding over all the globe, in all countries, and at all times."

There must be "liberty and justice for all." I think that were Abraham Lincoln to look upon the modern scene, he would revise his words to say, the *"world"* cannot exist half slave and half free. And any international settlement will fall like Babylon unless it conforms to "the laws of nature and of nature's God." The American Dream must come true for all peoples. One world, with liberty and justice for all. And it is coming. No power or organization can withstand it. Any nation, church, or system that gets in its way will be crushed to dust before it; even if this, our own, our native land gets in its way it also will likewise perish.

To the well-wishing delegation of divines that hoped for the cause of freedom that God was on their side, Lincoln replied that it was not important that God was on our side, but that we were on God's side. So it is. His truth goes marching on. It goes on with us or without us. Its triumph is sure.

What a mighty surge of enthusiasm should possess us to feel with deep reverence, that in making the American Dream come true, we are on God's side—that we are allied to that which will triumph, and that God may order that it triumph through us. How knightly we should feel and rightly noble when we take our stand against bigotry, intolerance, discrimination, and the evil and blight of racial hatred. How like a prophet we should feel when we make "liberty and justice for all" come true in action.

Barney Ross, champion boxer, lay in a slit trench at Guadalcanal after having fired his last bullet in defense of his three wounded buddies. "We were praying," he said. But I will let Barney, who is sitting beside me tell you the story himself:

"Yes, Ralph, we were praying. Somehow you learn how out there whether you know how or not. You don't care who hears you either. In that whistling hell I heard all our voices; realized we were all praying. I was praying to the Jewish God; Atkins, my pal, with a mangled leg, was praying to the Protestant God; the kid with the hole in his body and middle finger of his right hand stuck in it to stop the flow of blood was praying to the Catholic God. Suddenly, I realized a strange thing, we were all praying to the same God. We were all using about the same words, asking for the same things, and it struck me that there was no real difference between us at all, and I couldn't help but wonder if people have to come so close to death to realize that we are all on the same side and all trying to get to the same place."

Yes, Barney, you were helping make the American Dream come true! Is it just a dream? Maybe it is. But this I know, there is within me a very law of my being which says it ought to come true; come true for the whole wide world. And what ought to come true, could come true; and what could come true must come true; and what must come true, will come true.

Better still, it is not only my dream. It is not only your dream. It is God's dream!

> "Dreams are they—but they are God's dreams.
> Shall we decry them and scorn them?
> That men shall love one another,
> That white shall call black man brother,
> That greed shall pass from the market place,
> That lust will yield to love for the race,
> That man will meet with God face to face—
> Dreams are they all.
> But shall we despise them—God's dreams?

Dreams are they—to become man's dreams.
Can we say nay as they claim us?
That men shall cease from their hating,
That war will soon be abating,
That the glory of kings and lords shall pale
That the pride of dominion and power shall fail,
That the laws of humanity shall prevail—
Dreams are they all.
But shall we despise them—God's Dreams?"

                                        —Thomas Curtis Clark

=== ◇ ===

THE MEANING OF PEARL HARBOR DAY . . .

THE REVEREND C. R. FINDLEY
Evangelical United Brethren Church, Newton, Kansas

I NEED HARDLY REMIND YOU that just six short years ago something
very crucial happened to all of us. For the second time within a
generation our nation was plunged into war. Newsboys were on
the streets with their extra editions shouting, "Japs attack Pearl
Harbor." Radios were blaring the fateful information that we
were now at war. Sunday afternoon naps were rudely interrupted
with the startling news. Knots of curious citizens gathered on
street corners and commented on the turn of events. One of
them said, "We can go over there and whip the Japanese any
Wednesday morning." A group of boys playing football on a
vacant lot stopped their play for a little while in awe of what
had happened. A young soldier ready to go home to be married
had his leave canceled that night. A leading churchman preaching to a great union service that Sunday night prayed for our
president and for our nation. We were at war.

In that war something very precious in human experience was
laid on the line to see if it could survive. The American dream
was at stake. Could democracy, as we knew it, stand the shock of
two great wars within one lifetime? Would we win our battle on

the war front and lose our battle on the home front? Would the forces of fear and hatred engulf our nation in the wake of the war and effectively destroy our democracy? My reason for repeating these questions after six years is that they are still in the process of being answered. The hate-mongers are very much alive today. Old groups and new that cater to racial and religious hatred are mustering their forces in an attempt to capture America.

That such hate-mongers would throttle democracy is apparent to the most casual observer. For while there is much confusion about the meaning of democracy, and the word is frequently used in a deuces-wild sort of way, our American dream of democracy does have a certain specific content and meaning. Democracy means that many kinds of people can live together in peace. It means that we give more than lip service to the declaration that "all men are created equal; that they are endowed by their Creator with certain inalienable rights; that among these are life, liberty, and the pursuit of happiness." It means that America is "one nation, indivisible, with liberty and justice for all.

Democracy, as we know it, means that men shall be judged as men, and not as members of a certain race or religion. It means that Albert Einstein, a great scientist and a Jew, who had to flee from the Nazis early in their regime, could find not only a refuge but a place of honored citizenship in the United States. It means that George Washington Carver, a Negro, who in slave days was once traded for a horse, could rise to become one of the greatest scientists of our generation. It means that that neighbor of yours or mine who happens to be a Catholic is no less a good neighbor because he believes in a creed that we do not share.

Such a way of life must have strong foundations if it is to survive the attacks of the hate-mongers. And the history of our nation proves that democracy roots itself deep in the practice of religion. Civil liberty has followed and has been the product of religious liberty. And the demand for religious liberty was based upon a high ethical conception of God and a just estimate of the worth of man. The two great commandments: "Thou shalt love the Lord thy God . . . thou shalt love thy neighbor as thyself," have been the motivating force in the soul of many a pathfinder as he blazed the way to freedom of conscience. Love to God presumes that God is worthy of love. And to be worthy of love, he must be the Father of all men; as Peter said in his address to the household of Cornelius: "I see quite plainly that God has no favorites, but that he who reverences him and lives a good life in any nation is welcomed by him." And love to our neighbor presumes that every man has in him a native dignity and worth that can be brought out only through goodwill. And this goodwill must not be partial; it must include all men. "If ye love them that love you, what reward have ye? And if ye salute your brethren only, what do ye more than others?"

Men holding such conceptions of God and their fellow men could not long acquiesce in any system that made slaves of men's consciences. The Pilgrims broke away from their native England, first to Holland, then to America, in order that they might worship according to the dictates of their own conscience. The Puritans followed them. But this latter group especially were not willing to take their own medicine. They wanted liberty of worship with the further liberty of making everybody else worship as they did. They came to an open clash with Roger Williams, an energetic young clergyman who believed that no civil magistrate had a right to punish a man for his purely religious practices. Williams was driven out of the Massachusetts Bay colony and established the colony of Rhode Island at Providence. There for the first time in history, a commonwealth was planted whose fundamental constitution included a guarantee of religious liberty. So wisely was the charter of Rhode Island drawn, and so securely was liberty provided for, that it served the colony and state for 180 years.

About the same time that Williams was having his troubles with the Puritans of New England, Lord Baltimore settled the colony of Maryland as a refuge for Roman Catholics. The early laws concerning religion were very liberal, allowing all Christians to worship in their own way, and even making it against the law to call a man a derogatory nickname because of his religion. An irony of history was that the Catholics later lost control of the colony of Maryland, and their religion was completely banned until after the Revolution.

Establishment of the colony of Pennsylvania by the Quakers under William Penn was another high-water mark in the history of American liberty. All creeds were placed on a footing of complete equality. Peaceful relations were established with the Indians, and during the Quaker rule there were no wars or massacres such as plagued the other colonies. The most just and humane laws ever known up to that time were passed by the people's own representatives. Penn and his followers literally translated religious liberty into civil liberty.

Our generation needs to re-examine and to re-think these fundamental conceptions of democracy as we have inherited it in America. We need to see anew that there can be differences without violence; that there can be sincere loyalty to our deepest convictions without hatred and bigotry toward those who differ from us. Indeed, there are many fundamental differences of belief and religious practice among Jews, Catholics, and Protestants. And those differences have loomed so large in many parts of the world that they have built a complete barrier to understanding. But it must not be so among us. We must resolve our differences in the American way—in the forum of reason and persuasion, and not in the arena of force and fear.

All of us believe in the golden rule. We are all indebted to the prophets of Israel for their teaching of justice, without which the worship of God is mockery. "Let justice run down as waters, and righteousness as a mighty stream." "What doth the Lord require of Thee, but to do justly, and to love mercy, and to walk humbly with thy God?" All of us know something of the message and ministry of Jesus, our Jewish friends receiving him as the great prophet and teacher, one of their own race, and Christians acknowledging him as their Lord and Saviour. And his message for America, with its divisions and hatreds today, could well be the retelling of the parable of the Good Samaritan.

And when it comes to differences of race which the apostles of hate use so effectively, we would do well to ponder the answer given by Jan Masaryk when he applied for permission to enter the United States. On the form which he filled out in the space opposite the word race, he wrote "Human!" And we could also remember with profit the words of Roy L. Smith: "The race problem will never be solved by those who always see red."

In a spirit of humility and appreciation I would now like to speak a word in behalf of each of the groups in America around which or from within which tensions are forming. Perhaps I can best do this by imagining myself a member of each of the groups.

"I am a Negro. I am an American, but not by choice in the original instance. My fathers were brought here as slaves, as you well know. But I love America, and my greatest hope is to remain here and to make a worthy contribution to American life. I have done my part already as I had opportunity. I have given you the Negro spirituals. I have given you an example of child-like faith and of undaunted cheerfulness in the face of overwhelming miseries. I have given you scientists, educators, musicians, artists and writers, not to mention farm laborers and household servants through all the years of my sojourn. I do hope you will include me when you speak of liberty and justice for all."

"I am a Jew. They say I am different, and I am. I have been scorned through the centuries by the so-called superior races, Egyptians, Babylonians, Romans, and some that you know about more recently. I have outlived my past persecutors. I may outlive the present ones. I have given the world its greatest prophets and lawgivers. I have written your scriptures. I gave the Christians their great leader. In American history I helped Columbus discover the western hemisphere by providing him money and by five members of my race accompanying him on the voyage. One of my race helped finance the American Revolution. Millions of my people came to America to escape the oppressions of the Old World. I am now making my contribution in every walk of our national life. I worship the same God you do. I obey the same Decalogue that you do. I am wistful as I contemplate the American dream, and sometimes I am terribly afraid. I want to be your friend."

As a Christian, what shall I say to these friends in minority groups? What can I say? Perhaps I should pray the prayer of the publican, "God be merciful to me a sinner." Perhaps I should remind myself that I can best be loyal to the Christ whom I worship by practicing his laws of justice and charity. Perhaps—nay, surely—I can serve my day and generation best by trying to avert the coming of another Pearl Harbor day. And for this task there is only one strategy and only one word. It is a divine word. It is a human word. Its real meaning can only be spoken by those who live a life of understanding. The word is *love*.

9. The False Slogan:
"The Jews Killed Jesus"

THE REVEREND W. NEVIN ELLIOTT
Shiloh Presbyterian Church, St. Mary's, Pennsylvania

"There they crucified him." JOHN 19:18

No SLOGAN OF HATE AND IGNORANCE has been more persistently exploited than the false slogan: "The Jews Killed Jesus." It has been the choice invective of the merchants of mendacity of bigotry and fanaticism.

The picture of the incorrigible street urchin caught in the act of pilfering by the Jewish merchant and, having broken away, standing at a safe distance and shouting in pugnacious defiance the epithet "Christ-killer," is both familiar and tragic. But it is no more tragic than the ghastly spectacle of millions of adults who harbor the same or kindred untruths about our Jewish brethren.

The statement is not only outrageous because it is an outright falsehood against the people of God and therefore a reflection upon his judgment, but it is a direct lie about God himself. Murder, like all sin, is the visible manifestation of a spirit alien to God. Every crime and every evil, whether individual or social, blossoms in an atmosphere of antagonism to God. But the seed

161

is first to be found within the hearts of men. It was the hostility
of men to the spirit of Jesus which was responsible for the death
of Jesus.

The Jews played a very minor part in the death of Jesus. It
was so negligible that one might almost call it incidental. With
racial and international ill-will and misunderstanding so prevalent today, there is an urgency about the need for exposing
falsehood, and for bringing truth under the spotlight.

Now, the falsehood that "the Jews killed Jesus" has been, unfortunately, fostered by the Christian Church itself. A great
many Christian teachers and ministers have overemphasized the
part played by the Jews in Jesus' death. Half-truths, inadequate
presentations, slipshod scholarship—all these, have been com-
pounded into a gigantic injustice until this Frankenstein monster of opprobrium has attached itself to a great branch of the
human family.

There is no time like this present hour for Christians everywhere to begin to re-state in terms of unmistakable truth their
indictments of those responsible for the death of Jesus.

Intolerance Killed Jesus

This spirit was found principally among some of the leaders of
the Church in Jerusalem. That it happens to be the Jewish
Church is incidental. Jesus has been killed by a multitude of so-
called Christian leaders for 1,900 years. Whether they were pharisees, theologians, professors, or scholars, their fundamental attitude was one of intolerance. They were so ultra-ultra-conservative
that new ideas were abhorrent to them. Nothing must deviate
from the letter of the law.

But Jesus was a liberal. He broke the shackles of the letter,
and obeyed the spirit of the law. His ardent democracy, and his
utter defiance of cherished traditions were shocking. He feasted
with publicans and sinners; He healed the sick on the sabbath.

There was only one way to eliminate this innovator, only one
way to silence this rebel. He must be liquidated. It was intolerance that killed Jesus. *Not the Jews.*

Commercialism Killed Jesus

On the first day of the Passover when Jesus entered the Temple
and upset the tables of the money-changers and drove out the
crooked traders, he incurred the enmity of this group. Here it

was the spirit of greed and covetousness in the hearts of some would-be theologians who cared nothing about theology, but everything for money.

How often has the Church, since that time, committed itself to the specious doctrine that the end justifies the means. To provide necessary animals for the sacrifice was the end. To profit by the convenience afforded, at a four per cent brokerage fee, was the means. The Church has never been free from commercializing the things of religion.

When Jesus condemned this process and called it by its true name, robbery, only one course was left open to those who profited thereby. Jesus must be liquidated. The spirit of commercialism in the hearts of selfish men killed Jesus. *Not the Jews.*

Corrupt Politics Killed Jesus

Jesus was brought to the bar before Pontius Pilate. Pilate was a career man. He had sold himself to a system of Empire in which he was inextricably entangled. His selling price was power. Whatever would bring him into greater favor with Rome, that he would do. He was always engaged in weighing influence and eventualities. The possibility of having to get along with certain people weighed heavily against Jesus before Pilate. If he handled this case in the wrong way he could be put in a very uncomfortable position. When his loyalty to Caesar was appealed to, he was left no choice. Somehow he had to prove his loyalty and satisfy these evil forces. Truth, right, justice—what mattered these, if he could buy personal comfort and future preferment?

> "Lo! freedom weeps.
> Wrong rules the land
> And waiting justice sleeps."

So, for his personal comfort, Pilate must liquidate this rabble-rouser. The spirit of corrupt politics killed Jesus. *Not the Jews.*

Despotic Power Killed Jesus

Although a king in name, deriving his authority from Rome, Herod Antipas represented more than this. He was the leader of the social upper-crust in Jerusalem. He was a sophisticate who flouted conventions. He was an autocrat who played fast and loose with morals, lavish living, and political power in his daily life. But he kept his chicanery cloaked well by craft and subtlety.

When Jesus once called him a "fox," and denounced his murder of his brother Philip in order that he might marry his sister-in-law, Herodias, the King was displeased.

The appearance of Jesus before Herod on Good Friday morning offered a splendid opportunity for retaliation. Before Herod Jesus stood silent. The King could endure almost anything but the silent, accusing gaze of Jesus. So he eagerly seized this opportunity. First he must have his sport. So Jesus was crowned with thorns and robed in red and called by Herod's own title, "King of the Jews."

But Jesus must be liquidated for Herod's peace of mind. It was the spirit of wicked, despotic power in Herod's heart that killed Jesus. *Not the Jews.*

Cynicism and Greed Killed Jesus

Shakespeare made one of his characters, Iago, say of Othello, "He hath a daily beauty in his life, which makes me ugly."

This was the feeling of Judas Iscariot toward Jesus. Judas was a disillusioned idealist. When he found that Jesus was not to set up an earthly kingdom where Judas himself might become prime minister, he vented his disappointment and disgust with himself upon Jesus. Jealousy and greed were the logical concomitants.

What happened to Judas sometimes happens to disillusioned idealists today. They fail to see that

> "Still as of old
> Man by himself is priced.
> For thirty pieces, Judas sold himself,
> Not Christ."

Make no mistake, the spirit of disappointment, of jealousy, of cynicism in the heart of Judas killed Jesus. *Not the Jews.*

The Mob Killed Jesus

That crowd in Pilate's courtyard—whoever dared to state that it was made up solely of Jews? Jerusalem was a metropolis. This mob was little more than a rabble. Yet it was composed, in all likelihood, of respectable people.

Now crowds are only capable of action. There is rarely any sane collective thinking. Emotion rules mobs. This mob wanted an execution. It needed only one man to cry "Crucify him!"

How true the pattern runs. Whether it be in Jerusalem 1,900 years ago, or in Georgia only yesterday, it is the same. How easily do angry, thoughtless rioters lynch one of our Negro brothers today? The irresponsible spirit of the mob killed Jesus. *Not the Jews.*

Militarism Killed Jesus

> "The fairest soul that ever dawned in Galilee
> Was crucified by Roman soldiers on a tree."

In an imperfect world, I suppose, soldiers will probably always be a necessity. But these Roman legionnaires were minions of the empire-building spirit. Their household god was blind obedience to duty. They were the puppets manipulated by the agile fingers of a nefarious system no less culpable yesterday than today.

The spirit of militarism and force by might in the heart of the world killed Jesus. *Not the Jews.*

Indifference Killed Jesus

In the multitude assembled in Jerusalem to celebrate the Passover were many obscure faces, many confused voices. The tragic events of Good Friday are played out to a ghastly finish against the somber backdrop of this indistinct blur of sight and sound. These "uncaring nobodies" who were untouched, unmoved by Jesus' desperate plight; these human nonentities who "passed by on the other side" declaring, "It is none of our business"—all these thousands helped to kill Jesus.

. Again, and yet again in human history this spirit of indifference in the hearts of men kills Jesus. *Not the Jews.*

What think you, then? Did the Jews kill Jesus? His murderers were not confined to one place, one people, one age, one day. The cyclorama of the crucifixion is the result of the work of sinister forces in the life of man. Let us brand forever the responsible agents of Jesus' death. Make no mistake. It is the evil of bigotry and hatred in the heart of man that kills Jesus. If it was present then, it is no less with us and in us today.

If we are going to place the guilt of Jesus' death, let us place it squarely where it belongs. Away with this false calumny about the Jews. They no more killed the Son of God then you and I.

How truly Edwin Markham puts it in his poem, "A Cry for Brotherhood?"

"Yes, from the trembling lips of many a seer
The whole wide world has heard, and still can hear
The Psalms, the Torah, and the Talmud speak
Protection for the plundered and the weak.
Shall not the race whose gifts have been so great
Have some protection from the tooth of hate?

Protest this cruel wrong
In thunders of the sermon and the song.
Let cries go forth in shrill, tempestuous note!
As if they rose from Tempest's roaring throat.
Let there be thunders in the world; let be
A protest that will shake the ruler's knee.
Let there be protests till the happy hour
When Justice shall unclothe her arm of power."

10. Mother's Day

MOTHERS OF PEOPLE OF GOODWILL . . .

THE REVEREND JOHN I. DANIEL
First Congregational Church, Union, New Jersey

"She riseth also while it is yet night and giveth meat to her household." PROV. 31:15

AMERICANS ARE IN A TENDER MOOD TODAY. In millions of homes, sons and daughters are trying to tell their mothers what she means to them. We set aside this day to express our gratitude— for her devotion and love, for her wise and understanding counsel, for her sharing of our joys and sorrows alike. With the glow that comes from doing something that comes straight from the heart, we shower our American mothers with messages and flowers and gifts.

Today the lot of many of our mothers is a hard one. They are the homemakers, the housekeepers and cooks, nurses and spiritual guides, shopping experts and controllers of our family budgets. In many families, the mothers of America must also work at some job outside the home to augment the family income.

In the best of times, the average mother has her hands full. But in times like these, with food and clothing at record-breaking prices, she labors under terrific handicaps. It is hard to plan nourishing meals for growing bodies, with some cuts of meat reaching for the dollar-a-pound mark. It is hard to keep youngsters neatly clothed, when children's garments cost as much as those of grown-ups, and are quickly outgrown.

Families nowadays cannot put much extra money away for the schooling of their boys and girls, or for security in old age. Millions of men and women have already cut into their savings to meet the rising cost of living. In all this, the burden falls heaviest on the mother of the family, because it is she who has the main responsibility for making ends meet.

And I am ashamed to say that the mothers who suffer most from this needless situation are the very ones who deserve the best that a grateful nation can give them—the mothers who were widowed by the war. Today their pensions barely provide the sheerest necessities. A war widow receives $60 per month, plus $18 for the first child, and $15 for every additional child. If her husband carried a full $10,000 GI insurance policy, and she is under thirty years of age, she receives an additional $55.10 per month. $133 per month for a mother and child! $4.44 a day, for two people's rent, clothing, food, heat and light.

Where are the extra pennies for a movie, for the small luxury that takes the grind out of living? No wonder many of these gold-star wives have been forced to move in with relatives, or leave their children with parents or in-laws, or to take a job to make ends meet.

Some, who succeeded in borrowing a few hundred dollars, have gone into small business enterprises of their own. They put in long hours, usually for meager returns. The hazards of a small business today confront hundreds of thousands of American families, including many veterans, who wonder whether our system of free enterprise means freedom for big business only.

These are some of the realities faced by millions of our mothers, and no Mother's Day tribute to them is worthwhile unless it helps lessen their burden. If we are sincere in our desire to give some measure of return for their devotion to us, we will do all in our power to stop inflation, to bring prices down, to put better housing and more consumer goods within reach of the average family purse.

We are people of faith. We believe in a Divine Being of goodness and mercy. We know that we can make our prayers come true, if we work to provide more comfort, more security, and more happiness, for more of the people everywhere throughout our great country—and throughout the world. That's everybody's responsibility.

Every good mother worries about the physical care of her children. But that is by no means all. She wants her children to be healthy in every sense of the word, and health is no longer a physical concept only. Every reputable psychologist and psychiatrist agrees on that. In fact, the new constitution of the World

Health Organization, an agency of the United Nations, starts with this principle: "Health is a state of complete physical, mental, and social well-being and not merely the absence of disease or infirmity."

Every intelligent mother knows this, and does everything she can to give her child a healthy, well-adjusted personality. She wants him to keep the friendly, trustful attitude of childhood. She wants him to get along well with his companions, all through life.

But, unfortunately, even the most thoughtful mother cannot always protect her youngster from the baneful effects of social evils in our society today. For instance, imagine how a mother feels when her child comes home crying because he has just been taunted by his playmates for his race or religion. Imagine how the child feels! Some youngsters never get over the bitterness of being scorned for the color of their skin or for the country their parents came from, or the church their families go to.

In this America of ours, no mother should have to worry about protecting her child from the shock of racial prejudice or religious bigotry. In a country founded on the premise that "all men are created equal," that human dignity is inviolable and sacred, no mother, whatever her race or religion, should ever have to apologize to her child for the ignorance and malice displayed by some of our neighbors or fellow citizens. Yet many of them are forced to do just that—even those whose husbands and sons fought and died for human rights.

There is no finer way of paying tribute to our mothers than to fight the ugly evil of religious and racial prejudice whenever and wherever we meet it. We learn about the fatherhood of God in our churches; our schools teach the brotherhood of man. But until we practice real brotherhood with all our neighbors, we have not really heeded the lesson, nor accepted God.

And the victims of prejudice are by no means the only sufferers. A wise mother understands this, and tries to keep her child free from emotional ill-health and maladjustment. She wants him to grow up a sensible, well-balanced individual, capable of getting along with all kinds of people—able to appreciate and enjoy the differences which give zest to human relationships.

More and more of our school programs are put forward with this in mind. Education in democracy is education for life as an American citizen. But character-moulding, we know, begins long before schooldays. It begins in the home, with our mothers.

No wonder we say that "the hand that rocks the cradle is the hand that rules the world." Unfortunately, of course, this is not so. For, if the mothers of the world had their way in the council-halls of nations, no son would ever kill another woman's son in battle. If mothers could always make serene and beautiful lives for their families—unhampered by poverty, overcrowded homes, and degrading slum neighborhoods—what white child would ever look with scorn upon a colored child? If mothers could always bring the true message of religion to their firesides, what child would ever sneer at the faith of his playmate? If mothers were free to fulfill their mission, the bigots and tyrants of this world would never make headway with their vile appeals to prejudice and rancor.

Motherhood is indeed a sacred charge—and it should also be a joyful one. But too many mothers are so harried and loaded down by drudgery that they arrive at middle age worn out, unable to enjoy their well-earned leisure. For these tired and overworked women, motherhood never ceases to exact a penalty. Nothing in the laws of God or mankind justifies this.

American sons and daughters are privileged beyond all others to change this state of affairs. We have abundant physical resources and a government that must follow our mandate—if only we will express ourselves. If our moral drive is strong enough, we can start today to better the plight of all of our mothers, and their families, whose happiness and prosperity mean so much to them. Inflation, high prices for the essentials of life, racial discrimination and religious bigotry—all these are millstones around our necks, hampering us in the fulfillment of sacred aims and responsibilities.

The American mother, rich or poor, black or white, Christian or Jew, wants to bring up healthy children, who will become God-loving, law-abiding, happy men and women. She wants to know, too, that her sons and daughters will be able to live out their lives free of the scourge of another war. She looks to a world of peace and freedom for all people everywhere—and she wants her children to be the kind of men and women who will build it.

She deserves our help—not just on Mother's Day—but every day. For as we pray for a world that will offer a decent future to every mother's child, we must dedicate ourselves to the practical tasks before us today. And this way will our millions of American mothers, who have a right to hope for a better world—be *truly* honored.

11. The Way of Understanding

THE LIBERAL MIND . . .

THE REVEREND JACK DAVIS
The Methodist Church, Sarasota, Florida

HISTORY IS NOT A LEVEL, monotonous flow of events; it is not a steadily rising tide of intelligence, morality, and culture. Rather it shows a pattern of change. Significant periods of reform and apparent progress are followed by devastating times of reaction. Eras of good feeling, prosperity, peace, and democracy are followed by times of unemployment, discouragement, loss of faith, curtailment of liberty, approval of cruelty, willingness to accept some form of dictatorship and to go to war.

We have come to accept these changes as inevitable. But are the extremes to which they go inevitable? Normal human beings experience times of elation and times of depression; but when these moods go beyond certain limits, we say the persons affected are insane—they have a "manic-depressive psychosis."

It may also be true that when the condition of human society moves violently from one extreme to another, society itself should be pronounced insane. At any rate its effects are so disastrous to the institutions of society, and to the bodies, minds, and souls of individuals, that if there is any way to moderate these extreme heights and depths in the changes of our common life, we are under obligation to find it.

We have been enjoying a period of national prosperity, with full employment. In spite of the war, it has been a time of unprecedented liberty of thought and speech, and opportunity for a large segment of our nation. But today we are entering a period of nationwide reaction. The first of these indications is the one-sided fight against Communism. Every student of world affairs knows that Christianity and democracy occupy a middle course. It has been from the depressed working masses of the world that Communism has arisen. Fascism and Nazism came as reaction to its threat.

It is easier to fight Communism than American fascism, because Communism is a foreign importation, while fascism is social reaction wearing American clothes, and called by American names. Charles P. Taft, president of the Federal Council of Churches, a Cincinnati lawyer, says of this: "My concern primarily is with the fact that most business men, faced with this situation, join in a witch-hunt against the Communist bogey, instead of learning to understand our system, and learning to promote and defend it." I agree with Mr. Taft that the only way to combat these and all other "isms" is to practice democracy, and to strengthen the reality of a truly Christian way of life.

The second fact indicating a period of reaction is the strong anti-labor sentiment sweeping the country, and finding expression in the labor bills that have been made law by Congress. It is not surprising that our Congressmen would be trying to define the limits of the power of organized labor. But apparently the intention is not to correct abuses, but to impoverish the working class. These bills are full of the venom of reaction.

The third fact suggesting reaction is the practice of trying to solve peace-time problems with military power. If we put together the appointment of military men in top diplomatic posts, and the Truman Doctrine, committing us to military intervention anywhere in the world, they add up to the fact that we are looking to military power to solve our problems to an extent that is alarming. We like to think that we use destructive weapons only for the defense of our homeland and freedom. But we should not forget that we are still human, and throughout most human history, weapons and armies have been used as much to deny liberty to citizens as to protect citizens from enemies.

The only way Adolf Hitler could militarize Germany in peacetime was to suppress the liberties of the people. There are countries today, including some to which our country is giving military aid, in which military power is used to hold down the people who want the kind of liberty that we enjoy.

The fourth fact that indicates the coming of reaction is the increasing friction between racial groups in our country. Sometimes, as in Germany, reactionary elements deliberately create race tension. But if the reaction is a part of an economic depression, the tension is increased by the competition for jobs. As jobs become scarce, the competition becomes a contest between groups formed on the basis of race. There are signs of deep racial unrest. The antidote for reaction in all its forms is the open liberal mind. That is what education is supposed to give us. But education sometimes fails, because people keep forgetting that all true liberalism is religious in its origin. Liberal minds want freedom to seek the truth, and they believe that the truth when discovered will make them free. Liberals, wanting freedom for themselves, do not want to limit the freedom of others. They don't want to be dominated, and they don't want to dominate anyone else. They have faith in the power of free men. They do not think of freedom as doing what they please, for they know that in any society, freedom is restricted.

The best guide and support for the liberal mind is the quality of religion found in the Jewish and Christian traditions. Jesus drew men to him, because in his presence men knew themselves to be free. It was he who said, "Ye shall know the truth, and the truth shall make you free." And the common people heard him gladly. Time and again in human history, those in power have forgotten the common man. And in forgetting him (they have forgotten Jesus), they have lost the liberal mind, and they have plunged their nations into periods of reaction and bitter suffering. So the liberal mind can be recognized by these qualities: it is persistent to get and to proclaim the truth; it believes in freedom for itself and for all men; it has faith in the common man, and it believes that he can be trusted with liberty.

As we seek to cultivate the liberal mind, our greatest obstacle will be the love of money. The gravest warnings that Jesus ever uttered were against the corrupting effect of the love of money. He never condemned money as evil, yet he said, "With what great difficulty shall they that have riches enter in the Kingdom of God," One of the hardest things to understand is how the religion of Jesus could continue as the dominant religion in a civilization whose motive power is the worship of money. The primary cause of reaction in this and every period of history is the men and women who love money and prestige so dearly that they will sacrifice everything, including their immortal souls, to acquire it. It was the blindness of such people which was the immediate cause of the crucifixion of Jesus. He loved the common people too much to see them fleeced by the money-changers in the name of religion. A true liberal loves people more than he loves money, and no amount of material goods can induce him to do that which will hurt people. The test comes when we have a decision that may on the one hand improve the security of a lot of average folk, or on the other hand improve our own financial status. Our decision will indicate whether we are liberals or reactionaries—whether or not we are willing to damn humanity for our own private gain.

In closing let me sum up the things that are important to do if we would cultivate a liberal mind. We should resist those forces dominated by the subtle idolatry of money-worship. We should enter wholeheartedly into the practical application to everyday life of the religion of our choice. Encourage the free discussion of all public matters. Tolerate every voice; do not condone the suppression of any, even those we fear. Grant to every citizen the liberties you seek for yourself. Judge every change in our nation or the world by whether it increases the freedom and well-being of the common man. Do not tolerate any discriminations based on race. Oppose reactionary restraints on the rights of workingmen and women in their unions. Stand for the supremacy of the civil power in our government against all militarism. Demand and work for the unity of the world.

Each in his own way, however slight, can thus testify by word or act, to a search for a working liberalism in the faith that its truths will help free mankind from evil.

THE AFFIRMATION OF LIFE . . .

THE REVEREND WILLIAM HOWARD MELISH
Holy Trinity Church, Brooklyn, New York

IN WHAT DOES THE ATTRACTIVENESS OF JESUS LIE? Is it that he was a stern prophet of things to come? A disciplinarian who subordinated the things of this world to the hope of heaven? A puritan who taught self-denial as the first rule of life? There have been many who would have it so. Yet the gospel record states emphatically otherwise. Jesus and his followers practiced no such self-denial. In a day noted for religious ritual and ceremonial observance, Jesus rebuked the legalists and placed his emphasis upon the living spirit. If there is any single phrase in the gospel record that sums up the purpose of his ministry, it is his proclamation: "I am come that you may have life, and have it more abundantly." Is it not in his constant affirmation of life that there lie the undying atractiveness of Jesus and the appeal of his movement?

Jesus loved the natural world. His mind was saturated with impressions of its beauty and vitality. He lived in Nazareth, a village sct on a hillside overlooking the fertile plain of Esdraclon where the river Kishon threads its way westward to flow into the visible blue waters of the Mediterranean. As a boy he may well have found relief from the care of four younger brothers and two younger sisters by flight to the fields. On the Roman road that traversed the valley moved the caravans of the Syrian and Phoenician merchants. On the hilltops were the flocks of the white sheep and the black goats, so easily distinguished and divisible on the right hand and on the left; in the vineyards were the husbandmen and the laborers; in the fields the sowers and reapers and gatherers-into-barns. The strength of Jesus was drawn from the earth. In later life his illustrations and parables were of the earth—earthy.

Jesus also knew the attractiveness of village life. He saw how immersed a man can be in the buying and selling of cattle, in the taking of a wife and the making of a home. He watched the children in the market-place with their singing and dancing games.

Jesus respected work and honored workmen. He was himself

an artisan-craftsman who made a living for himself and that large family for which, as the eldest son, he was responsible, by making yokes and plows and wheels and furniture and joists and beams for cottages and barns. It was with a workman's sarcastic humor that he said, "Why do you see the speck of dust in your brother's eye but fail to see the rafter that is in your own?" It is probable that Jesus was so sympathetic toward the poor because he had known so much poverty in his own family household. Eight mouths are many to feed, and only a man who has known the pinch of hunger and the bitterness of scarcity could use the illustrations Jesus constantly employed—of mending a patch on a garment so often repaired that this latest patch proved its final undoing—of a woman who lost a silver coin and searched the whole cottage until she found it and was so relieved that she called in her neighbors to rejoice with her; of a man who had so little in his own cupboard that when a friend summoned to a midnight journey asked for the loan of five loaves of bread, he had to go out into the night and rap on a neighbor's door. Such illustrations stem from the simple annals of the poor. Jesus the carpenter had eyes to see and ears to hear.

Beyond his concern for the workers and the poor, Jesus had an unusual interest in all sorts of people. When we think of the limitations of small-town life and the provincialism and narrowmindedness of the small-town mind, isn't it something of a miracle that this small-town carpenter had in him none of the racial or national bigotry so prevalent in his day? Compare him with his own fellow citizens when he preached his first sermon in the little Nazareth synagogue. He commended a Phoenician woman who had sheltered Elijah and he spoke of a Syrian leper whom Elisha had healed. The good pious church people of Nazareth were so incensed at what they considered a reflection upon them that they threatened to run the carpenter out of town. In fact, there was a first-class riot. And Jesus was constantly criticized for the friends he made and the company he kept. The Galilean farmers naturally disliked the tax-gatherers and they resented it when Jesus entered the home of a Levi and had dinner with him and his friends. As religious men they particularly looked down their noses at their northern neighbors with their alien, heathen views, and they flamed with anger when Jesus told a story of a certain man who hailed from Samaria.

Jesus was interested in people. He saw in his next-door neighbor the hunger for better things, and in the alien stranger he recognized the same leaven of the spirit of God at work. When he befriended the outcast, and welcomed the emotionally distraught and mentally unstable, and preached good tidings to the poor, he was carrying out only different aspects of one single task—to make men whole, and to release in humanity its divine potential wholeness. We begin to understand something of the mass-dynamic that Jesus unleashed in Palestine; why the gospel says so simply that "the common people heard him gladly." It was because of Jesus' great credo: "I have come that you might have life, and have it more abundantly."

We stand in a day when men and women need that same *affirmation of life* which was the proclamation of Jesus. He saw the earth in all its bursting beauty, its laborious toil, its crippling poverty and ignorance, its incredible possibilities. This world is no blind, meaningless, mechanistic process; it is a gift and a privilege; it is "new every morning"—a poet's dream, a builder's vision, a craftsman's delight, an artist's creation! This is no world to be blown to atomic smithereens.

It is disturbing to the sedate and comfortable to see whole peoples on the march today. Many in America look with bewilderment and antagonism upon the multitudes in China, in India, in the Soviet Union, in Indonesia, and in Africa. We fear their differences, this self-assertion of new group-interests, this competition of a vast dynamic and a youthful vitality. Do we ask with Jesus if the spirit of the divine creation may not be as much at work in them as we like to believe it has been in our own historic emergence as a people and a nation? Christ commended a heathen from Samaria because, although he did not acknowledge God in his thoughts or with his lips he nevertheless better exemplified obedience to the law of brotherhood than the priest or the layman whose days were spend in the Temple.

Jesus understood the needs of people and sought wholeness for them by bringing them within his movement to realize the kingdom of God. The truth is that men and women become whole, in body, and spirit, as they sense a reason for living, and as they are caught up in the great causes of God in their day and age. Let that happen and they will turn the world upside down, beginning with themselves; there is no discipline they will not accept; there is no self-denial they will not face and transcend.

Look what Jesus and his disciples did! They gave up many things. They worked. They shared. They distributed. They suffered. But the point of all this is that these trials and sufferings were things accepted as part of a greater affirmation of life. That is why any man or woman who comes to care supremely about the use of his life, and the use of the lives of others, will always discipline himself, that he may have self-control to be useful. Such is the discipline and self-denial which accompany and flow from the affirmation of life which stems from Christ. It is put in its clearest form in the book which, above all others, the Master loved to read and quote, in the fifth and sixth verses of the fifty-eighth chapter of Isaiah:

"Is not this the task that I have chosen?

"To loose the bands of wickedness, to undo the heavy burdens, and to let the oppressed go free, and that you break every yoke?

"Is it not to deal thy bread to the hungry, and that thou bring the poor that are cast out to thy house? When thou accost the naked that thou cover him; and that thou hide not thyself from thine own flesh?"

Can we of the organized churches give voice to the affirmation of life which was Christ's proclamation, and inspire in people that faith in themselves working together which can transform human life into the Kingdom of God?

=====◆=====

THE WAY OF UNDERSTANDING . . .

THE REVEREND ELWOOD ERICKSON
Congregational Church, Haworth, New Jersey

THE TEXT IS FROM THE THIRD CHAPTER of Ezekiel, 15th verse: "Then I came to them of the captivity at Tel-abib, that dwelt by the river Chebar, and to where they dwelt; and I sat there overwhelmed among them seven days."

A British officer, not a chaplain, during the war commented on the failure of many of the chaplains to get a responsive note from the soldiers, and explained it by saying that they did not have "the dimmest foggiest notion of what the ordinary soldier thinks about." In the vast variety of experiences that comprise ordinary careers, we do not have the foggiest notion of what others are really thinking. Every life has its own secret, often an enigma to others, sometimes a riddle to oneself. To interpret that secret is a difficult task, requiring precise knowledge and a consecrated imagination.

The psychologists have an interesting word to describe this power of a consecrated imagination—the word empathy. Empathy is the power of seeing in, a stronger term than sympathy, the power to see with. The latter may end in a fine and noble sentiment, may stir the heart and stop there. Empathy slips the key of understanding into the closed door of a man's life, enters into the deep-down-under perplexities, fears, and aspirations. For instance, in true creative writing, an able author sees into the lives, motives, and aims of his characters. One of them, Willa Cather, wrote that at the age of eight she rode around her father's farm and became acquainted with her polyglot neighbors —Swedes, Norwegians, Danes, Bohemians, Germans and French Canadians. "I used to ride home in excitement. I always felt as if they had told me so much more than they said—as if I had actually got inside another person's skin." That is empathy—the power of a living and consecrated imagination which made the books of that fine writer creep into so many lives with penetrating understanding.

Though the old prophet Ezekiel never used the word, he did use the technique. He had come to his people at the time of a great national crisis. Yet, like so many in high position, only dim echoes of his people's heart-breaking anguish came to him. He really did not have the foggiest notion of what his people were thinking about. But he went down to learn more about them. He went with them in their captivity at the river Chebar, lived with them, shared their food, their thoughts, entered into their sufferings. "I sat where they sat." Then there came an astonishing revelation. With this more precise knowledge which let him slip the key of understanding into the closed door of his nation's mind, a feeling of awe, wonder, oppressive humility swept over him. "I was astonished—overwhelmed."

What is he saying? In our intricate human relations, the only way really to understand people is to sit where they sit. That means the only way by which we can enter into living and vital communication with our fellows is to enlarge this pitiful little

ego of which we are so proud into an extended and expanded
personality. It is when we can think ourselves into the inner
life of others, get at their lonely center, that we arrive at the
beginnings of a true relationship. Figures—alien, remote, dim—
then become human, become brothers. With this new knowledge
comes astonishment, indeed an oppressive humility. We learn
in Laotze's fine words: "The deeper insight into human beings
becomes, the more sacred does every individual being seem to
us." Gone are all those doctrines that imply that God selects a
chosen few. Of course the mean, the self-admiring, the unlovely
is hated by the best of men, as it should be. But is that the real
person? May there not lie within that man something lovable
which is slowly fading under the fierce heat of an all-consuming
passion or choked by an overwhelming selfishness? But if we
could get at the lonely center would we not be astonished? To
feel ourselves related to all souls, to be able to address ourselves
to humanity, is to sit where others sit and is to share the Christ-
like spirit of a consecrated imagination.

Yet few of us do. We go through life and never sit where
others sit—never learn what life means to others or what they
want of it. Whence this reluctance, this blindness?

It may be because knowledge is disturbing and we do not want
to be disturbed. We like to build retrenchments around childish
prejudices to ward off new or different convictions. For instance, in drawing up our blueprint for a Christian society,
most of us approach it not to find out what Christianity says,
but rather to support our own view or the views of church or
party. So faith can create blindness through piety, cursing where
it thinks it blesses or adores. Sacred error has a tougher life
than truth and is exceedingly difficult to overcome. What priest
and church have blessed is embalmed for centuries. To disarm
faith of its poisoned fangs is a major operation.

Knowledge is disturbing, but the intolerance which separates
is due to our dangerous ignorance. This fanaticism which refuses to sit where others sit grafts stupidity upon superstition
and makes the jungle that chokes all modern life.

Our reluctance to enter into the lives of others with a consecrated imagination may be due to the fact that it not only
disturbs us, but it also hurts. The more we know the more we
ache. Shakespeare's Miranda says, "Oh, I have suffered with
those I saw suffer." And so does every sensitive spirit. To enter
into the mystery of another's pain, to see what they endure, the

shames borne without a whimper, temptations overcome, dismal frustrations met, is a soul-wracking experience, and most of us avoid it if we can. When we extend ourselves into the lives of others, we invite strains and tensions.

> He who lives more lives than one
> More deaths than one must die.

This ripened intimacy with life can hurt when it breaks through our dismal pride. We may discover in our self-adulation that we can loathe a thing for years only to find in the end that we have been guilty of that thing in our own person. We all condemn intolerance. Most of us know that it is due to ignorance. Yet a man can carry intolerance under his cloak, caress it gently and hide its meaning to himself, never really know it for what it is because he calls an ugly thing by a fair name. To be disillusioned is painful and usually avoided. But an honest man will ask himself some searching questions, however painful. Do I so love truth and right that I am willing to submit to an exposure of what in me is unknown to myself, though it make me humble and ashamed? Am I willing to be made glad that I was wrong when I thought others wrong? Am I ready to sit where others sit even though it be the seat of self-judgment? This is the astonishing purging of a Christ-like, consecrated imagination.

Consider this experience of the prophet in the intricate problems of international relations. The "red hot ploughshare of international politics" is sundering society into wide chasms of thought which are fearful and alarming. Ours is a world of controversy, tension, and suffering. National aspirations, subdued during the war, are now breaking out in a fierce flame of violence and destruction. Despite global communication and transportation, other peoples are still dim and alien to most of us. We know so little about them—about their aspirations, their traditions, their fears. How desperate is the need now for an imaginative understanding which is able to put us in the place of other peoples across the world, to sit with them where they sit.

Like an individual, a nation has its own secret. The key to that secret is to be found not only in the sectarian skills and acquisitions but in slipping the key of understanding into the nation's culture, aspirations, needs, and hopes. Half of our confusion is due to the fact that we read about people instead of reading them. Even that which we read is woefully inadequate, too often distorted and dangerous. No system explains itself

save from within. When we have listened to the voice of a
people's soul, at the lonely center of a nation's life, we find that
here are all the emotions, the aspirations, the fears that have
stirred in our own souls. Everywhere the human heart, when we
get to it, is homelike. To understand a people one has to understand its soul.

Only as such inner knowledge is more widely and wisely
spread will we get some vast reconciliation in the time to come.
Hate is now answered by hate, resentment by resentment. Something else is needed—intelligent goodwill which alone can break
this awful chain. This is not easy either to believe or practice.
But hate can never overcome hate. In the words of the Master:
"How can Satan cast out Satan?" He cannot. When we can
enter into the lonely center of a nation's soul, sit where they sit,
then these dim, fugitive figures become so like ourselves that, with
the prophet, we are astonished.

"But who is sufficient for these things?" No one. We have
never seen life as gracious and fair and noble as it really is. We
have also never seen it as distorted and twisted and deformed as
it really is. No man could know all that evil means and live,
for the vision would break his heart. Jesus had that vision and
it drove him into the black anguish of Gethsemane. One cannot
do these things by the mere exercise of the will. In God alone
can man meet man. The whole system of the universe seems to
rest upon this divine law of driving men upward toward the
center to the one great life, the Infinite God. Our failure or
our success in life is a matter of relationship with God. The
verdict concerning Christ is an inner verdict. Success or failure
is an affair of what is going on within us. The outside events
have the power to bless or curse only by reason of what we are.
So a society under the reign of God, with its understanding,
tolerance, and intelligent goodwill is going to arrive only when
we ourselves have become worthy sons of God. The secret of
victory is in our inner training. In the words of the Imitatio,
"He to whom all things are one, and who draweth all things to
one, and seeth all things in one, can be steadfast in heart and
remain peaceable in God."

IS TOLERANCE ENOUGH?

THE REVEREND JOHN R. BODO
Wolff Memorial Presbyterian Church, Newark, New Jersey

THE OTHER DAY, in leafing through the Modern Library's *Anthology of American Negro Literature* I came across the little poem called "Incident." This is how it read.

> "Once riding in old Baltimore,
> Heart-filled, head-filled with glee,
> I saw a Baltimorean
> Keep looking straight at me.
>
> Now I was eight and very small,
> And he was no whit bigger
> And so I smiled, but he poked out
> His tongue, and called me "Nigger!"
>
> I saw the whole of Baltimore
> From May until December;
> Of all the things that happened there
> That's all that I remember."

Fate has seen fit, in this case, to indulge in a little irony. For that little colored boy was Countee Cullen, one of our finest American poets, whereas the white boy who slighted him is a forgotten man. Were it not for the despised Negro's poem, he would not be remembered at all.

There is among the masses of mankind a grudging, work-a-day, live-and-let-live tolerance. It is based on the instinct of self-preservation. Its motto is the negative Golden Rule, "Don't do to others what you wouldn't want them to do to you."

But there arises the question, "Does tolerance of this kind have the moral strength to win a lasting peace? Is such a tolerance the answer to our quest for national and personal security? Is tolerance enough?"

It is a great art to tolerate anything that is too different. Anyone who differs too much from us tends to be irritating or even shocking. The common reaction, then, is to hang a tag of condemnation on anyone whose color of skin, religious belief, political thought, or manner of speech is too different from our own. Such tags as "Nazi," "Communist," "foreigner," "wop," "mick," are a dime a dozen. But rare is the man, and blessed is the man, who can boast a wide-open mind!

Most of the time the possibilities of tolerance are not realized. Instead, it becomes a pose, to be struck whenever expedient; a profession of faith without corresponding action. I have in mind certain catch phrases bandied about by the ignorant and the intolerant, which reveal them at once for just what they are. Let me name some of them.

"I wouldn't want America to be overrun by foreigners. We always get the scum of Europe."

This one crops up whenever immigration is being discussed. After striking a pose of tolerance toward distinguished foreigners like Albert Einstein, the intolerant man hastily qualifies his statement for fear that the Department of Justice might hear him and relax the rules. He likes foreigners, he says, but not too many of them and only the very best, of course!

Why, in the name of common sense, should we sift immigrants so carefully when in our own nation we allow criminals and morons to raise large families? What is more, there would be no American patriots today if once upon a time the American mainland had not been overrun by foreigners.

"I wouldn't want to see any harm done to the Jews. Some of my best friends are Jewish."

In Nazi Germany there was hardly a man or woman who did not have at least one good Jewish friend. This friend seemed to be an exception to the rule that all Jews were enemies of the German nation. But the rule held fast: the Jews had to be liquidated. And they were.

"I wouldn't want my daughter to marry a Negro."

This statement is popular with people whose show of tolerance seems very convincing to the naive observer. What kind of argument is that anyway? My daughter will marry whomsoever she chooses. The only reason I might discourage her from marrying a Negro is my fear of the punishment her white friends—even the most "tolerant" ones—would inflict on her for doing it.

Tolerance may be a virtue. Often it is merely a pose. Sometimes it degenerates into a vice. I am referring to the tolerance practiced by large sections of the Christian Church.

The sham of the average church's tolerance appears clearly on at least two fronts—in its pattern of racial or national segregation, in the social snobbishness of the membership.

The Christian Church preaches the doctrine of human brotherhood under God, the Father. In the local church, however, the national and racial prejudices of the members prevail so completely that the moral tone of the church becomes the same as that of a club where membership is restricted by law, whether written or unwritten. Where some of these divisions are not so apparent in the Sunday morning congregation, they are very obvious in the societies of the church. Invitations to join a certain society may be extended to all, but the very texture of the society shows who will and who will not be welcome.

Tolerance is not enough! It is not enough to make allowance for whatever difference there may be between our fellowmen and ourselves. It is not enough merely to let them live; we have to help them live!

In a sense, Jesus was the most intolerant man who ever lived. His shattering blasts at the self-righteous pharisees are monuments of righteous intolerance. He was thoroughly intolerant of all sham, but more than tolerant of human weakness.

When Jesus met Matthew, the social outcast, collecting his crooked gains at the customs table, he could have said to him, "My good man, I don't blame you. You are part of a rotten system, that's all. People despise you, but I, for one, sympathize with you." That would have been tolerance. Instead, Jesus said to Matthew, "Follow me!", and the tax collector left everything behind to become a new man.

When Jesus met the woman who was a moral outcast he should not have taken note of her at all. Even the most tolerant have to watch their reputation, and talking to a prostitute in plain view of everybody is most unwise. But Jesus was more than tolerant. He appreciated her foolish gift, the expression of her desperate quest for forgiveness, so deeply that he held her up in front of the entire company as an example of the beauty of repentance.

Mere tolerance is not enough. At its best it is a negative virtue. At its worst, a positive vice. What is needed is a fighting tolerance. Our world is shrinking rapidly. Every twenty-five years or so we launder it in blood, which makes it shrink all the faster. Brotherhood is no longer an ideal or a dream. It is an imperative for the survival of the human race. Lukewarm, insipid, passive tolerance is inadequate. What we need is a restatement of the gospel of Christ in terms of fighting, saving helpfulness, in terms of uncompromising brotherhood under God —no strings attached!

> "Live and let live!" was the call of Old
> The call of the world when the world was cold—
> The call of the men when they pulled apart—
> The call of the race with a chill on the heart.
> But "Live and help live" is the cry of the New—
> The cry of the world with the Dream shining through.
> The cry of the Brother World rising to birth,
> The cry of the Christ for a comrade-like earth.

═══◇═══

BELIEF IN OUR FELLOW MEN . . .

THE REVEREND WINSTON L. KING
First Congregational Church, Waterville, Maine

THERE IS NOTHING MORE DIFFICULT than to maintain a balanced but vital faith in men. The extremes are all easier than the good middle road.

For instance, it is perilously easy to *dis*believe in men. The ordinary wear and tear of living does things to our faith in men. Remember that man who borrowed five dollars from you, and returned you abundant but worthless promises to repay? Or that friend of yours who betrayed your deepest confidences? Or perhaps in your business you run into the seamy side of human nature—the trickery, the meanness, the graspingness of people. Perchance the spectacle of the continual struggles of men against each other, each and all in the name of truth and right, makes you ask: What does this all mean anyway?

But we are not faced alone with *dis*belief, but also *mis*belief in man. It is perhaps impossible to believe in man too strongly, but it is perfectly possible to believe in him wrongly. Rousseau, the French writer and philosopher whose ideas did so much to influence the French Revolution of 1789, was one such. He believed blindly and uncritically in the native goodness of man. It is society's vices (he said) which spoil men. Let each child be brought up naturally, that is, largely free from the so-called "civilized" conventions, and he would be a perfect creature. Strangely enough the revolution which his ideas inspired ended in a dictatorship and produced a fierce appetite for conquest and military glory which bathed Europe in blood for a generation.

Our own public documents sometimes seem to believe in man without qualification: "Created free and equal" is one phrase. Of course when they wrote that they probably had only *white* men in mind. But even for white men several tons of law books have not sufficed to guarantee even the most elementary equality in our society.

It is also possible to believe in *man* but not *men*. This is the original sin of Communism. Much of what it says about Man is wonderful. But somehow in the concrete process of achieving this glorious destiny for man, individual men get ground to pieces. Somehow in the name of Man, individual men are betrayed.

Somewhere between these extremes lies the Christian faith in men. The Christian belief in men goes deeper in its disbelief and rises higher in its faith than any other philosophy of man.

Christianity is very realistic in its appraisal of men's failings. Too realistic, some people tell us—realistic in the way a man is when he tells you that your shiny nose is a veritable beacon light; that your trousers, which have lost just a little of that knife-edge crease, look as if they had been slept in; or realistic like the person who calls a spade a steam-shovel and shouts it aloud at least twice every time he talks about spades.

Yet paradoxically Christianity is also optimistic about men, far more optimistic even than those who naively believe in man's unquenchable goodness. This creature who is a deep-dyed sinner is also capable of sainthood. He who sins against God in word, thought, and deed can also glorify God by word, thought, and deed. He is not a helpless pawn of fate, but the master of an eternal destiny. His name, son of man, is only an alias; his true name, whatever subdivision of mankind he may belong to, is son of God. Here is an optimism, at least of possibilities; here is a belief in the stature of man, which far exceeds any other optimism of which I have ever heard.

Frequently enough, stirred by some tale of heroism, some music, or inspiring words, we sit back, close our eyes, and conjure up the image of noble Man—noble man fighting against terrific odds, carrying on his endless battle against his ancient foes—fear, superstition, disease, pain, and hunger. He has the proportions of a Greek god, and the courage of a Christian martyr. And we say fervently: I believe in man! I am on his side!

Then we open our eyes and see the real people about us, those we meet on the street or do business with daily. And they don't look like Man. It is difficult to think of them as belonging to the same species. For *men* are not all godlike in build or martyr-like in character. They are tall and short, fat and thin; they bulge at both the right and wrong places. They do not ordinarily look heroic, but more often just medium—busy, worried, sometimes pathetic, sometimes irritating. And the question stares us in the face: Do we believe in Man, or men? The ideal dream-man, or real flesh and blood men? Can we believe in these latter as builders of the Kingdom of God? What of the wrongs done in our communities? How do we treat the people who work for us, or those who serve us in garage, elevator, or store? Do we treat them as though they were animated pieces of furniture placed there for our use and convenience? Or do we treat them with fine Christian condescension, a "my good man" attitude? Or is it that we proudly tell newcomers: The *best* people come to *our* church? It may even be that we can speak feelingly of the shame of large city slums and the corruption of political machines, but live comfortably within sight of small town menaces to health, or sound of small-time grafters!

Much of our "love" for man is without respect. The Friends (Quakers) can show us the way here. They have a fine record of active but respectful doing good to their fellow men. One example is a recent project of theirs in Mexico. A number of recruits—doctors, nurses, social workers, placed themselves at the disposal of Mexican authorities in certain communities. And the words "at their disposal" are literally true. They did not go in and set up their own kind of center, saying politely but firmly: "We have come to work for your good—in our way." They actually let the Mexican workers put them where they would and take over direction of the social centers. Perhaps the arrange-

ments and methods were not always those they would have
chosen, but they adhere firmly to their policy: We are here to
help you, in the way *you* want to be helped. It takes far more
grace, much more real belief in men, to work with them as
equals to accomplish the good we desire, than to hand it down to
them from heaven, ready made on a golden platter.

Despite our best efforts we have our blind, prejudiced spots
and pass them on to others without thinking. The individual,
no matter how worthy, never has a chance to prove himself but
is put in the groove that prejudice has carved for him as soon
as he is sighted. And, be it said to our everlasting shame, it is
adults who pass on the poison virus of prejudice to our children
—for race or faith mean little to them till we inoculate them
with our vicious habits of mind.

Where shall we begin to practice our love for man, or as the
Christian says, for *men?* Let us believe in them and love them
as our friends and neighbors; without possessiveness or dictatorial
spirit; without prejudice as to race or creed; and extend this
living faith and hope as far as our human might and the fellowship and prayers of the church of Christ can carry it!

===◆===

THE POWER OF EXAMPLE . . .

THE REVEREND ROWLAND A. DAVENPORT
The Veterans' Hospital, Portland, Oregon

IF ANYONE SHOULD ASK ME what New Testament character lived
most fully the gospel Jesus preached, I would say without hesitation, Barnabas. When it came to presenting Jesus in the universal language of love, we must consider Barnabas as a standard
bearer. His life was so attractive that people forgot what he
preached and remembered him for what he did.

Barnabas was by nature a retiring character, the kind of person in whom the world finds little journalistic interest. What
this type accomplishes is not apt to be spectacular, and humility

prevents the individual from appointing anybody as publicity agent to advertise his acts of love.

We first read about this Christ-like character in the fourth chapter of the Acts of the Apostles in connection with the social program of the early church. This congregation was evidently a broad cross-section of the community, bordered on one side by people of means and on the other by people of poverty. Those who lived on the crest were unusually conscious of the needs of those who lived on the flats and endeavored to banish their immediate economic wants through a program of voluntary gifts.

During a season of unemployment, with its pressing need for help, our friend Barnabas, the record shows, "having land, sold it, and brought the money and laid it at the apostles' feet." If we were to judge Barnabas' generous gift in the light of present-day giving, our materialistic minds could readily understand why it was written into the records. When we want to raise several thousands of dollars for the relief of the less fortunate, we go to our largest contributors to church activities and secure their gifts and pledges. We advertise these front-window givers and use their apparent generosity as a psychological prod to raise the balance of our needs. From this standard, Barnabas' gift rightly belongs in the story.

But we cringe at this interpretation of Barnabas' generous gift, for we know this was not the spirit in which it was given. Luke would never have used it as a great example of giving if it had been. We must look for a motive elsewhere in the nearby story of Ananias and Sapphira.

Here is a couple who saw the response of the church to generosity and desired for themselves such praise and goodwill. The Scriptures tell us that they, also, sold possessions and gave to the church. But where Barnabas gave all the proceeds, they gave only a part, claiming they were equally generous. They wanted all the glory but were unwilling to pay the price connected with it.

Barnabas gave with no earthly praise to stimulate him and he gave through no pressure other than need. Barnabas gave because of the love of Christ which controlled his heart and hand. Only one other giver has excelled our generous friend in the matter of finance, and that is the widow who gave one cent. If her story was not in the Bible, we would no doubt have Barnabas as the standard of generosity.

We next hear of Barnabas in the Ninth Chapter of the Acts.

Saul, who had been the most aggressive of the opposition, had met his Lord on the road to Damascus. After this revolutionary experience, he spent several years of meditation in the nearby Syrian desert. Now he was back in Jerusalem knocking at the door of the room where the disciples were assembled. You can see them scurry into a close huddle upon hearing who was seeking admission. "Is it the hated Saul, the persecutor?" "Can it be true that he has accepted our Lord as his Christ?" "Can we trust him?" These questions were rapidly asked within the group, and over the last one they were more than troubled. They were not ready to court added trouble.

Attached to that group was one who had the generosity of forgiveness that was somewhat lacking in the others. "If Saul claims to have seen the risen Lord," argued Barnabas, "and is now a fellow-traveler in the way, why not give him a chance to prove himself?" So through the ever-extending arms of Barnabas the little giant secures an admission into the inner circle of those he once despised, hated, and persecuted and who, in turn, had feared him. It calls for a bit of divine grace to see the good in the worst of men. Barnabas possessed this grace.

I have often wondered what would have happened to Paul if Barnabas had not had this insight and made this stand. With Paul's innate drive when possessed by a challenging cause, he no doubt would have accomplished great things for Christ. But with the active opposition of both the Jerusalem Church and the Hellenists, it is doubtful whether he would have got started as soon as he did. The church would have been a poorer institution if he had not, for the New Testament would have been a different Scripture. Approximately half of the books, containing thirty percent of the wordage, came from the pen of Paul.

If there is any single human factor that saved Paul for the Church and gave us this large portion of the Holy Word to guide our thinking and conduct, that human factor was Barnabas, a man who could see good in the worst of men and had a generosity of forgiveness.

We have another window opened for us in the Eleventh Chapter of Acts which lets us see into another section of this divinely controlled heart. The church at Antioch in Syria was growing. Barnabas and Stephen were busy early and late teaching and organizing these new Christians. There were not enough hours in their days to accomplish all that should be done. There was needed a man with greater ability.

Five or so years had passed since Barnabas had appeared as Paul's defense attorney in Jerusalem. "Here is our man," Barnabas says to the leaders at Antioch, and promptly sets out to bring Paul again into the active circle of the Christian Church. It takes more than most of us have to step down, when we still have many years of constructive effort ahead of us, and let a more capable man take over.

Barnabas had this quality.

The fourth and last incident we have of Barnabas is found in the Fifteenth Chapter of the Acts. Barnabas and Paul had finished their first missionary journey and were getting organized for the second one. As part of this preparation there was the matter of who were to be their traveling companions. It started as a question raised by Paul, but soon developed into a warm discussion. Barnabas wanted to give another chance to John Mark, his young nephew who had failed them at Pamphylia on their first missionary journey. Paul said sternly and uncompromisingly, "No, I won't have a man with me who can't take it." Paul, motivated by a spirit of efficiency, and Barnabas motivated by the spirit of generosity of judgment, now part company. Paul chose Silas and set his face toward Syria and Celicia, while Barnabas took young Mark and sailed for Cyprus. As far as the records go, this incident marks the final separation of the great heart and the great brain.

A normal young man can be struck down several times by adversity and he will arise and start anew. But let a friend whom he admires turn against him for lack of understanding and appreciation of his true self, and we will often find him depressed and defeated for the rest of his life.

It was Barnabas who possessed this understanding and appreciation of Mark's true worth. We can be grateful that he did. For, approximately twenty years later this same young man was to give us the first written Gospel of our Lord, one of the four most widely read books in the world.

There is a bit of irony connected with this story of Barnabas, Paul, and Mark. It is not the last meeting of the latter two. In Paul's letter to the church at Colosse, written while in prison at Rome, we read that this swaying sapling had grown into a giant oak and was one of the pillars of strength Paul was leaning so heavily against in his imprisonment. We must admire Paul for his ability to recognize his hastiness and graciousness to fuse old breaks. But it was Barnabas who could see strength in weakness and who possessed the patience to develop it.

These four somewhat isolated stories are enough to show us the great heart of Barnabas, responsive always to the needy, despised, and rejected, was keenly sensitive to the human possibilities about him.

The rest of his life is shrouded in tradition. He left us no sermons, no great and powerful churches, no writings from his own pen to help us fill the gaps. But he did leave along the roads he traveled others who loved Christ because of what they saw in him.

═══◇═══

THE HIDDEN INGREDIENT . . .

The Reverend Charles C. G. Manker
Pilgrim Church, El Paso, Texas

A FEW YEARS AGO leading drug stores throughout the country displayed in their windows large cards advising their customers to look for the hidden ingredient in their products. As you read on down the card you found that the hidden ingredient, so precious to the product, was the reputation of its maker.

As we look around us today, it is surprising how many "hidden ingredients" are contained in almost every commodity. In every walk of life, in every business, in every dealing which we have with others, there is a hidden ingredient far more precious than that contained in the product of the drug store. And the ultimate success of that business, that dealing, or that transaction depends on this hidden ingredient. As an illustration of the value which business places on this particular hidden ingredient, let us review an instance in the life of two companies, each manufacturing the same product, in a certain city.

The one had a beautiful modern building, all the latest machinery and equipment, and plenty of raw materials, while its competitor across the way was rather cramped for space. It did many operations by hand that could have been done better and more efficiently by machine. And many of its machines sorely needed replacing. Yet the modern plant was for sale, and at a bargain. Whereas a large syndicate was offering the owners of the plant across the way several times the physical value of their plant, plus a nice bonus, in its endeavor to purchase it. Obviously, the value which they were looking at was not in the plant, equipment, and stock of materials. As a matter of fact they intended to junk the entire physical plant the moment the transaction was completed. What they were really buying was the "hidden ingredient"—the goodwill of that company.

Goodwill is an eternal principle without which nothing can operate, for long, successfully. With the unfolding of the first nebula, this principle came into evidence. Each heavenly body is a living demonstration of this principle, for it eternally keeps to its way, exerting just the right amount of attraction and influence on its neighbors, yet never trespassing on their rights or their territory.

There is no peace without goodwill. And where goodwill is in evidence you will find that strife is absent.

According to the World Book Encyclopedia, there are more than five hundred million Christians in the world. And according to the Encyclopedia of Religion and Ethics, there are some one hundred million Christians living in Russia alone. Does it not seem that five hundred million people, who are committed to one religion and who are disseminated as the Christians are throughout the world, should be a sufficient number to influence and lead the world into the paths of peace, understanding, and co-operation, that is, if their religion means anything and is worthy of the name? We must admit that something is radically wrong: either the religion itself is impotent and woefully lacking, or those who profess to espouse it are masquerading under a banner to which they have sworn no allegiance.

Let us look at this Christian religion. What is it? The World Book Encyclopedia tells us that it is the religion of Christ. It is a belief in the one God and Father of us all. But certainly the religion of Christ did not stop there. His religion was not easy, and the people of his day had no more desire or intention of living up to his precepts than have the five hundred million people who profess to be his followers today. His religion was the very exponent of "the eternal principle of goodwill."

Goodwill is an intangible something, a sort of feeling or emo-

tion. Like "beauty" and "love," it is beyond definition. It must
be experienced. It must be felt. It must be shared and it must
be lived. Goodwill is a universal God-given gratuity. The creator
must have been brimming over with it when he planned the
universe and started the forces of evolution on their way to
the creation of a kingdom of heaven here on earth.

It seems strange that in all his teachings, Jesus never once
mentioned the term goodwill. Yet his every precept, his every
action was motivated by the spirit of goodwill. Think not for a
moment that his admonition to turn the other cheek was occa-
sioned by weakness, or a surrender, or an abject submission to
the forces of evil. Can you imagine any man who could say,
"Call no man your master," submitting or surrendering, for a
second, to brute force? That admonition was born of an innate
goodwill that enabled him to look through and beyond the deed
with a compassion born of understanding. For the very act
of violence, of attacking an adversary, is a confession of weakness
and an acknowledgment of defeat. It is an escape mechanism.
It is resorted to to cover up the fact that you cannot match the
wits of your adversary. It has been well said that one need not
kiss the hand that smites him, but rather grasp it in cordial good
feeling and thereby let the electricity of his own high resolve and
goodwill find its connecting current, which often exists where
we least expect it.

Five hundred million people, imbued with such a spirit of
goodwill, could change the course of history and reduce the
instruments of war to the role of relics of a barbaric past. The
barriers of race, nationality, and class prejudice all melt and
disappear in the presence of this eternal spirit of goodwill.

If five hundred million Christians today would allow this
spirit of goodwill so to possess their beings as to dissolve the
barriers of prejudice, intolerance, suspicion, fear, and hate, our
United Nations would soon be well on its way to the realization
of its mission. It would be folly to say that the United Nations
has been successful. But one should be slow to accuse fifty-five
great nations, or any one or group of them, of deliberately trying
to circumvent or defeat the purposes for which the United
Nations was formed. It seems inconceivable that these fifty-five
nations would spend billions of dollars and send their keenest
minds to its council, for the *avowed* purpose of securing to the
world international peace, co-operation, understanding, and
brotherhood, when *actually* they were trying to destroy it.

What is the matter?

The members of that council represent more than two billion people and eight great religions, only one fourth of whom are Christians. But all of them believe in and worship one God. One may call him God, another Yahweh, another The Enlightened One, and another Allah; but he is still God. Perhaps this Mohammedan parable, contained in the Masnavi, is pertinent:

A man gave to four hungry men a coin. One of them, a Persian said, "We shall spend this coin for (angur)." But the Arab said, "No, you rogue. I want (inab), not (angur)." Whereupon the third, a Turk said, "No, my friends, we don't want (inab) either. We should buy (usum)." By this time the three were getting angry, so the fourth, a Greek said, "Stop this altercation; we'll buy 'istafil'."

Tempers arose and soon fists began to fly. The parable goes on to say that they were fighting because of ignorance, ignorance of the secret of the names. If one who had knowledge and was versed in the various tongues had been present, he would have reconciled them. He would have taken the coin and said, "With this one coin I can satisfy fully each of your desires. Had you but known, you were each demanding grapes, but each in his own tongue."

Forms of worship may be as different as they are in our own Christian denominations; but the fact remains that the only true worshipers in any religion are those who worship him in spirit and in truth.

Men of the United Nations, arouse yourselves! One thing only stands in the way of fulfilling the dreams and hopes of billions of people and thus accomplishing your purpose. You have overlooked the hidden ingredient! Though your deliberations are not opened on bended knee in Christian prayer, the very fact that you are meeting to deliberate, to strive to promote "peace on earth, good will to men," is in itself a prayer far more eloquent than mortal tongue can frame, and it is understood in every language and every religion.

Men of the United Nations, Christianity is not the sole possessor of this gracious hidden ingredient. Followers of Zoroaster, listen to your teacher: "To save ourselves we must teach others to be saved." Hark to the words of your Avesta: "Our duty is to teach friendliness to the enemy, righteousness to the wicked, and wisdom to the ignorant." Know you not that Zoroaster's righteous man was "he who shall establish the life of his fellow man upon the three-cornered foundation of good thoughts, good words, and good deeds." In the face of such teaching, how can you continue to be blind to this precious hidden ingredient?

Followers of Confucius, what are you doing to uncover this hidden ingredient? Did not your teacher say, "Let us not trouble ourselves with supernatural things and beings while we do not know how to serve men?" Was not his one formula for human conduct based on the idea of reciprocity? Did he not say, "What you would not others do unto yourself, do not unto others?"

Followers of Buddha, did not your teacher exhort you to "flush the world with love," and "never shed a drop of blood for the glory of God?"

Followers of Mohammed, have you forgotten the eighteenth of the Forty-two Traditions of An-nawawi which says, "Fear Allah, wherever thou art; and follow up bad actions with good, so as to wipe them out; and behave in a decent way to people"? Listen to the words of your Masnavi: "Bitter things become sweet through love; copper things become golden through love. Dregs become clear and bright through love. Through love a dead person is made living; through love a king is made slave."

Men of the United Nations, if you will but scratch the surface, you will find this hidden ingredient. It is there as a spark—as a red hot coal. If you will but give it a little air it will break into a roaring flame.

Men and nations are like unto a mirror. Look into their souls' eyes and you will see the reflection of yourself. Look with eyes of sincerity and honest resolve, devoid of deception and subterfuge. Look into their eyes with genuine goodwill and you will see reflected only goodwill.

In our one world, millions of persons are still displaced, hungry, sick and ill-clothed. They are looking to you for help. Their bodies demand food, clothing, and medicine. But if these people are to be salvaged for the benefit of human kind, their souls demand also that hidden ingredient. If they are to continue to exist, physically, they must accept of your physical bounty. Give it, not in a spirit of patronage, but in a spirit of brotherly love. Their souls are crying out for your goodwill. Peoples of all races and nationalities desire to be treated only as men. They want genuine goodwill, not patronage.

Goodwill is a cosmic largess. It is from everlasting to everlasting. In its presence comes brotherly love.

GOING A LITTLE FURTHER . . .

The Reverend Wesley H. Hager
First Methodist Church, Mount Vernon, New York

IT WAS ON A VERY HOT DAY in the summer of 1787 that George
Washington sat at a desk in the State House in Philadelphia,
looked at the document before him, picked up the quill pen and,
with trembling hand, scrawled his name. Thirty-eight other men
followed him in signing. As he watched them, he thought of the
long bitter months of argument and debate and ill-feeling.
Rising above their differences, those men had taken part in
forging the imperishable words of one of the great documents
of freedom and now had affixed their signatures under the words,
"We, the people of the United States . . . do ordain and establish
this Constitution."

The last man to sign was Abraham Baldwin, kind-faced
lawyer from Georgia, who said, "God has willed that we make
this instrument for the people."

Governments exist for the people. The glory of a nation is
always in its people. The peculiar glory of America has been
the fact that many people from many lands have come together
here to make something new. The individual contributions of
the peoples of many lands brought into being a strong nation
where all people might live together in freedom. It was a new
idea in government and the idea was explosive. It sent a tremor
through the world. Men asked in wonder, "Can this thing
really be?" When they came from distant lands they found it
true. More than that, they found a welcome. On the base of
the Statue of Liberty, they read the words of the Jewish poet,
Emma Lazarus, "Give me your tired, your poor, your huddled
masses yearning to breathe free. . . . I lift my lamp beside the
golden door." Here was the practical application of what
Malachi had said 2,500 years before, "Have we not all one Father?
Hath not one God created us?" Here was the political acceptance of the truth the Apostle Paul had uttered on Mars Hill
when he said to the people of Athens, "God hath made of one
blood all the nations of men."

According to our Christian gospel and the Jewish tradition

out of which it came, we the people see and respect the divine image in every human being and recognize our common brotherhood with all people.

We the people are all God's children. That simple but tremendous fact is the foundation upon which the new world of peace and brotherhood must be built.

In a letter written by one of our G.I.s who was stationed "somewhere in the Philippines" he said to his dad: "Living as I am now, finding out how much I value life, learning how much human kindness is a part of the black tribes of New Guinea, of the Filipinos of this island . . . people, friends and enemies alike, take on a new significance. They are not personalities for whom one entertains predilections or against whom one holds enmity, but rather people who are sharing the earth with us. I have thus come to realize there is no place for prejudice . . . ."

The great tragedy of earth is the simple fact that we the people have not yet learned to see all people as they really are, the children of God. We have allowed prejudice and hatred to raise barriers between us, barriers that are difficult to break down. In one of our elementary schools where the children were writing essays about their parents, one little girl is said to have written. "We get our parents when they are so old it is very hard to change their habits." But we must change. The barriers must be broken down!

Into the same hospital room where I was waiting for a fever to go down so I could return home, came little Nickie, ten years old. He had been taken ill at a summer camp far from home and had been brought to the hospital for treatment. We became good friends. It mattered not that he was a Jew and I a gentile preacher of the gospel of Christ. His mother came from New York and I watched them together through the days. She was a good mother and did everything a good mother would do to comfort a disappointed lad, surround him with love, and fill the long hours with interest. We have a great deal to learn from the Jewish home and from Jewish family life. There are very few with Jewish names who ever enter our penitentiaries.

One day Nickie's mother loaned me Marie Syrkin's book, *Blessed Is the Match*. I read it with awe and reverence. Here was the heroic story of the brave struggle made by the European Jews against their enemies in Europe. Here was the story of

their brave leaders who made the Warsaw ghetto holy ground.
Here was the story of the slaughter of six million people. Here
was the story of a far nobler spirit than my own, that of young
Hannah Senesoh, nineteen years old, who could write, before
she faced the firing squad,

> "Blessed is the match that is consumed in kindling flame.
> Blessed is the flame that burns in the secret fastness of the
>   heart.
> Blessed is the heart with strength to stop its beating for
>   honor's sake.
> Blessed is the match that is consumed in kindling flame."

It reminded me of the words of a far greater Jew who once
said, "He that loseth his life shall find it."

We the people must remember these things when we try to
understand the so-called "Jewish problem." And most of all we
must remember these things when the poison called "anti-
Semitism" threatens to creep into our minds.

In all of our life together, we the people all need each other.
America grew to strength and power because all the people
added their contributions to the building of the nation. Yet
some of us still forget it. One of our Negro poets has described
a scene he witnessed in New York: "Down in Columbus Circle,
I heard a fellow shouting 'America for Americans.' I stopped
to learn what he meant by Americans. He didn't mean Negroes,
Jews, Italians, Polacks, Chinese, Russians, Greeks, or Mexicans.
I wondered if he'd learned arithmetic. Subtract them all—the
people he didn't mean. Subtract them all—how many would be
left? They'd scatter sort of thin across this land, with a lot of
space between them . . . and they'd start hollering . . . for other
folks to come and do a lot of work those other folks are doing
right now."

In all the world it is true. There is important work for all.
We need each other. Life would be lacking in many of its
richest and most beautiful qualities if any were missing. A
blind man said, "Look at the kikes." And I saw: Lillian Wald
establishing the Henry Street Settlement; Adolph Ochs publishing the New York Times; Julius Rosenwald establishing 5,000
schools for Negroes; Serge Koussevitsky directing the Boston
Symphony. A blind man said, "Look at the Dagos." And I saw:
Columbus discovering a new world; Francis of Assisi filling Italy

with the love of Christ; Leonardo painting the Last Supper; Dante writing the Divine Comedy. A blind man said, "Look at the Chinks." And I saw: T. Z. Koo, great Christian thinker of China; Bishop Chen, heroic leader of a brave church; Lin Yutang writing of life and its meaning; Madame Chiang Kai-shek interpreting the Orient and the Occident. A blind man said, "Look at the Niggers." And I saw: Dr. Carver working in his laboratory with God; Haile Selassie mourning the lack of love in the world; Paul Robeson playing Othello; Marian Anderson bewitching continents with her voice. We the people are all God's children and we need each other. We also determine what tomorrow will be by what we are and say and do today.

Bobby Burns could sing:

> "It's comin' yet for a' that,
> And man to man, the world o'er
> Shall brothers be for a' that."

It will come when we the people recognize that we are all God's children and that we need each other.

Elizabeth Waugh tells of visiting a little Negro chapel in the town of Beaufort on the Sea Islands, just off the coast of South Carolina. Brother Abraham, six feet, six inches tall, rose to preach. He read the text from St. Matthew's Gospel and then said,

" 'And he went a little further.' That is a beautiful text, my dear friends. "Not much further, just a little further. 'An' he went a little further.' Now, dear ones, that's all anyone going to expect of you. That's all they can expect. Each day just go a little further, and some day see where you gets. Now you takes Pasteur, Louis Pasteur. He was fooling around with some little bugs in a jar and he went a little further and he gets a microscope an' he looks an' he looks. Now what? Why we is immune. We has Pasteur-ized milk. All he done, he jest went a little, just a little further. . . . An' you take George Washington. His father says to him, 'George, you-all cut down that cherry tree?' An' George Washington went a little further, he tole the truth. He went jest that much further. You-all know what we think of him today. Brothers and sisters . . . you don't have to go far. All you has to do each day is jest to go a little further . . . just a little further."

Then Miss Waugh tells us there was singing here and there,

then everywhere, then a little prayer and the service was over, except that everyone turned to everyone else and shook hands. All God's children shaking hands.

That is it—all of God's children shaking hands in the spirit of prayer and worship, going a little further than self, recognizing that God has made of one blood all nations.

It was one hundred and fifty-eight years after the Constitution was signed in the city of Philadelphia that another body of people met in San Francisco. But here there were not only thirty-nine representatives of one people but the representatives of fifty nations. They too signed a document—this time under the words, "We, the people of the United Nations . . . do hereby establish an international organization to be known as 'The United Nations'."

The world began to grow up that day.

We, the people must go further than we have ever gone before—further than self, further in prayer and in faith, for God has made of one blood all the nations of men.

———◆———

FIT FOR TOMORROW'S WORLD . . .

The Reverend Edwin T. Buehrer
Third Unitarian Church, Chicago, Illinois

Before asking ourselves whether or not we are fit to live in tomorrow's world, we might ponder whether there will be a tomorrow's world in which we will be permitted to live at all. The world is one world, today, but only in a geographical sense. It is not yet one world in terms of goodwill and mutual understanding. In order to achieve that final goal of oneness we must turn our backs on all those processes and activities, and all those states of mind and provincialisms which have given the world fifty-seven centuries of war out of sixty. Now the full dimensions of our peril must be frankly recognized. Now we must do what we have never been able to do before, we must eliminate war or forfeit all that men have hoped for or dreamed of regarding tomorrow's world. It is like the voice of Jehovah speaking to the Israelites in the desert: "See, I have set before thee this day, life and good, or death and evil." No one who is apathetic on the question of war or peace is fit to live in tomorrow's world.

There is another test, and I want to suggest that we place two facts side by side. Fact number one: From the birth of Christ to the year 1800, our basic ways of living changed hardly at all. The chariots of Julius Caesar rolled over Roman cobblestones just about as fast as did the carriages of a British King on his way to Parliament. People ate much the same food; they heated and lighted their homes in much the same way; they shared a similar philosophy of life, and they accepted much the same plan of salvation. Moreover, they cured their illnesses by similar remedies. In those days they had some 100,000 horse-power, consisting not of steam or electricity, but of horses and camels. Fact number two: Today our mode of travel and communication has changed very radically. Our food and clothing and living habits have changed, and our power has increased to upward of a billion horsepower generated by our machines. This power, if properly harnessed and distributed, might possibly reduce our daily working time to a matter of minutes.

Man modifies the very life of nature today. He makes ten blades of grass and ten ears of corn and ten bales of cotton grow where only one grew before, and he harvests them with proportionate speed and efficiency. He destroys whole species and tribes of living things, and he brings new forms and patterns into being. He does not just accept nature; he reverses many of its processes and its trends. The American Indians accepted their environment and used, in a primitive sort of way, the raw materials that were there to be used. They were often without food, and they were sometimes on the verge of starvation. Then came European man. He modified his environment to serve his own ends, and with the result that today, with a population twenty times that of the Indians, there is still room for many millions and more than enough food resources to go around.

Always starvation in every century! Tomorrow's man will say, or may say, "There will be no more starvation!" Always disease! And tomorrow's man will say, or may say, "Disease will be brought under control!" Always war! And tomorrow's man has it in his power to rule war out. The price of war is now— almost now—self-destruction. With his very survival at stake and fear gripping his heart, man may restrain his warring nature before it is too late. Many times in history, says Arnold J. Toynbee, when it was a question of survival man could change his habits and, ultimately, also his nature. The test of our fitness to live in tomorrow's world is our ability to believe that man can eliminate war before he will submit to self-destruction.

Among other things we need the will and the power of constant renewal. The tragedy of modern man is that he is so slow and unresponsive to the changes that are so urgent. The city in which I live and work has been frustrated for forty years or more by its transportation system. When I first saw this system twenty-five years ago, it looked just about as obsolete as it does today. The concept of private enterprise—now reduced in many areas of our economic life to a mere ghost and an abstraction—constantly blocked a program of public ownership, until all hope of benefit to the owners had to be abandoned. It required bankruptcy and city-wide inefficiency to bring about at long last what vision and statesmanship should have accomplished a generation ago. And already representatives of competitive industry have given notice that we shall not see the practical application of atomic energy for general use for years to come. They oppose its use because it will upset the economic structure which is now their vested interest, precisely as they opposed the development of the Chicago transportation system, the Tennessee Valley Authority, and other large-scale public enterprises.

Very well, this leads us to the fourth test of our fitness to live in tomorrow's world. It is in our power to see and to desire the larger situation in which the smaller situation finds itself. The mind is not something you can take hold of and look at. It is not a thing that has shape and form; it is a process of far-reaching movement and change. Locked up in its mother's womb, the brain could never produce a mind or a personality. The mind is communication of man with man, and a constant outreach into the farthest reaches of space and time. Wholeness, togetherness, integration, all for each and each for all, that is the watchword of tomorrow's world.

Consider the human body. Doctors now believe that many people have diseases of many kinds, including the dreaded polio, and never know it. For with an attack on one part of the body, the rest of it concentrates upon the enemy with all its health-giving power. Injury in the brain, even, is compensated for by other parts of the brain which take on extra duties. In that manner does nature, outside ourselves and within, come to our assistance. The strength of the whole is the strength of each part.

To be fit for tomorrow's world we must believe without question, and accept as a principle altogether inviolate, that all human beings—whether black or white or brown, whether talented or handicapped—all of them, belong—and on equal terms.

In the natural, inanimate world this principle of wholeness means that nothing is ever wasted, nothing ever lost. Transferred to the world of man it is the divine principle that human life must be preserved, respected, honored, cared for, trained, educated, defended, and, if necessary, salvaged. This is the practical meaning of love . . . the ultimate concept of fellowship and of communion. Life must increasingly become a solidarity of mutual living and helping to live, in joy and sorrow and aspiration and hope and fear. The man required to build tomorrow's world is the man who believes that. Disaster always comes when that principle is violated.

Modern man must ultimately adapt himself to the necessity of finding his greatest good and his greatest freedom in togetherness. Each of us is infinitely freer than we could possibly be if we occupied the continent alone. Only in togetherness can we create those goods and services, those intangible values and relationships in which human personality can find its best growth and happiness. But that togetherness must not exclude a single human being who is willing and able to make such contribution as his talents permit. Co-operation has always been necessary, but it has never been necessary on so large a scale. Unrestrained competition has always had its elements of danger; but with so much power available to the strong competitor, it has never been so dangerous. To recognize that, and to order our lives accordingly, is to qualify for citizenship in tomorrow's world.

There is a great conflict raging, with the line of battle running through every land, and through every human heart. Life is a struggle of opposites. Here is the individualist, strong, resourceful, confident, laboring under the illusion that he can live his life apart. And here is the man among men. On a world scale he is the internationalist; locally he has different names; but always he is characterized by his desire for mutual goodwill, helpfulness, and co-operation. We have also, on this side, the man who must either obey or command, the man who somehow cannot take his place as an equal among equals. And here is the man of liberty who knows that only in freedom—freedom of inquiry, of movement, and action, freedom of expression—can the highest levels of human achievement be realized. Here is the man who is conscious and proud of race. In his pride and self-consciousness he excludes "lesser breeds" from his home and neighborhood. He prefers not to have them in his schools and churches. And here is the man who measures men, not by the circumstances of their birth, but by the dimensions of their minds, the eagerness of their spirit, the integrity of their life, their willingness to enter into the pattern of mutual living. He has no other measurements.

Well, this world conflict somehow runs fairly consistently through these opposing lines. You and I cannot be everywhere on the battle front; but unless at least in mind and spirit we can be found somewhere, giving aid and encouragement to the man of liberty—at least that—we may well ask whether or not we have qualified to live in tomorrow's world.

Tomorrow's world will cost a price. It will require the effort of countless men and women, and only those who pay the price and put forth the effort will be fit to enter. We must adapt ourselves to change more drastic and more rapid than man has ever faced before, changes of thinking, feeling, and living. We must educate and discipline ourselves to see every thought and every deed of man within the larger world setting. We must desire and practice mutuality of living, and we must thrill to it as the great untapped reservoir of a freedom man never before has known. And somewhere on the world battlefront, as the great issues are being contested, we must play our part, even if our part consists merely in giving aid and encouragement to those who carry the brunt of the struggle for human advance.

These are the qualifications which constitute our password into the world of tomorrow. These are the things which must inspire new music, new art, new marching songs. These are the things which must produce new constitutions and new bills of rights.

But whether we live to enter that world of tomorrow or not matters not too much; for by our very acceptance of the struggle we create tomorrow's world in our own hearts, and we will behold its mountains on the far horizons. Moreover, we will help prepare the way for others to occupy the land toward which we ourselves have journeyed.

12. The Kingdom Is Coming

THE POWER OF INCARNATED IDEAS . . .

THE REVEREND ROY MARTIN HOUGHTON
Plymouth Congregational Church, New Haven, Connecticut

"If a house be divided against itself that house cannot
stand." — MARK 3:25.

IS THE WORLD RULED BY GREAT MEN or by great ideas? During
the war decade was Germany ruled by Hitler or by an idea of
racial purity and world conquest by the master race? Was
Italy ruled by Mussolini or by an idea of the divine mission of
the state? Was Russia ruled by Stalin or by an idea of government by the proletariat? Was England ruled by Churchill or
by an idea of human freedom with a tradition stemming from the
Magna Charta? Was the United States ruled by Franklin D.
Roosevelt or by an idea of better living conditions for the common man under the slogan: "The New Deal"? Most of us would
agree that the world is ruled by a combination of these two
forces—men and ideas.

When incarnated in moral beings ideas are irresistible. Luther,
embodying the idea of man's individual approach and personal
responsibility to God, gave the world a free Church. Abraham
Lincoln, incarnating the idea of brotherhood, inaugurated a
world-wide movement for human rights.

Lincoln's career organized itself about that one dominant idea. While in the legislature, he put himself on record as opposed to slavery, declaring the institution to be founded on injustice and bad policy. As a lawyer he won the reputation of standing for justice and honesty; refusing to take a case for a client he believed guilty, but defending with relentless determination one who was unjustly accused. He engaged in those memorable debates with Stephen A. Douglas, which developed an impulse into a grounded philosophy of social justice and gave him a national reputation. In those debates he took his stand firmly on the side he believed was right, regardless of personal consequences.

The supreme hour of his life arrived when he was elected president. He saved the Union, and he saved Democracy by his adherence to the basic principle of his life: "Let me die in the advocacy of what is just and right." The power which dominated his life and made him an apostle of brotherhood to all mankind is revealed in his second inaugural:

> "Fondly do we hope, fervently do we pray, that this mighty scourge of war may speedily pass away. Yet if God wills that it continue until all the wealth piled by the bondman's two hundred and fifty years of unrequited toil shall be sunk, and until every drop of blood drawn with the lash shall be paid with another drawn with the sword, as was said three thousand years ago, so still it must be said: 'the judgments of the Lord are true and righteous altogether'."

He recognized the mercy of God, but also his justice and righteousness, and a sure retribution.

This idea which Lincoln personified has been the energizing force of human progress from the dawn of civilization. There have stood face to face two opposing forces: class privilege and common rights. Abel, embodying the one, will share the fruit of his toil with God and man. Cain, representing the other, will take the life of his brother that he may possess the earth. Every step in the upward climb of the human race from that time to this has been crowned by the triumph of that eternal principle which says: "I am my brother's keeper."

Moses delivered his people from bondage, led them through the wilderness into a land of promise, and ushered in a glorious new day for humanity.

Settled in the land of plenty, class privilege and oppression gained ascendency. The Prophets, those men who speak for God, called them to account: "He has showed thee, O man, what is good, and what doth the Lord require of thee but to do justly, and to love mercy and to walk humbly with thy God." It took defeat and exile to make the people humble and obedient to the word of God.

The Church itself was corrupted by power. In spite of St. Francis of Assisi and many other saintly men, the hierarchy made the Church an institution of avarice, oppression, and extortion. Luther challenged the power of the Pope and publicly defied his edicts. It was a long and bitter struggle, but it issued in the redemption of the Church, and in the freedom of man to make his individual approach to God. That conflict has not yet ended. Eternal vigilance is the price of continued religious freedom.

What the Reformation was to the Church the French Revolution was to politics and social justice. The common people met face to face in bloody conflict with royal despotism and class privilege. The clash shook the world. When the power of the king was broken and the voice of the people prevailed, a new highway of social progress was opened with the slogan: "liberty, equality, fraternity."

The forces of class privilege and oppression were not conquered. Their field of action was transferred to the North American continent. Our war between the states was the result. Lincoln allied himself with the Prophets and the gospels. He took his stand on the eternal truth of the Fatherhood of God, which implies the Brotherhood of man. Justice and humanity triumphed, and by the Emancipation Proclamation slavery received its death blow.

But Lincoln did more than abolish American slavery. Through the victory here won a mighty wave of enthusiasm for common right was set in motion.

The tide of brotherhood seemed to roll on with increasing power. Our heroes and heroines were men and women with a passion for service to the neglected, the afflicted, the downtrodden. They were the Livingstones, the Grenfells, the Florence Nightingales, the Maud Ballington Booths. Mr. Gladstone said, "The safety of our country is not in law or legislatures, but in Christian gentlemen like unto Lord Shaftsbury."

The theory of evolution in science penetrated the social consciousness. Men believed that some blind impersonal force was moving man upward and onward. Society would be saved automatically. Men were saying with Swinburne:

"Glory to Man in the highest
For man is the master of things."

There was no longer need for God and divine redemption. Man was sufficient unto himself.

Then came the shock. Man, separated from God, proved that he could be more brutal, barbaric, sadistic, and depraved than anything the older theologians had conceived. When many good people were convinced that there never would be another war, little groups of godless men, relying on human force and material weapons, plunged the whole world into two of the most terrifying and devastating wars of all time. It was the same old struggle of selfish greed and lust for power against human rights and brotherhood. Man against God. Men with their mechanized weapons prepared for sudden attack and swept over unprepared nations with crushing power. From all human calculations victory was within their grasp. But again the "enormous right hand" was extended athwart the nations, and a voice spoke. "Thus far and no farther."

The lesson is written large on the pages of history: Racial, religious, and class prejudices; cruelty, inhumanity, greed and lust for power are enemies of God. All who ally themselves with those forces will find themselves fighting against God. Sooner or later they will be crushed. What Carlyle said more than one hundred years ago is true today: "At the center of the world whirlwind, verily now as in olden time, there lives and speaks a God. Forget that and thou has forgotten all. Success can never more attend thee. How can it now? Thou hast the whole universe against thee."

Leaders in Church and State, in labor and industry, in science and education, and especially all church members should listen to that voice out of the past. It is a trumpet call of no uncertain sound: Whoever and whatever—individual, institution or nation —attempts to fight against God is doomed. The war of abundant life and world peace is God's way of justice, mercy, humility, and brotherhood. There is no other way!

Nineteen hundred years ago there walked by tranquil Galilee a humble peasant, poorly housed, poorly clothed, poorly fed. He went about doing good, teaching by precept and by example.

He said: "Thou shalt love thy neighbor as thyself." His followers were few. A crown of thorns and crucifixion were his reward. But the influence of his life has leavened the world.

Less than a century ago the spirit of the Nazarene possessed the soul of a humble son of the wilderness. He, too, was of lowly birth. He, too, embodied the idea of brotherhood and sacrificed his life on the altar of humanity. That same spirit carried Lincoln from the cabin to the capitol. His cause triumphed, a race was set free and mankind made better because the little group of Galilean disciples had become a world community. This then is the goal of history.

> "The crest and crowning of all good,
> Life's final star is brotherhood."

When God's people in every nation are possessed by that spirit and impelled by that ideal the goal will be reached, and the prophecy of the Scottish bard fulfilled:

> "For a' that and a' that,
> It's coming yet, for a' that—
> That Man to Man the warld o'er
> Shall brothers be for a' that."

God wills it and, as Lincoln said. "The will of God prevails."

———◆———

HOW MUCH, THEN, IS A MAN BETTER ...

THE REVEREND HOWARD L. BETHEL
First Presbyterian Church, Plymouth, Ohio

GEORGE BERNARD SHAW is quoted as saying, "After reviewing the works of human events for sixty years, I am prepared to say that I see no way out of the world's misery except the way Christ would take were he to undertake the work of a modern statesman." The picture of Jesus as a modern statesman is a striking one. Of course he is much more than a statesman, but it is not amiss for us to think of him in that capacity this morning. He has at heart the welfare of all men and is concerned about the entire man. Surely he feels a keen interest in the healing of the world's wounds; alleviating the world's misery; bringing to all mankind security and peace. It is entirely proper for us to inquire what great underlying principle would motivate him in dealing with the world today. What would be his attitude to democracy and to our democratic institutions today? How far would he go in compromising with totalitarianism? How would he deal with our labor problems? What would be his stand on universal military training? Is Bernard Shaw right in his contention that Christ's way is the only way out of the world's misery?

It would be the height of presumption for anyone to try to say just how Jesus would act on the many confusing problems that face the modern statesman.

All we can do is to seek a clue to his attitude in dealing with a very complex and confusing situation. That clue, or at least one clue, is to be found in the words he used when faced by a man with a withered hand. This man had been planted there by Jesus' enemies. Would he heal on the Sabbath? He met that situation, as he met every situation, fairly and squarely. They rescued a sheep that had fallen into a pit—"How much better then is a man?" In these words we get a glimpse of the mind of Christ and some intimation at least of how he would approach today's work as a modern statesman.

In the first place, we may be assured, every act Jesus would take would be based on his high regard for the value of man and the sacredness of personality. He never treated a man as a means to an end. He gave man a high place, feeling assured "God so loved the world that he gave his only begotten Son" to redeem the world. By the world he meant man, not matter. Bent on establishing the Kingdom of God, he often said, "Follow me," but always left the way open for a man "to go away sorrowful." In a word, Jesus was not a despot, forcing men, but a friend, wooing them. Obeying Jesus never means the loss of one's personality, but rather that all his powers are enhanced. The disciples of Jesus amazed their contemporaries by their courage and insight. The truth had made them free. Jesus' way was found to be a way of liberation. It was not unnatural but in harmony with man's nature. It did not hamper their lives, but released inherent powers. Jesus came to give life, and his true disciple is buoyant, happy, fully alive.

As a modern statesman, Jesus could never give his sanction to any action that would make a man a mere pawn in the hands of a few favored ones. He would support in every way any law that would bring out the best in man. As the Sabbath was made for man, so he would maintain that the state, industry, school are to serve man, not make man a slave of state or institution. "How much then is a man better?"

In every age there has been a tendency to place some limiting adjective before the word man. In Jesus' day, too, people erected high walls about themselves. A part of the task of the Master was to break down these walls of separation. Race prejudice, however, does not yield quickly and even Peter must receive a vision that opened his eyes on this question. He "perceived quite plainly that God has no favorites, but that he who reverences him and lives a good life in any nation, is welcomed by him."

The Church, however, at its best, must always accept the teaching that, "There is neither male nor female; for ye are all one in Christ Jesus." We sing, "In Christ there is no east or west, in him no south or north, but one great fellowship of love throughout the whole wide earth." The church in our day is finding it difficult to put in practice these lofty ideals. We shy at the idea that "all men are created free and equal." We smuggle in the word "some" for "all" or make it "white." But religion and science join hands in demanding there be no limiting adjective. "How much then is a man better?"

Today we are experiencing a great upsurge of racism. Fascism was defeated on the battlefield, but the idea is not dead. Science has exploded the theory of race superiority but the prejudice is so deep-seated that we are clinging tenaciously to it. Anti-Semitism is as prevalent as ever, perhaps even stronger than before the war. It should be the task of the true Christian to fight this evil thing as hard as he can. Men defame the name of Christ when they use that name to persecute their Jewish brothers. We cannot pretend to love him, and then attack the very people who gave him to us.

The friction between Negro and white has been on the increase since the end of the war. The Ku Klux Klan has raised its ugly head and is trying to intimidate the black man. Jimcrowism prevails in far too many places where the Negro is made to feel that he is a member of an inferior race.

We are living now in a very small world. A century ago we

were a long distance from China; the Orient seemed like another
world. Today our acts are quickly known in what we still call
the "Far East," and tend to raise the hopes of oppressed people
seeking freedom or increase their suspicion and hatred of the
white race. We are entering the atomic age and that means great
changes in living conditions. Science has made us a neighborhood
and Christianity has the imperative task of making that a
brotherhood.

The world longs for brotherhood. It alone holds out any hope
for peace, and without peace our civilization is doomed. In
India there is bitter strife between Muslim and Hindu. The
keen mind of Gandhi said that in the friendliness of genuine
brotherhood is the only salvation for his beloved India. China is
torn by a civil war and only a spirit of real brotherhood can
bring the two parties together and build a great nation. The
machinery for world government is being forged in the United
Nations, but machinery alone will never bring peace and goodwill. We must undergird the nations of the world with that love
which "knows no jealousy, makes no parade, gives itself no airs,
is not rude, selfish, irritated, nor resentful." Love and brotherhood cannot go out from the church till it has become an inherent part of the church. She dare not stand irresolute and
complacent in a world of chaos, of hate, and of fear. Like her
Master, she must be willing to say, "And I, if I be lifted up, will
draw all men." The lamp that too long has been concealed beneath the bushel of sectarian strife must be placed on the stand
that the world may receive the light.

By denying the rights of other races, we are not only holding
them down and making life for them bitter and often unproduc-
tive, we are hindering ourselves. What the world would have
lost had George Washington Carver been "kept in his place!"
Where he won distinction and made a great contribution to the
progress of the race, how many others were kept down by an
unfavorable environment and by Ku Klux Klan methods! The
black man has lost by being handicapped, but the white man,
too, has been crippled by his prejudice. A deep-seated prejudice
acquired in childhood is most difficult to get rid of. All one's
thinking is influenced by it. Only the courageous will be able
to cast it aside and achieve freedom. Racial hatred injures both
the Negro and the white man.

If Jesus were to undertake the work of a modern statesman,
he would be guided by one great underlying principle, the value

of man. "How much then is a man better . . ." In his enfolding
love, "There is no room for Jew or Greek, there is no room for
slave or freeman, there is no room for male or female; you are
all one in Christ Jesus." The development of democracy, the
advance of humanity must ever be hampered till the Christian
church stands squarely on the teaching of Jesus.

Today we are entering the atomic age. That age can mark
most rapid progress or most terrible destruction. If the church
can discover how Jesus would act if he were to take up the work
of a modern statesman, and then go forth with buoyant hope
to make him and his teaching a reality, then peace can come to a
frightened world. We doubt not that Jesus has the answer, for
in his way the principles of democracy are firmly established.
These principles must be sought, found, and put into practice
by Christians of this generation. He gave us the clue when he
faced his enemies that day in the synagogue and said, "How
much then is a man better . . ." Only in that way can we create a
nation and a world of "goodwill and better understanding among
all peoples."

=====◇=====

WE CANNOT ESCAPE OUR FELLOW MEN . . .

THE REVEREND S. EDWARD YOUNG
First Presbyterian Church, East Aurora, New York

> "Woe to him who—seeks to set his nest on high, safe
> from the clutches of calamity."

IT IS SAFE TO SAY that mankind's most persistent rebellion has
been its rebellion against the brotherhood of man. Of all the
truths that Jesus preached we choke most violently over his
statement to the effect that we are all tied up one to the other,
in the common bundle of life.

There are few people on earth who so pride themselves on
being democratic as we Americans. We began our national
existence by declaring that "all men are created equal." Our
Fourth of July oratory crackles with paeans about the dignity of
the common man. Still we rebel, way down deep, against treat-

ing all men as brothers. Some, such as the Negro, we segregate; others, such as the Jew, we slyly persecute, and others, such as vast portions of the yellow race, we exclude from ever becoming citizens. We have our slums and our mansions, and it is becoming increasingly difficult in America to move from the first into the second. This rebellion is not confined to the antagonism of one group in American life toward another; the white toward the black, the gentile toward the Jew, the stockholder toward the laborer. It is much more personal than that. In one way or another each of us as an individual tries to escape his fellow men.

Consider what we are saying now in terms of something the prophet Habakkuk once declared. He writes, "Woe to him who stores ill-gotten gains, seeking to set his nest on high, safe from the clutches of calamity." So the prophet writes of the sure punishment that follows ill-gotten gains. By a little re-editing we can make our text preach a broader truth. Not only ill-gotten gains but well-gotten gains are not safe from the common lot. Let then our text become this, "Woe to him who—seeks to set his nest on high, safe from the clutches of calamity." Or, to put the same truth in shorter form: *We cannot escape our fellow men*.

We have come a long way, to be sure, in realizing that we cannot make our home safe, if our neighbor's home is in danger. I once knew a wealthy man who was the stingiest man in town when it came to supporting the good causes in his community. He did everything for his family and nothing for anybody else. He was continually saying, "Charity begins at home," and for him that was not only where it began but also where it ended.

He is not typical of most us. We have learned the hard way that all the fences in the world cannot separate our homes from the homes of our neighbors. Their diseases, poverty, troubles have a way of leaping over fences and landing in the middle of our hearths. We have learned that the only way to rid ourselves of such a devastating plague as infantile paraylsis, is to join forces to defeat it. But too often we have learned that we must share these burdens. We are not happy about it. It is a source of annoyance.

Again, we have come a long way in recognizing that we cannot make our community safe, if the nation is in danger. But some of us still sit in such comfort here in our favored communities that the problems of the nation still seem far away. There are not many such, for we know now that coal miners in Pennsylvania and a railroad boss in Chicago can make life difficult in our home town, and that a war five thousand miles away on one side, and three thousand miles on the other, could necessitate practice blackout here. We have found out, too, through such great agencies as the Red Cross, that when disaster strikes anybody, anywhere, it becomes the concern of everyone, everywhere. Only by sharing in such responsibilities do we build up a common reservoir of security and relief in times of emergency. So too, we are just discovering that we cannot make our nation safe when the world is in danger. I believe that some day history will write about us that no nation ever changed so rapidly its thinking on foreign affairs as America did between 1941 and 1946. From Vermont to Iowa and the Pacific, from the Dakotas to New Orleans, the minds of men changed from isolationism to internationalism. The world cannot quite believe it yet.

But it would be a mistake to believe that the transformation in our thinking is complete. If the commentators are right, we may yet see a considerable retreat in economic internationalism. There are forces that would cripple, in the name of economy, the International Bank, the Bretton Woods and Trade Agreements, and the feeding of countless starving millions in Europe and Asia, and thus sabotage the economic machinery without which the political machinery cannot survive. No, the battle for a real peace is not yet won. We have come a long way in discovering that no nation can be made a nest on high, safe from the clutches of calamity, but there is a lingering rebellion in human hearts against the brotherhood of man that still keeps victory for brotherhood from being securely won.

Let us then take a new look at the brotherhood of man. It is the only fact in human affairs that promises any hope. We have finally come to the point where, able to destroy civilization altogether, it is imperative that we join hands and minds in a common effort to build a better world.

That leads us to ask what is the ground for hope that it will ever happen? All the hope, yes, is contained in one truth—men are brothers under their skin—hearts alike, desires and impulses alike, some goodness, some evil, some faith, some doubt shared in common. Were it not for the fact that larger than their differences are their similarities, there would be no hope at all. I look at a fellow man; perhaps what repels me about him is that his clothes are tattered, perhaps that his English is fearful, or perhaps that his skin is another color. But then I remember, or ought to remember, that all the promise of the future lies in my shaking hands with him and seeing him as a brother man. If I brush him aside, I am brushing my future aside and the future of my children. If I want to believe in tomorrow, I must come to terms with this fellow. I must not seek to escape my fellow men, but seek to live with them. The brotherhood of man a burden? On the contrary, it is a happy thought, for the simple reason that all our hopes and faith ultimately depend upon it. Edwin Markham wrote a spritely carol of great good news:

> "There is a destiny that makes us brothers:
> None goes his way alone:
> All that we send into the lives of others
> Comes back into our own."

Yes, brotherhood we must express, concretely and practically, in smashing the walls of bigotry and intolerance within the very fabric of our own social structure—the tragic blight of anti-Semitism in some of our so-called enlightened communities, the evil of the Ku Klux Klan with all its menacing threat to our democracy. These are symptoms of social sickness that only the true practice of brotherhood can correct.

I do not believe that the main problem in morals, in our time, is simply to convince men of the brotherhood of man; rather it is to teach them to be happy about it, to lead them to discover that the deepest thrill in life is not to escape one's fellow men but to join hands with them.

There is no nest on high safe from the clutches of calamity. But I would speak of a kindred truth. What a calamity to try to build one's nest on high. It is a lonely as well as a futile business. The laughter in the hearts of man that does not burst, only to die quickly, is the laughter in the heart of man who, shoulder to shoulder with his fellow men, sees the promise that goodwill and better understanding can fulfill, and finds the warmth, the sheer nerve-tingling good news of this abiding fact—we are brothers all, each one tied to the other by a silken thread of common humanity under one God and Father. "Woe to him who—seeks to set his nest on high, but *blest be the tie that binds.*"

13. The Healing of the Nations

PREJUDICE AND ITS CURE . . .

The Reverend Lloyd Ellis Foster
Old First Presbyterian Church, Newark, New Jersey

A PREJUDICE IS A MODERN CROSS used by unthinking men and women upon which to crucify those who differ from them in race or in religion. A prejudice is a warped idea whose genius it is to mar and to distort human relationships. Racial and religious prejudice paints people who differ from us in race and creed as being inferior and inhuman. It exists in the world today as one of the most sinister and destructive forces which threaten both individual and world peace.

The urgency to realize racial and religious understanding has been sharpened and intensified by our entrance into the atomic age. Science has placed in our hands a terrifying instrument—the atomic bomb. The outcome—catastrophe or co-operation—will be determined by our control of atomic energy. Control, however, rests upon character, the kind of persons we are, what we think of other people who differ from us in their religious and racial connections, and, basically, how we treat them. In the light of this ominous threat of world conflagration, racial ill will and religious hatred may be the igniting forces that will start the flames of war, disease, and economic collapse. Our only hope is in a fresh realization of the inviolable sanctity of all human beings and in a realistic attempt to establish a brotherhood in the life of our world. For our world is destined to become either a brotherhood or a battleground!

The basis of racial and religious prejudice seems to be a violent emotional recoil to people who are different. That which is strange or new often arouses fear and distrust. When the object is a person whose convictions and practices are in sharp variance with our own, it is easy to acquire an attitude either of latent suspicion or of open hostility. When these social tensions are dramatized and intensified by conflict, either in the community or in the nation, they inflame passions and incite mass reactions that may be blindly disastrous. And yet how ridiculous and provincial these prejudices are when seen in their true perspective!

What we do not always realize is that prejudices have a demonic power to destroy. A prejudice is an evil thing—an admixture of hates and lies. All evil is by nature actively destructive. The genius of prejudice is to destroy both the object of its venomous dislike and its possessor. The man or woman who harbors racial or religious hatred is seldom aware that the possession of such a demonic passion may destroy his own inner life.

But is is not enough to give awesome warnings as to the demonic destructiveness of prejudice. The problem must be faced positively and courageously. Two allies, resourceful and powerful, stand by. They are education and religion. Education reminds us that little children are born without racial or religious bias. The raucous, raging individual, who, under cover of night, mingles with the murderous mob in the lynching of a Negro, was, as a child, free from such fierce animosity. In this fact is our hope for the future. Education must rally all its resources in the training of a generation capable of living in social harmony with people of varying and multiple antecedents. It must teach brotherliness not so much as a theory as a practice.

Our second ally, religion, has a major contribution to make. It must provide the philosophical ground for racial and religious understanding. Such a basis cannot be established by an emotional appeal or by sentimental regard. The reasons for racial and religious goodwill must be found to root in the scheme of things—in moral and religious conviction—else they will topple over like a child's blocks.

It is necessary, therefore, that we should recognize the profound moral ground underlying the necessity of racial and religious goodwill. What is the central Christian teaching at this point?

Christians today, as well as during the centuries of the Christian era, look to Jesus Christ as their interpreter of moral and spiritual truth. What he said and did should be the norm for Christians everywhere. His teachings have authority for us, not because of any compulsive decree, but because they appeal to our moral and spiritual understanding when it is at its best. What did Jesus teach about racial and religious goodwill, and how did he live out his insights? The gospels are crystal-clear. Jesus taught that all men are brothers because they compose a society of sons whose founder is God, the Father. Jesus proffered the water of life to all men without regard to their racial and religious dissimilarities.

Recall that Jesus lived in a small world of smoldering prejudices. The racial and religious antagonisms of his day were deep-seated and threateningly active. Groups employing the weapons of violence were arrayed against each other in bitter hostility. Yet against the darkening skyline of his day, Jesus towers dramatically and convincingly as the champion of human values. In his sight a person was of supreme value. The color of his skin or the inherited religious mores of his peculiar group in no way excluded him from sonship in the family of God. He was a person, a human being endowed by God with the capacity to think and to love and to achieve; he was akin to God in his spirit; he was a son of destiny included in God's majestic plan to establish the divine rule in heaven and earth. When challenged by a certain lawyer, Jesus crystallized his entire teaching into two terse requirements: "Thou shalt love the Lord thy God and thy neighbor as thyself." The neighbor we are required to love was given no racial or religious labels by Jesus. To harm or to hate one weaker than oneself was, Jesus insisted, the worst sin in the catalogue of human infamy. For Christians, therefore, the moral and religious ground of racial and religious goodwill is in the teachings and practices of Jesus. To claim to be a follower of Christ and yet to express in feeling and in action narrow and mean prejudices is a contradiction beyond one's power to grasp.

It is comparatively easy to admit that prejudice has a demonic power to destroy both the object and the possessor; it is not too difficult to agree that in Christianity we find the ground whereby we conclude that a human being is of supreme significance. But the hardest thing of all is to gather up all the splendid insights of Christ's teaching as to the treatment of others, and to live them out with patience and courage in the frenzied maelstrom of a war-embittered age. The patience we must have is the patience of understanding. Only as we understand how the rapier-like thrusts of prejudice lacerate and inflame the inner lives of those in the minority groups, can we understand their abnormalities of thought and conduct. To patience must be joined courage. We shall need a courage that is stalwart enough to enable us to stand as a minority in periods of racial and religious tension.

Lincoln remains the greatest exponent of democracy in our republic because his humane treatment of human beings was an integral part of his philosophy and of his practice. Frederick Douglass, a colored man who had known the cruel punishment of slavery, after having tea with Lincoln in the White House, confessed: "Lincoln is the first white man I ever spent an hour with who did not remind me that I am a Negro." In the eyes of Lincoln, Douglass was not primarily a man whose skin was black, but a man whose spirit was aflame with wisdom and courage and moral purpose.

How can we more aggressively establish this pinciple of human worth in our American life? There must be aggressive effort both to interpret and to defend democracy. The school, the press, the radio, the pulpit, and the forum, must be mobilized to set forth the principles of democracy. Social pressure and legislative action must be used to make discrimination a crime. Moreover, democracy must be defended by exposing the Fascist groups at work in America. Their twisted thinking and their cunning propaganda must be shown to be a diabolical perversion of American traditions. The battle of bullets and bayonets is over; the battle of ideas and ideals rages more fiercely than we suspect under the deceptive cover of a half-won peace.

At the heart of our planetary crisis is the simple yet complex matter of human relationships. How we evaluate other people and how we treat them *will* determine the outcome. In this grave emergency, the Christian must be an ambassador of Christian goodwill. To be such an ambassador, the Christian must confer dignity upon human beings; he must practice the principles of democracy in his own community; he must strengthen the forces of democracy from within through educational and legislative action. To measure up to these high demands is indeed the supreme challenge.

=====◇=====

OVERCOMING PREJUDICE . . .

THE REVEREND J. KENNETH CUTLER
Rosewood Avenue Presbyterian Church, Toledo, Ohio

PREJUDICE, INTOLERANCE, AND HATE are three of the greatest enemies of the human soul and of human society. And they are all related to one another. The line between prejudice and hate is very thin. Few attitudes are more destructive to human personality.

When I read the newspapers these days I read with a pair of scissors in my hand, for upon almost every page I find a sermon of some sort. It may be in a news article, an editorial, or a cartoon. Psychologists who have examined people belonging to "anti" groups have discovered that hate shrinks the human intellect, feelings, and imagination. "Hate," this report says, "exacts great cost in physical and mental illnesses."

So modern scientific research is bearing out the words of Jesus spoken many centuries ago. He it was who told men not to hate but to love and to keep on loving their fellow men no matter what happened. Hate and prejudice exact a terrible price from those who indulge in them. Every time we hear men and women giving vent to their bitter prejudices and hates we ought to cry out to them: "Stop! Give them up or they will destroy the highest and best that is in you." When we add up the cost of hate in the lives of those who hate and those who are hated it is terrific.

This story came out of Germany when the Nazis were systematically liquidating the Jews. A Jewish father and mother heard unaccustomed sounds coming from the room of their seven-year-old child. Tiptoeing down the hall they heard their little daughter sobbing out these words in her sleep: "O, dear God, please do not let me be a Jew." Such is our world!

Prejudice and hate are like a contagious disease which spreads from mind to mind, from group to group, from nation to nation until they infect the whole world unless they are stopped. Any one who disseminates prejudices and hate is an enemy of both God and man, and deserves, more than most men who commit crimes against society, to be placed behind prison bars.

How then can we be delivered from the shriveling, blighting, poisonous effect of hate upon us?

We must, first of all, acknowledge the fact that prejudices are acquired. We are not born with them.

One of our current magazines relates this incident: Every day, six-year-old Tommy brought home breathless accounts of the prowess of his new friend, Joe. With wide-eyed admiration, Tommy would report that Joe was the smartest boy in the first grade. Joe could make the biggest bubbles with his bubble gum. Joe had taught the other kids how to make paper airplanes. Then one day, over a bridge table, Tommy's mother was asked, "Did you know that your son's closest friend at school is a Negro?" That evening while Tommy was again regaling his mother with the wonders of Joe, she said, "But Tommy, you never told me that Joe was colored." "Colored?" the child asked, "What's colored?" "Why, his skin is darker than yours isn't it?" Tomy paused thoughtfully to ponder the question. Then he answered, "I don't know, but I'll look tomorrow."

This white child had God's view of the situation. He was not trained to see black or white. He only saw a friend. The responsibility rests squarely upon the shoulders of parents to see that their children do not catch from them their cherished prejudices.

In a recent newspaper column entitled, "Don't allow prejudices to ruin your life," Elsie Robinson emphatically states that our narrow horizons can be broadened with real effort. She writes, "They are the horizons which you have built yourself out of your own prejudices and fears, out of your hates and feuds, out of your possessive love, out of your ignorance, out of your greed and foolishness. Those are the real horizons of your life. Those horizons which have twisted and warped your own nature are not easy to cross. They will stick to you as long as you live and they will cripple and frustrate you unless you push them back. Push back your horizons. Cut your hates and prejudices and

fears. Do a job on that ignorance. . . . Leave your petty walled-in
world and become a citizen of the greater world. It may not be
so comfortable. It may not be so secure. It will certainly smash
a lot of your cherished notions to smithereens, but it will give
you a new spirit and a new pride and a new power. . . . Get to
work on some of your racial prejudices and religious bigotry.
. . . You can begin right now to be a citizen of the world."

We can overcome prejudice if we will learn the art of putting
ourselves in the other fellow's shoes.

It is good and true advice which has come down to us from
some rabbi of old who said: "Never judge a man until you have
stood in his place." If we cannot actually become a Jew, or a
Negro, or a foreign-born person we can at least enter through
imagination into their experiences. How would we feel if
theatres, and places of recreation were forbidden to us, if hotels
and restaurants refused to admit us, if some professions were
closed to us?

In the third place, we can overcome our prejudices if we will
look for the good in others and emphasize the good.

It is much easier to see peoples' faults and to criticize them
than to see their good points and praise them. But we can train
ourselves to be constructive, positive, helpful in our thinking
and our relationships.

Remember, running someone else down never built you up.
We shall never build up ourselves, or our own race by running
down someone else or some other race. That sort of thing is a
boomerang, for there is a moral principle of justice and fair-play
in the universe which we violate when we do it; it will back-
fire on us and we will eventually get the worst of it.

My fourth suggestion to help us overcome prejudice is this:
that we value highly the things we have in common.

Actually we have much. Rabbi Morris Lazaron has put it
beautifully in his book *Common Ground*. He writes: "All men
are moved by the same dreams, inspired by the same ideals,
plagued by the same problems, uplifted by the same hopes,
driven toward the same goals. The same fears haunt you. The
same intimate personal hurts wound you. Learn to know each
other and to understand each other. Your appreciation will be
deepened, your horizons will be extended, your lives enriched
and who knows what subtle yet potent forces you may stir into
being that shall make ours a nobler nation."

I have always made it the practice of my life to make friends

with people of other races and nationalities. For an entire year
during the war, four young Japanese-Americans shared our
home. We have entertained for extended periods a Persian, a
Korean, a French refugee child. People of many other races and
nationalities have been our guests. We have found in these
contacts, and in numerous others outside the home, that what
Rabbi Lazaron says is true. We have much in common, enough
to build enduring friendships. Rabbi Lazaron testifies that his
life has been made richer by his Christian friends. "They have
helped me to be myself in fuller measure," he writes. His
counsel to us is: "Christians get a Jewish friend . . . Jews get a
Christian friend. No Christian who has ever had a Jewish friend
has ever felt the same toward Jews and Judaism. And no Jew
who has ever had a Christian friend has ever felt the same
toward Christians and Christianity. Perhaps these strands of
friendship, when there are enough of them, shall weave the
pattern of the new world."

Let us, my Christian friends, build a bridge of friendship over
the yawning chasm of prejudice and hate across which future
generations may pass with safety.

I have just one further point and it is most important of all.
We must overcome our prejudices and hates because God wants
us to.

It seems perfectly clear to me that one of the first things that
Jesus tried to do was to outlaw from the minds and hearts of
his fellow Jews all idea of prejudice. He told the story of the
"good" Samaritan. He healed the servant of a Roman centurion.
He taught men to believe in God as Father of Jew and gentile
alike. No word of hatred for the gentiles ever escaped his lips.
And if ever a people had reason to hate their conquerors the
Jews had reason. But Jesus taught men not to hate, but to love
and pray for their enemies. When he told the people to go the
second mile, to turn the other cheek, to overcome evil with
good, was he not referring to the hated Romans?

The story from which our text is taken relates an experience
of Peter and the struggle which he had to wage to overcome his
deep-rooted prejudices. Like many Jews then, he had been
taught from boyhood to shun Samaritans and gentiles. But God
took Peter in hand and showed him through a vision that no
man was "common or unclean."

What did Peter do? Did he say, "Lord, this is too much for me.
I don't mind the gentiles as long as they keep their place?" No.

Peter welcomed the messengers of Cornelius, the Roman centurion. He obeyed God and went to Cornelius' home and said: "God hath shown me that I should not call any man common or unclean. Therefore I came to you without delay or hesitation, as soon as I was sent for. Of a truth I see that God is no respecter of persons. But in every nation he that feareth him, and worketh righteousness is accepted with him."

It must have been with considerable trepidation that Peter returned to his fellow Christians in Jerusalem. He knew their prejudices. But he told them the whole story of his vision. Then he spoke these words: "What was I, that I could withstand God?"

We are fools if we try to withstand God. God wills to build on earth a co-operative fellowship among men based on Christian principles of brotherly love. Jesus called it the Kingdom of God. I want to be working with God, not against him. Don't you? If a man believes God wants him to change his attitudes he can do it. That is life's greatest incentive to progress. "God hath shown me . . . Therefore I came. . . ."

=====◆=====

ONE GOD O'ER ALL THE EARTH . . .

THE REVEREND GORDON POTEAT
First Baptist Church, Lewisburg, Pennsylvania

The word *religion* had the original meaning of "binding fast." Religion represented that central loyalty which held people together in a tribe, a community, a nation, an empire. It has served this purpose effectively in various times and places even down to the present.

Our present need of some bond of union to hold the world together is desperate, for a greater variety of peoples and cultures has been brought into closer contact than ever before in human history and, instead of recognizing a common bond of loyalty, they are separated from each other by local loyalties which tend to produce conflict rather than concord. The world has become a neighborhood, but it is far from neighborly. Successive councils and conferences are being held to create treaties, economic agreements, and legal instruments which are intended to reduce the incidence of conflict, but these are all unstable devices if they are not undergirded by mutual good faith.

But can religion perform this essential function (in the situation which we face) today? We have "one world" as far as communication is concerned, but we have no one world religion. Instead of a more or less homogeneous group of people held together by a single religious faith, we have a wide variety of peoples separated from each other by diverse languages, customs and religions. The diversity of religions makes religion itself a part of the problem of world unity rather than a factor in its solution. Motilal Nehru, the father of the head of the Indian Congress Party, said some time ago that "religion is the chief barrier to the political independence of India" and we have seen that the prospective withdrawal of Britain from India has been the occasion of riots between the two chief religions of that country. Religion has undoubtedly sharpened the conflict between Jews and Arabs in Palestine, even though other factors are involved. In our own nation, we have three main religious faiths with many subdivisions which subtract from rather than add to our national unity.

Dr. William E. Hocking, in his book *Living Religions and a World Faith,* says that "The need for understanding among men and the need for identity of religion are not two needs, but one. The identity of the ultimate object of thought and value *is* the possibility of understanding. . . . If the free adjustments of reason are ever to replace the adjustments of force and fraud (in international relations), two conditions are necessary: First, that this very heterogeneous mankind shall be able to *discuss* their issues, that is, shall be able to think together because they have in common science, logic, and the standard of right; they must *have* the same God. Second, that they shall come to feel together in regard to what is good and what constitutes human welfare; they must *worship* the same God. . . . Ultimate agreement means caring for and serving the same cause, worshiping the same God."

Is such a spiritual unity as Dr. Hocking suggests beyond all possibility of achievement? Has any discernible progress been made toward such a goal? Let us limit our attention for the moment to the state of religion in our own nation. Immediately obvious is the multiplicity of denominations into which church

and synagogue attending folk are divided. But there is a greater
unity than appears on the surface. When our forefathers repudiated state-supported and state-enforced religious establishments
and espoused the principle of religious liberty, they made room
for a variety of individualistic expressions of religious faith. But
at the foundation, these various expressions of faith hold to
much which is shared by all alike. In a recent symposium entitled
The Religions of Democracy, in which leaders of Jewish, Catholic, and Protestant groups participated, the editor introduced
the discussion of these words: "Without minimizing the importance of conscientious convictions wherein each differs from the
others, we need constantly to bear in mind that Jews, Catholics,
and Protestants possess a valuable fund of common faith and
wide realm of common ideal and purpose." He was right. Take
note of some of these common elements: Do not all of us agree
in the worship of one God whose character is benevolent and
in whose will is our peace? Do we not all share together a body
of scripture? Do we not all of us agree that the two greatest
commandments are "to love God with heart, mind, and soul, and
one's neighbor as oneself?" The Psalms are the prayer-hymns
of all of us. In a book entitled *A Jewish View of Jesus,* Rabbi
Enelow has written: "The Jew cannot help glorying in what
Jesus . . . has meant to the world, nor can he help hoping that
Jesus may yet serve as a bond of union between Jew and Chris-
tion once his teaching is better known and the bane of misunderstanding is at last removed from his words and his ideas."

Our division into denominations is not wholly reprehensible.
It is one result of freedom of religion and a refusal to be
regimented by the state. It also represents a recognition that
religion to be vital must provide for change, experimentation,
and adjustment to new conditions. Moreover, the historical
causes which produced many of the original divisions become
less and less significant as time goes by. Many of these divisions
go back to struggles in Europe which are no longer important
here, or they go back to national traditions which were trans-
planted to American soil and are rapidly receding into the
background as these traditions combine to form a common
culture.

The major denominations are more and more being associated
together in such organizations as the Federal Council of Churches,
the Home Missions Council and the Foreign Missions Council
and in more than 500 city and community united church coun-

cils. There is increasing collaboration between Christian ministers and Jewish rabbis. When the Mormons made their trek
to Utah several generations ago they were attacked by hostile
religionists along the way, but on a commemorative tour over
the same route last year they were banqueted in the towns
through which they passed. We have still a long way to go, but
the progress accomplished promises something for the future.
If there are some who fear that increasing tolerance will reduce
the intensity and power of religious convictions, there are many
who believe that the centering of attention upon the most important convictions of faith—the love of God and of our fellows—
will cause conviction and tolerance to grow together. Love is
inclusive, not exclusive.

When we look at the rest of the world, what hope is there that
religion will be a bond of union rather than a bone of contention? In America our beliefs have a common historical source,
but this is not the case with other parts of the world. Shintoism,
Buddhism, Confucianism, Hinduism, Mohammedanism, and the
rest: what hope is there that this conglomeration will contribute
to the making of one world?

First: There are important moral and spiritual truths which
have been discerned in all the living religions and these constitute points of contact between the religions.

Second: The Bible has been translated into over a thousand
languages and has been circulated in all the regions of the world.
It has become the most universally read of all religious classics—
read by people of every religious tradition. And it has become a
dynamic factor in the modification and purification of many
religious practices, as is seen, for example, in the career of
Gandhi. He remained a Hindu and cherished the Hindu Scriptures, but he was also a student of the Bible and in the light of
its teaching repudiated the Hindu religious conception of
"untouchability."

Third: The spread of science and the scientific method of
thought has powerfully affected all peoples and their religions.
The universities of the Orient have the same curricula as those
of the Occident. The polytheism and animism of ancient religions are being surrendered for a conception of truth as one
and universal. The possibility of thinking together is far less
hopeless than it seemed half a century ago.

Christ said that he did not come to destroy the law or the
prophets, but to fulfill them; he did not come to compete with,

but to enhance and to enlarge upon the ancient insights into man's relation to God and to his fellows. In Christ's name we have no call to erase the memory of Confucius or of Buddha any more than his early followers feel called upon to obliterate the memory of Moses or Isaiah, of Socrates or Plato. The real conflict today is between godlessness, materialism, cynical selfishness, narrow loyalty to class or nation on the one hand, and faith in God the father, belief in the infinite value of the individual, and recognition of unlimited moral responsibility in the world community on the other. Nothing less than the acceptance of a universal spiritual loyalty and a common moral obligation transcending all local or particular loyalties can save us from the suicidal struggle for dominance and power which arrogant egoism produces in individuals as well as in nations. It is for this we pray when we say: "Our Father who art in heaven: may Thy name be hallowed everywhere: may Thy Kingdom come and Thy will be done on earth." It is for this practical end we must strive—one world of fellowship—if we are to be worthy of this hour in which each of us is called to play his part.

=====◆=====

WHO IS RELIGIOUS? . . .

The Reverend Merodach Green
First Congregational Church, Waseca, Minnesota

> "Inasmuch as ye have done it unto one of the least of these my brethren, ye have done it unto me."

OUR LORD REMAINS FOREVER the great realist. He allows neither tradition nor form of religion to obscure his vision of great moral and spiritual realities. He speaks with final authority. The good Samaritan is to be preferred to a selfish pharisee. The prayer of the penitent is heard, that of the self-righteous is not blessed.

Nowhere in literature is there a more graphic and arresting

portrayal than his description of the Last Judgment. Writers
and preachers have turned to it for inspiration. True, it appears
in the apocalyptic chapters of the gospel, but nevertheless it is
the Master's own matchless account of reality as he knew it to
be. It is the very quintessence of the meaning of living. It is
simple, vivid, and conclusive. Here is the very soul of all worthwhile religion. To this immortal chapter we turn as we seek to
find the answer to our quest as to what Christianity really is and
what our present world needs in its confusion, slumbering hatred,
and ugly attitudes. What is the great requisite in our Christian
faith?

It is not the edifices or architectural structures.

In all our cities, towns and villages are churches, and we are
glad of their presence and meaning. Yet nowhere in the description of the "Last Judgment" scene is there a word as to edifice
or architectural structures. The essence of religion is independent
of all this. Cross, altar, pulpit, font—how much they symbolize,
and what great value we set on these, and how much we derive
from them. But the Last Judgment scene omits them.

Even sacred literature is not of primary concern.

The literature of the Church means so much to us. On our
pulpits and desks rests the Bible, the book of books, the inspired
Holy Word. The centuries have read it avidly. The saints
have sought its inspiration, direction, and comfort as for hidden
gold. What help and hope our souls have gleaned from the
sacred pages! Yet not a single word concerning all this that we
hold so dear appears in the Last Judgment.

Theologies, doctrines, and creeds are not the great imperative.
All our churches are based on these. They decide how one
church or denomination shall vary from another. Because we
are human, we shall always have differences. There will be the
emphasis that some place is a veritable "Jerusalem," and another
but a "Mountain of Samaria." Which is the right church, and
where is the right place to worship? The Last Judgment scene
makes it clear these are not the vital essentials. Our theologies
are deep and complicated. Our creeds are ancient and venerable,
and we shall continue to repeat them. The great doctrines of
the church are far reaching and significant; they contribute much
to our spiritual life and the great hope set before us. Yet in
this Last Judgment scene not one question is asked concerning
these. The important matter there is, how did we deal with
human kind in their trials—the hungry, the needy, the poor, the

stranger, the unfortunate, and discouraged? What did we do
to alleviate their misery and ameliorate their lot? It is an astound-
ing thing that in this great scene not one question of doctrine
is raised. Doctrines have received so much emphasis in all
churches that it is difficult to believe that our Lord makes not
a single reference to them in the Last Judgment. To me, as
pastor, it comes with urgency and tremendous heart-searching,
that some one thing is very necessary in the mind of our Lord,
and all else is secondary. Here with unquestioned certainty,
he determines the issue which we must not fail to place in the
forefront of our aims, purposes, and preaching.

In India, Hindu and Moslem are opposed in deep hatred.
In Palestine, the Holy Land, Jew and Arab in opposite camps
display bitter hostility. Yet to the master, Islam is nought,
Buddhism is nought, Greek Catholicism is nought, Roman
Catholicism is nought, Protestantism is nought, Lutheranism is
nought, Nonconformity is nought. Something else is the determining factor in his mind.

A quality of heart and spirit is the determining factor.

It remains forever true that "he that hath not the spirit of
Christ is none of his." We must emphasize anew the Master's
uncompromising demand of us all—a quality of spirit and heart.
The doctrines must find their incarnation in us; the great creeds
must breathe life and power in us. Here is the final test. How
are we in this matter? How do we react to the need and sorrow
of humankind? How far do we go out of our way to bless, to
help, to heal the open sores of the world? We believe that much
of the misery and sorrow today could be alleviated were all our
Christian churches to rediscover this Judgment scene and see
the Master's emphasis.

"Neither in this mountain nor in Jerusalem," but everyone
that doeth the will of the Father. Only in this spirit can the
Christian world rise triumphant above prejudice, intolerance,
racial discriminations, and war.

In the book, *Madame Curie,* there is a powerful illustration
which we may well use to show what Christian people should be
in this world, if it is to be made a better world. Several months
before the discovery of radium, Pierre Curie had told his wife
that he hoped that when the mysterious element was found it
would have a pretty color. One evening, when he returned from
the university, she told him about her discovery and that radium
had something better than a beautiful color. After supper they

went into the shed to see the marvelous element. "Don't turn on the light, we'll sit here in the dark and observe. Look toward that corner. See, it has a glimmering radiance all its own, and seeks to make the jars, the wall, and even your old coat reflect its uncanny splendor. It is radium, Pierre, seeking to make everything else, life itself, radiate light and influence."

Christianity in the mind of our Lord was to be a vital power in this world. It supersedes edifices, creeds, doctrines, and denominations. It is life, light, and power. We catch the sacred light from our living Lord, the light of the world. We become incarnation of his spirit.

To me, it is a matter of grave concern in a world teeming with churches, and with millions of men and women professing Christianity, that war, intolerance, racial hatreds, and bigotry should lift their heads so high, and cast dread upon all. It is imperative that we become greater realists in our faith. I know of but one way to do this, and this morning I lead you beyond all secondary considerations to the very presence of our living Lord, the master of life, the conqueror of death, the Redeemer of the world. From his presence let us go into the world, and in our daily life and actions, reveal his eternal spirit.

For "inasmuch as ye have done it unto one of the least of these my brethren, ye have done it unto me."

<hr />

THE ACCEPTANCE YEAR OF THE LORD . . .

THE REVEREND A. L. KERSHAW
Christ Church Parish, Bowling Green, Kentucky

MY LAST SERMON as your rector is much like the first. I have been aware that between that first sermon almost four years ago and the last one today, there have been complaints that I have harped too consistently on the social problems confronting our world and our religion, while not preaching very often about more "spiritual" matters.

Once the distinguished clergyman, Robert Norwood, was gently rebuked by one of his parishioners for always preaching the same sermon. "The text varies," said this gentleman, "but the message is ever the same." "My dear friend," Dr. Norwood replied, "There is but one sermon!"

Actually, there is but this one sermon! The will of God. Our world, our civilization within it, and our individual lives within that, find peace and happiness and security only in the direct proportion they find the will of God.

Our text is from the prophet Isaiah—"To preach the gospel to the poor, to heal the broken-hearted, to preach deliverance to the captive, and recovery of sight to the blind, to set at liberty them that are bruised, to preach the acceptable year of the Lord." This Jesus took when he read from the prophets in the synagogue as the purpose of his ministry—and what is this passage but God's will forcibly portrayed in concrete terms!

Three years ago, thousands of men invaded France on D-Day for the purpose of giving to our world the chance for lasting peace. Countless men and women were transported from their homes and loved ones to spend valuable years of their youth on tiny geographic pin-points far across the world. In the Pacific, in Africa—on the great seas—in the air—men were laying down their lives so we could sanely build a different kind of world where such tragedies do not happen.

Surely some of you know that war poem by Archibald Mac-Leish?

> "The young dead soldiers do not speak.
> Nevertheless they are heard in the still houses
> (Who has not heard them?)
> They have a silence that speaks for them at night,
> And when the clock counts.
> They say,
> We were young. We have died, remember us.
> They say,
> We have done what we could
> But until it is finished, it is not done.
> They say,
> We have given our lives.
> But until it is finished no one can know what our
>   lives gave.
> They say,
> Our deaths are not ours,

> They are yours.
> They will mean what you make them.
> They say,
> Whether our lives and our deaths were for peace, and
>   a new hope
> Or for nothing
> We cannot say.
> It is you who must say this!
> They say,
> We leave you our deaths,
> Give them their meaning.
> Give them an end to the war and a true peace.
> Give them their meaning.
> We are young, they say.
> We have died.
> Remember Us . . ."

It is hard to imagine a person so casual or self-absorbed that he does not feel within himself at times the burden and power of the legacy these four years have left us. "We leave you our deaths. Give them their meaning!" When men look back on this time, what will they say that these lives meant? That will depend on what people like us make them mean.

Four history-packed years! We saw man look into the mind of God, and split an invisible atom, and then desecrate God's love by using the new truth for the destruction of myriads of human beings. We realized at least for a few days, that for the first time in the history of man, his civilization was in imminent danger of total extinction, and for perhaps the last time in history, he had the one chance to reorder his life and world.

We saw one more war end, and we seemed more thankful that our petty inconveniences of rationed sugar and coffee and meat were at an end than we were eager to realize what attitudes we had to change and create if we were, as Mr. MacLeish put it, "to give these lives meaning." We saw the birth of a world organization of nations, and from the first too many people doubted that it would succeed. We saw America entering a period of waste, profligacy, and gambling, while millions of God's children were starving and homeless around the world. A fever to forget the war quickly and the veteran with it soon plagued our nation, and we deceived ourselves that there was peace within Israel while underneath the seething corruption boiled.

We saw some of the members of the United Nations behave like prima donnas, and saw how they often put their pride and bias before the primary purpose of world peace.

We saw, while lauding our freedom of speech, how anyone, disagreeing with what is popular, and at the same time patriotic, was labelled a Communist or a Communist Front.

We saw on the back of a war against the doctrine of a superrace, the revival of the Ku Klux Klan, the birth of the Columbians, and a great rise in the number of shameful lynchings.

We saw the growing encrustment of our age with materialism, and of our society more and more equating the good life with possessions, and the pursuit of wealth.

Four years packed with lyricism and loveliness! When above our heads like the sword of Damocles hangs threatening the destruction of human life itself, either we recognize our Christianity as virile and timely and as our one remaining hope, or else it is such a reluctant afterthought that it is actually boneless. Either the God whom we worship is omnipotent and omniscient, and can help us mightily to reorder and right our lives and world or else we have been suffering from grandiose illusions and really pay homage to a God of straw.

It seems to belong to the character of our age that we seek, child-like to escape from what really is, and from where we really are. We try to make of religion a pipe-dream about the glories of the next world and how much more righteous and worthy we really are when compared with those around us.

But religion, like life, is not made for escape and illusion. It is at its best and highest only when it is a structural part of reality. John Erskine sadly observed in one of his essays about Christians: "They make of religion not a pillar of cloud by day and a pillar of fire by night. Rather they make of religion an ecclesiastical apothecary shop, where sick souls may purchase drugs."

And so for these four years I have pleaded with you to remove the bromides and drugs from your faith, shake off the webs and dust, and use your faith every day in your life.

I have urged you fearlessly to apply the truths of your faith in every corner of your existence: School, recreation, business, work, attitudes, and desires; economics, politics, race relations.

I have repeatedly called on us to think of the kingdom of God on earth as the first, last and most important goal of this parish, and of the church as a whole: that we think of ourselves as

Christians far more vitally than as Episcopalians; that denomina-
tionalism in our world is too often a drag and actual barrier
to a fuller Christian brotherhood. I have called upon us to
seek out the most important things in our faith rather than
whether it should be immersion or sprinkling; grape juice or
wine; a white collar or red suspenders. I have exhorted us to
think more on the will of God as it speaks to us today than on
what happened in the church in 314 or 572 or 1197.

These things are fine, and if our world were secure and loving,
we could well afford to interest ourselves in the poetry, and
periphery of religion; but these four years drive us to seek a
Christian solution to our times, and look at our plight truthfully
and humbly.

I have stressed my sincere belief that the church, by running
drives for money, for members, for statistics, has prostituted its
calling in thinking more, worrying more, and spending more,
for its own institution than for the larger kingdom of God. In
our own faith we are too prone to take the liturgy, and beauty
of architecture and vestments and appointments, and traditions,
as final in themselves, and sometimes mistake them to be as
important as courageous work for the kingdom of God.

The institution of the church is only valid and justifiable
when it leads us to fellowship with Christ, and to brotherhood
with men; when it incites us with vision and strength and
sacrifice for the kingdom of God on earth. It is in error and
wrong when it becomes an end in itself and shamefully storms
the democratic right of every man to work out his own faith
in mental and moral honesty. Martin Luther was forever right
in saying that one single man can be right as against a whole
tradition, and history has proven it a thousand times, Tertullian,
a leader in the early church about 200 A.D., rightly remarked:
"Christ called Himself the Truth; and not the tradition; therefore, every new truth, no matter how foreign to past belief, is
truth of Him."

If together with the happy and warm friendships and profound joy of working together for something we mutually love,
if I have by this just a trifle extended your vision, incited you to
live your faith functionally every day of your life, and helped
you to see the urgency of our times and of our carrying fearlessly God's will into our family, social, national and world relations; if in any small way I have inspired you to seek first the

kingdom of God and his righteousness, then these years will always remain for us meaningful and happy.

In the parting words of St. Paul from his second epistle to the Corinthians: "Finally, brethren, farewell. Be perfect, be of good comfort; be of one mind, live in peace! And the God of love and peace shall be with you."